scraptherapy®

Scraps Plus One!

scraptherapy®

Scraps Plus One!

New Patterns to Quilt Through Your Stash with Ease

IRRESISTIBLE
20
PROJECTS

Joan Ford

The Taunton Press

The Taunton Press, Inc.
63 South Main Street, PO Box 5506
Newtown, CT 06470-5506
email: tp@taunton.com

Editor: Renee Iwaszkiewicz Neiger
Technical editor: Nanette S. Zeller
Copy editor: Candace B. Levy
Indexer: Cathy Goddard
Cover design: Alison Wilkes
Interior design & layout: Carol Singer
Illustrator: Joan Ford, with technical assistance by Tinsley Morrison
Photographer: Burcu Avsar, except for the quilt border on the back cover and
pp. iv, 8, 10–12, 30–178: Scott Philips © The Taunton Press, Inc.

The following names/manufacturers appearing in *ScrapTherapy Scraps Plus
One!* are trademarks: Katie's Scallop Radial Rule™, Mary Ellen's Best Press™,
Mettler®, OLFA®, Pigma®, Qtools™, Quiltsmart®, ScrapTherapy®, Square²™,
Tucker Trimmer™

Library of Congress Cataloging-in-Publication Data
Ford, Joan, 1961-
  Scraptherapy scraps plus one! : new patterns to quilt through your stash
with ease / Joan Ford.
       pages cm
  Summary: "This book reignites quilters' love of scraps and their creativity
by explaining how scraps plus one new element--a fabric, color, theme, or
technique--can breathe new life in to any tired but beloved fabric collection"-- Provided by publisher.
  ISBN 978-1-60085-519-1 (pbk.)
1. Patchwork--Patterns. 2. Quilting--Patterns. I. Title.
  TT835.F6675 2013
  746.46--dc23
                        2012051217

Printed in the United States of America
10 9 8 7 6 5 4 3 2 1

Quilting is a social sport. I made this discovery early in my quilting history, less than 10 years ago from this writing. As such, the opportunity to connect is ever present—in classes and workshops, on quilting retreats or cruises, or during "fabric acquisition road trips" (yes, it makes up a silly, not-so-polite acronym) to the local quilt shop. Every quilter has that special sewing circle. Those friends who have only to mention an all-day quilting get-together and, before you can drop a stitch, a pot luck meal is arranged and space is cleared in the dining room for the invasion of sewing machines, boxes of projects to finish, and gab.

This book is dedicated to those special friends with whom I quilt. Sometimes they lend a patient ear to the problems of the day over the whirr of sewing machines working. Sometimes, perhaps more often than the latter, they hear an earful of spits and rants from this energetic author. But always they are ready to laugh, smile, cry, and share.

Beth, Janine, Marcia, Melonie, Wenda, and especially Gail, who traveled to New York City with me for an eye-opening weekend of fabulous quilt exhibits and decadent fabric shopping, this one is for you. Thanks for listening and laughing at the appropriate cues. And it's for our spouses who quietly fade into the outer reaches of the house while the assault of fabric, thread, and storytelling takes over. Hey, at least quilters are good cooks, and the pot-luck leftovers are always available for an extra plate or two.

ACKNOWLEDGMENTS

Perhaps writing a book about making quilts can be compared to planning a big wedding. You start with a few lists, then check things off the list as they are completed. The big day comes, and then it's "happily ever after" from there on. No big deal, right?

Until you are in the middle of the process, you don't really consider all the behind-the-scenes people making each element perfect—the caterer, the venue managers, the musicians, the baker, and of course the dressmaker. Each person is an important member of the team; any one aspect goes awry, and the event can be flawed. It takes the talents of many to make a perfect wedding day.

Such is the case with the book you are holding. I owe sincere gratitude for the combined effort of an incredible team of talented individuals at The Taunton Press. Many, many thanks to each contributor to this book, including those involved in its design, its production, and its distribution. A big thank you to Tinsley who opened my eyes to a whole new level of illustration expertise. My sincerest thanks are extended especially to Maria, Shawna, and Renee, my biggest cheerleaders. And a wedding wouldn't be much of a celebration without guests. So thank you, dear quilter, for appreciating a favorite hobby as much as I do.

contents

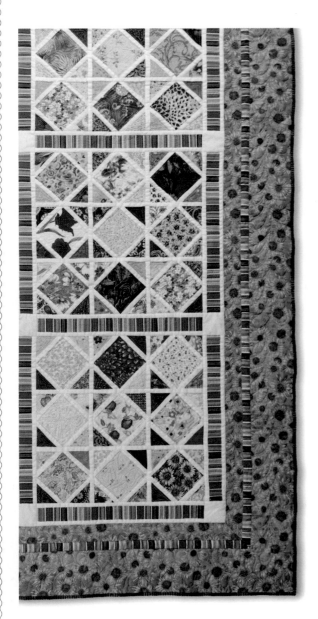

Your Scrap Plan

Ever been on a successful weight-loss program? In the beginning, it's pretty easy—once you get past the initial adjustment to a new lifestyle. The pounds seem to melt off during the first few weeks following a strict diet. You persevere and reach your goal weight. Yay! Celebrate!

But maintaining the goal—the second step—can be even more difficult than reaching it.

So, should you give up? Well, I suppose you could, but that gets you right back where you started, feeling defeated, overwhelmed, and unsuccessful. Instead, consider another approach. Try to change it up a bit. Add variety. Make it fun. Find sources of new energy.

And so it goes for your scrap fabric stash.

Does this sound familiar? You've been following along with the ScrapTherapy® process, diligent with the steps laid out in my first book, *ScrapTherapy Cut the Scraps!* You've been cutting, sewing, and cutting some more. The solutions from the first book really got your blood flowing . . . and then you stalled out. Now what? You need something fun to get you back on track. And that's what *ScrapTherapy Scraps Plus One!* is all about—changing it up and getting the creative juices flowing.

If you are expecting this book to be an expanded collection of more quilts that follow that simple seven-step formula laid out in *Cut the Scraps!*, you will be surprised. Yes, in this book you'll find a review of the ScrapTherapy seven-step program; you'll find more suggestions and projects to help you follow the steps, which motivated you before.

However, you will also find something new. A little twist to mix things up a bit.

ScrapTherapy Scraps Plus One! is the next step for your scrap fabric plan. Maybe you got off to a good start following the seven steps from *ScrapTherapy Cut the Scraps!* and you can use a little refresher. Perhaps you need a recharge for your scrap quilting batteries with some fresh patterns and ideas. Or, perhaps your ScrapTherapy plan is going strong, but you can use some new ideas, a challenge or two, and different project ideas. Or maybe this is your first look at a unique approach for your scrap stash. No matter what the reason, bottom line is your quilting hobby should be fun! Your leftovers from completed quilt projects should be a source of inspiration, not guilt. If you started down a path to organize your leftover scrap fabric stash, and it feels like the wind went out of the sails a bit, it's not too late!

Scraps Plus One! lets you pick up where you left off. Or start anew.

It's all here. The recharge, the review, and the next step.

THE RECHARGE

Right after *Cut the Scraps!* was published, I confess, my creativity took a hit. Things were feeling a little stale. The fabric inventory in the local shops didn't excite me. Sure, beautiful fabrics, in glorious new prints and colors, went on display, refreshing the merchandise available for sale on a regular basis, but my excitement was tepid. In their bins, my cut-up scraps looked dog-eared and stagnant. My heart wasn't singing.

Then I stepped on a train and headed to New York City for a weekend. For two days, I attended two fabulous quilt shows and visited three quilt and craft shops, and suddenly, I could feel the creative energy stirring again. My excitement was renewed.

RENEW YOUR ENERGY

A vacation spot, a new swatch of fabric, a pattern or book that excites you, a trip to the local quilt shop to breathe in the colors and prints. Sometimes that's all it takes to get the energy back on track. Your beloved quilting hobby should be fun, inspired, and gratifying.

ScrapTherapy Cut the Scraps! may be the inspiration for you to make a change. Or perhaps this book will offer you a new direction. At any rate, mixing things up a bit can be as simple as stopping, reflecting, and deciding what to do next.

For me, *Scraps Plus One!* is the result of a renewed energy toward using my own cut-up scrap stash. It is about approaching each new quilt from a fresh perspective. And it's about sticking with a plan that—I know from experience—works.

Sometimes, it's good to step away from the usual routine. By stepping away, you might even get a better perspective of why you liked your original routine so much.

THE REVIEW

Scrap quilts? Not me! It's funny, since I began quilting, I never thought that I would be much of a scrap quilt maker. I didn't like the way many scrap quilts tried to connect fabrics that didn't belong together. In the scrappy quilts I saw, there typically wasn't a cohesive theme or a focal print to tie colors and prints together.

It seemed that many of the scrappy quilt patterns and books had it backward: start with a pattern, and then go on a strange treasure hunt to unearth the right pieces of fabric from massive piles and bags of unkempt scraps, and finally assemble the project. In my mind, it makes more sense to start with the scraps, cutting them up following a simple plan. Then you are ready to select and sew the scrap pieces into *controlled scrappy* projects.

CUT THE SCRAPS

Since writing *Cut the Scraps!*, I've become known for scrap quilts. I realize that the quilts I make from scraps don't always look overly scrappy. Sure, I use scrap fabrics, but to keep them from looking overly scrappy, I often select a theme before diving into the cut-up scraps in my bins. I've been known to supplement my stash defiantly with the purchase of a fat quarter or two (or more!) if colors or value ranges in my own collection are depleted. And I love using notions and gadgets that make my hobby more fun, my results more accurate, and the sewing more efficient.

We all love fast results from big pieces of fabric, but if you have small pieces of scrap fabrics and don't want to throw them away, it seems sewing small pieces is inevitable. And yes, some of the piecing can be tedious. But it doesn't have to be boring or without reward. Tips and suggestions throughout the book will offer alternatives

to keep you moving forward and to make your sewing time efficient and fun.

The importance of making test blocks, sewing accuracy, and tips to complete and quilt your scrappy quilted project all are found here in this volume for reference and as a refresher.

As a regular fabric purchaser, I won't advise you to stop buying fabric. It's a treat to shop and buy, even if the goal is to work from what's on hand. Finding what you need in your fabric stash is a bonus, not a requirement to complete a scrappy quilt project. You are encouraged to head to the nearest quilt shop if the perfect inspiration fabric needs to be procured. Something old goes very well with something new!

THE NEXT STEP

So what's next? Okay. You're juiced up with new energy. The batteries are charged. The sewing machine is oiled and ready to sew. The only thing left is new projects to make.

I have yet another confession: I don't have a favorite project from this book. I simply cannot choose. They are *all* my favorites! So much variety. Something for everyone.

ADD A "PLUS ONE"

In this book, you'll find traditional methods and unexpected variations in construction. You'll also find classic quilt patterns and blocks, some with a twist toward the contemporary. The variety of shapes and modification of technique derived from using just three square scrap sizes is a source of endless fascination for me. Classic blocks get a scrappy interpretation. And scraps combined with one other element seem to have boundless possibilities. Variety is the secret ingredient that keeps working with scraps interesting and exciting. The *Scraps Plus One!* concept adds a little fun twist to inspire you to use your scraps plus one other element—a focus print, a solid background, a technique—to unify your scraps.

When choosing your next scrappy project, consider a project that will clear out the sizes or colors that seem to linger. For me, darker floral prints always seem to fall to the bottom of the pile, unused. So from time to time, I pull them out, pair them with a solid fabric that coordinates with what I've selected—basic colors like red, green, yellow, and blue often work nicely—and choose a project that combines the scraps plus one coordinate. After all, these fabrics got into my stash because I liked them. And using them gives me the chance to reminisce and make them into something even nicer.

WHAT ARE YOU WAITING FOR?

It's time to dig in. Just as *ScrapTherapy Cut the Scraps!* leads you through the steps to organize and use those leftover scrap fabrics from your finished quilt projects, *ScrapTherapy Scraps Plus One!* is all about recharging and inspiration.

So, let's get on with it. Roll up your sleeves, put in a fresh rotary blade, and to coin a phrase, let's "Cut the Scraps" and get sewing . . . again!

PART ONE

Scraps Plus One

CHAPTER 1

Scraps Plus One Inspiration

Inspiration is important. It's no surprise that the image of quilters gathered around a quilting frame has come to symbolize community.

A while back, I visited New York City to see the quilt show Infinite Variety: Three Centuries of Red and White Quilts presented by the American Folk Art Museum at the Park Avenue Armory. As I walked through the show, I made several pertinent observations. Many of the quilts were quite simple, two colors only: red and white. Patterns were basic, but not one was boring. If you think about it, some of the most common quilts are made from simple blocks, like a nine-patch or a four-patch. Add triangles and these blocks become stars or pinwheels. The more complex-looking quilts in the show were also inviting: The complexity was offset by the comfort of just two colors used to make the design.

As a casual observer, I was repeatedly struck by one thing as I took in quilt after quilt around the show floor: Many of the quilts were made several decades ago, and extraordinarily, each one looked as if it could have been created recently by any number of today's contemporary quilt designers. The quilts have been well preserved, for certain, but more important, the designs themselves were clean and timeless. Blocks were sewn in simple settings with uncomplicated border treatments, many without borders at all. Pieced and appliquéd samples were equally represented.

Armed with these observations, I started thinking, what if, in making a two-color quilt like a red and white quilt, one of the colors was replaced with scraps? So, a single-color fabric, red for example, plus light-value scraps would make an interesting combination. And vice versa: Choose a design and replace the color red with a variety of scraps, then pair the scraps with yardage in a neutral color, like white, cream, gray, tan, or black. So, there's the premise for the projects that follow. Scrap fabrics plus one "something else" provides the theme.

WHAT'S THE BIG IDEA?

So now you know that the "one" is the element that helps your scraps work together. Let's mix it up and dig a little further into what the "something else" might be.

And while you're at it, don't be afraid to take the blocks right to the edge of the quilt. Clean lines and a contemporary finish puts the focus on the simplicity or complexity of the quilt block elements. However, if making a quilt without a border makes you uncomfortable, go ahead and add one. Make the quilt top as directed, then take it to your stash or to the quilt shop to audition border options. Depending on how wide you want the border, 1 yard or 2 yards will usually be just the ticket. It's never too late to tweak the design direction, unless, of course, the quilt is quilted, bound, and labeled!

SCRAPS PLUS ONE COLOR

Picking the color is easy. Dig in your stash or head to the quilt shop and find yourself a nice chunk of color fabric. For example, **Prairie Porcelain**, on p. 74, started with 3½ yards of dark blue fabric. Then select scraps in a contrasting value to complete it—for Prairie Porcelain I used light-value scraps.

Prairie Porcelain quilt

For this category, it's important to start with yardage in a solid or solid-reading color. Big bold prints in yardage can get messy when paired with scraps in a variety of prints. If your color is solid, then your scraps can be a little more "printy." If your color is very printy, then be very careful that the scraps you choose read solid and are very similar in value to each other. Too many prints next to each other can get muddy and confusing.

SCRAPS PLUS ONE NEUTRAL

I love pairing scraps with white solid background fabric! Against it, almost every scrap fabric in my collection is darker and therefore contrasts more, so even a creamy scrap with a little calico print will show up when sewn next to white. It is so much easier to sort through my scraps knowing any scrap will stand up against my background fabric. The **Flower Bed** quilt, on p. 40, is a good example of using a white or cream background fabric plus scraps.

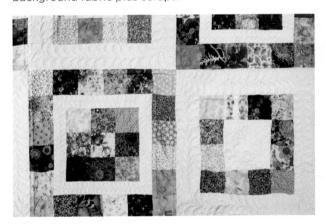

Flower Bed quilt

The same argument can be used for black. Almost every scrap, even if it's a dark fabric with a little print, will stand out against a solid black. Notice the use of black fabric in the **Sweet Revenge** quilt, on p. 102.

Choosing a neutral that is somewhere in between only means that you may want to avoid scraps that are of similar value to the neutral. Don't shy away from color, it's very trendy to pair color with scraps—tan, chocolate brown, blue, red, green, and gold all are fair game. As stated earlier, I tend to favor solid-reading neutrals and colors over prints that will be paired with scraps.

SCRAPS PLUS ONE FOCUS PRINT

Choose a focus print. Maybe it's for the border, maybe it's used for the block background, as in the quilt **From Little Acorns**, on p. 56. As a general rule, choose big bold prints for borders and small-scale toss prints for construction elements, but that's not a hard-and-fast rule.

Some scrappy quilts just need a solid color to calm them down, like the **Basket Case** quilt, on p. 36. The light gray inner border is a calm, solid color. When making the sample, I tried using more white fabric instead of the gray, and it made the quilt look like scraps in a snowstorm. And a repeat of the focus bold print for the inner border was just hideous.

Most often, when I choose a focus print, it becomes the border, and the scraps are selected to coordinate. That's perhaps the traditional way to use a focus print.

SCRAPS PLUS 1 YARD

You see it; you love it; you buy it. One yard, please. Now what? Maybe that yard is four fat quarters that coordinate. Or maybe you've had a terrible week and a trip to the quilt shop is in order, and all you want is a yard of fabric to lift your spirits. Have you overbought for a mystery quilt? Got a yard left? However that fabric got into your stash, seems to me it might be nice to add some scraps to make it interesting and call it good. The toddler-size **Magic Carpet** quilt, on p. 92, uses 1 yard of fabric, plus scraps.

Basket Case quilt

SCRAPS PLUS ONE FAT QUARTER

Sometimes I think the fat quarter fairy visits my stash and leaves gifts. How else did all those fat quarters get there? It's a mystery. Take one fat quarter, add scrap fabrics, and make it into something. What fun! The **Magic Carpet** table runner, on p. 92, for example, needs only scraps and one fat quarter.

Magic Carpet quilt

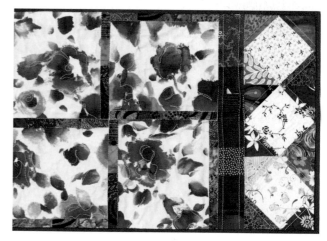

Magic Carpet table runner

SCRAPS PLUS ONE SHAPE

A square? A triangle? A circle? What's your shape? Scraps can do anything. Just look at the **Friendship Bread Runner**, on p. 116, for an example of triangles gone wild. For more triangle play, **Miracle Max**, on p. 30, takes nine patches made from square scraps and turns them into giant triangles for an end result that looks like nothing but triangles upon triangles. If squares are your thing, perhaps **Flower Bed**, on p. 40, or **Beach Blanket Bingo**, on p. 172, is just for you.

Beach Blanket Bingo quilt

SCRAPS PLUS ONE BLOCK

Take the nine-patch concept further and build a nine-patch within a nine-patch, using scraps and only one other color, and you can make something like **99 Bottles**, on p. 62. Four-patches, same idea. One block doesn't have to be repetitive or boring. Your scraps make each and every block unique and creative.

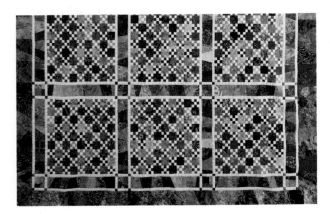

99 Bottles quilt

SCRAPS PLUS ONE NOTION

Sewing squares together can get boring. Sewing small 2-in. squares together can get boring *and* challenging. Tools and notions make the task more accurate, more efficient, more interesting, and more fun. Interfacing, trimming tools, scissors, and writing instruments are some of my favorites to make sewing scraps in all three sizes more efficient. For example, **Georgia's Garden**, on p. 121, uses fusible materials to make the scrappy pieced strips.

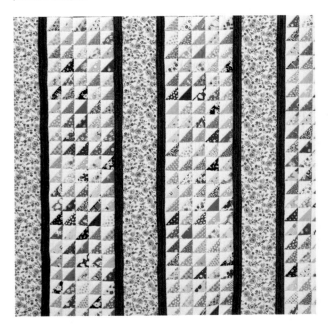

Georgia's Garden quilt

SCRAPS PLUS ONE SIZE

Basket Case, on p. 36, starts with nothing but 5-in. scrap fabric squares. No 2-in. scraps. No 3½-in. scraps. That means the pattern can be easily adapted for purchased pre-cut 5-in. squares. Believe it or not, the same is true for **Georgia's Garden**, on p. 121; all you need is 5-in. scraps to make this triangle-crammed quilt. **Flower Bed**, on p. 40, and the **Chruściki Tote**, on p. 164, both use 3½-in. scraps exclusively.

REENERGIZE AND RESTART

Everybody gets distracted sometimes. Even your favorite pastime can take a backseat to life's little ups and downs. Those scraps, organized and ready to sew, can get pushed aside for another day. And yet, the box waits, sending a message just by its presence in the sewing room on the shelf. Or maybe the scraps remain, wadded and tangled, in a bag. All good intentions to cut them up cast aside, just for a moment or two. The guilt persists. Let's face it, the scraps aren't going to sew themselves up into something warm and wonderful! If your fabric scraps are going to become something, other than a box of scraps, it's up to you to roll up your sleeves and dig in. Or the box of scraps will stay a box of scraps.

If you haven't touched your scraps in a while, maybe it's time to freshen things up a bit. It's hard to stay motivated when the same old dog-eared scraps keep surfacing. Challenge yourself to turn over some of the older scraps that don't seem to go with one quilt or another. Let the scraps in your bin determine the theme for your next quilt.

Bottom line—it all comes down to the person in the mirror. Scrappy quilts don't have to be scrappy. They don't have to be massive and intimidating. They don't need to be perfect.

In my mind, variety keeps the scrap quilter—or any hobbyist—excited and motivated. And variety is right in the palm of your hands. And in your scrap bins!

THE 2-IN. PROBLEM

I am guilty! I have stopped cutting 2-in. scrap squares. There, I have said it. I can't use them fast enough! And they started to take over my bins. It makes sense that I have more leftovers that are small and skinny that yield 2-in. scrap squares. Think of how many times you are left with only a small strip of fabric after the fabric is cut and used in a quilt. Now what?

Add one more bin to your collection of cut-up scraps. Keep odd lengths of 2-in. strips in that bin. Just as I consider that the 5-in. scrap square is a storage unit for four 2$\frac{1}{2}$-in. scrap squares, the 2-in. strips are storage units for future 2-in. scrap squares. When making a quilt that requires 2-in. scraps, go first to your cut squares and select what you need to coordinate with the theme. If you can't find enough that are already cut, then go to the 2-in. strips and start cutting from those. Truth be known, my strip bin also has a stack of 2$\frac{1}{2}$-in. strips. Like the 5-in. square, the strips are storage units for 2$\frac{1}{2}$-in. squares, too.

Several years ago, working with Quiltsmart®, Inc., I developed the ScrapTherapy Small Scrap Grid printed fusible interfacing. Specifically it was designed to be used for the really scrappy border on Bloomin' Steps, a quilt project in my first book. I have continued to recommend using the grid for additional projects that require 2-in. scrap squares. **Georgia's Garden**, on p. 121, and **Magic Carpet**, on p. 92, are projects that use the grid in a couple of different ways. While the grid interfacing isn't required to make any of the projects for which it is recommended, it makes sewing the small pieces easier, more fun, and more accurate.

THE TRUTH OF THE MATTER

Now that you have a better idea of the basis for the projects that follow, I have something to confess: I cheat. But it's usually for a good reason.

Some of the quilts combine concepts. Some are just plain nice quilts, and I had to include them, just to share. The quilts and patterns are meant to be idea starters. The concepts are available to explore further.

While I fully plan to stay within the parameters I have set—scraps plus one other element—you may find an exception or two in the quilt projects. I hope you forgive me.

By the way, you can cheat, too! It's your quilt, after all.

CHAPTER 2
The Seven Steps Revisited

STEP ONE: GETTING STARTED

Before getting swept away with the quilt projects in Part Two, a review of the seven steps used in my first book to cut, store, and use scraps seems in order. These steps walk you through the process of preparing your fabric, defining a theme for your project, and making it happen. Does every scrappy quilt project need to follow these steps? Of course not! But having a process keeps you focused and headed down a sensible path. This works particularly well when you are faced with a heap of messy scrap fabrics and have a hankerin' to make something of it. So, here we go.

It has been said that knowing that you have a problem is the first step in solving it. I'm not suggesting that any part of quilting is a "problem." The ScrapTherapy pattern series started as a result of my issues with unused scrap fabrics in my own stash, stored away in my basement. You shouldn't have issues associated with a hobby that you love to do.

When I started quilting, I kept several shoe box–size clear plastic bins full of fabric scraps—pieces of fabric, strips, half strips, quarter strips, rectangles, triangles, you name it. The bins were stored, out of the way, unseen on the bottom shelf in a dark corner of the basement. Leftovers from hundreds of quilts and samples created in less than 10 years of quilting experience. The bins were rarely touched. I wasn't using what I had and ran to the quilt shop to purchase a fat quarter or a yard or two of fabric when a piece of scrap fabric would have been fine.

Stored away in all those bins in the basement were treasured memories of quilts I made and had given away, commemorating a variety of life's passages like graduations, weddings, and births.

It made me cringe to think that someday, someone might be digging through my stash without me. They would wonder, "What did she have in mind for all this?" And it also drove me over the edge thinking that someone else might be using my favorite pieces of cloth—my memories, my investment! Yes, I am very selfish when it comes to my fabric stash. If I bought it, I oughta be using it!

So when I headed to a quilt retreat weekend with some friends, I brought those bins out of my basement. I cut for much of the first day of the retreat. I cut until I had lots of scraps stored right back in those shoe box–size bins, now neatly cut and ready to sew. Plenty to choose from in each size.

Once I had enough to choose from, I pulled out some background fabric from my stash, added a few specialty rulers, and started to work. By the end of the evening I had assembled four blocks into a small baby-size quilt, using background, accent fabric, a border, and of course, my scraps. Every thread of fabric came from my stash, and it looked great. And I felt terrific. I was on to something.

STEP TWO: CUT!

Now that you've decided to begin, where do you start? First and foremost, don't decide that you will change your habits overnight. Small steps and manageable goals will keep you on track. Rewards along the way are key. Next, keep it simple. I propose cutting your scraps into just three square sizes that store easily and play well together. And finally, cut more scraps than you need for the next project, so you can pick and choose scraps that go with your theme as you build your scrappy quilt.

DEFINE "SCRAP"

Everyone will have his or her own definition of what constitutes a scrap piece of fabric. While there are exceptions to every rule, and the rule of thumb may vary from one person to the next and from one piece of fabric to another, for me, it's a scrap if the piece of fabric is less than $1/4$ yard by width of fabric—9 in. by 42 in. Usually, my fabric scraps are much smaller than that—leftovers from a fabric strip, an extra rectangle or square, odd shapes remaining from mitered borders, and long, skinny strips of backing leftovers. These pieces are tossed into a basket as I work on the latest quilt project. In between projects, pull the leftovers from the basket and replenish my scrap bins with fresh-cut scraps. That way I always have new scrap squares replacing the ones I use. It's an ongoing cycle.

In my mind, if the leftover fabric is more than $1/4$ yard and is completely intact, it goes back into the stash to wait its turn as cornerstones, a small border, an accent fabric for blocks, or one of many more possibilities. My stash also has dedicated space for fat quarters (18 in. by 21 in.) and large, but odd-shaped fabrics—usually leftovers from backings. Running yardage is stored on several shelves, folded edge out for easy access.

THE RIGHT STUFF

Here's a list of tools you'll want to have on hand for your cutting session:

STRAIGHT EDGE RULER
Any straight edge acrylic ruler used for quilting will work. Consider a ruler that has strong, distinct vertical lines typically used to cut strips with dimensions shown clearly in whole and half inches. It's not about any one brand of ruler, it's about how comfortable you are with its accuracy and speed to get the job done. My favorite ruler sizes to use are 6 in. by 12 in., 4 in. by 14 in., and 6 in. by 6 in.—or in those size neighborhoods.

SEE-THROUGH STORAGE BINS
Shoe box–size bins allow the cut-up scraps to be stored neatly in stacks. See-through makes it easy to find colors later. Although plastic bins aren't optimum for long-term fabric storage, our goal is to use the scraps, not *store* the scraps for the long haul.

ROTATING CUTTING MAT
A 12-in. rotating cutting mat has an even cutting surface that turns or rotates. Because the surface turns easily, cutting is fast and accurate, plus its size makes it portable for cutting sessions on the go!

ROTARY CUTTER AND FRESH BLADE, 45 MM
A fresh blade at the beginning of a big cutting session makes the job so much more pleasant and allows you to cut through more layers of scraps with confidence and accuracy. To avoid fabrics that shift, don't cut more than six layers of fabric at a time.

VINYL FABRIC STRIP GUIDE
I like to use Qtools™ Cutting Edge and Sewing Edge. These orange and purple vinyl strips help make cutting fast and accurate. Put a strip on the bottom of the ruler, precisely on the cutting measurement line—orange for smooth bottom rulers, and purple for rulers with a rough or frosted finish. The orange vinyl clings to smooth surfaces, the purple vinyl sticks with a light adhesive to the ruler without leaving residue, and the thickness creates a guide that stops the ruler at the edge of the fabric and makes the cutting process nearly thought free.

LIQUID SPRAY STARCH ALTERNATIVE
If your scraps have long-term creases and wrinkles, spray a small amount of spray starch alternative on the fabric, then iron out the wrinkles, without leaving starchy stiffness.

SCRAPTHERAPY SIZES

Gather your cutting tools and from the basket of fabrics to cut, pull out a small clump of scrap fabric. Grab just one handful without being selective about size, color, or value. We'll discuss sorting later. Go to your ironing board and press each scrap neatly, and make a stack of ready-to-cut fabrics near your cutting area. Make sure they are in the way so you are motivated to clear them out. A short 10-minute or 15-minute cutting session should do it.

The ScrapTherapy sizes are 2-in., 3½-in., and 5-in. squares. Every ScrapTherapy quilted project starts with scraps cut into one, two, or all three of these sizes. Why these sizes? The logic starts with squares—not strips, not triangles.

The 5-in. scrap size was the first one I decided on; it's a versatile size with lots of potential. Next, came the 2-in. size, because a 2-in. square was about as small a piece of fabric that I wanted to fuss with, in terms of stacking and storing. If I needed a smaller scrap piece, I could always trim it down, as you'll see in the **99 Bottles** quilt, on p. 62.

It felt like a size in between the two was missing. Then, doing a little math, I realized that a 2-in. scrap will finish to 1½ in. (subtract ½ in. for seam allowances). A

four-patch made from 2-in. scrap squares will finish to 3 in. (1½ in. + 1½ in. = 3 in.), which is 3½ in. unfinished. That's how 3½ in. became the third ScrapTherapy size.

Storing these sizes is easy, because they fit nicely into the shoe box–size see-through bins. Two stacks of 5-in. scrap squares fit perfectly into one bin. Three stacks of 3½-in. plus five stacks of 2-in. scraps fit very well into a second bin.

The three ScrapTherapy sizes make sense, because they play well together; it's as simple as that. Quick quilts appear like magic from your scrap bins when you sew four-patches from the 2-in. scraps and then sew them alternately with 3½-in. scrap squares. Likewise, nine-patches made from 2-in. scrap squares can be sewn alternately with 5-in. squares. Quite by accident, I recently determined that nine-patches made with 3½-in. scraps are the same size as four-patches made with 5-in. scraps. Now, why didn't I discover that sooner?

PALMING THE RULER

Many quilting classes teach us to place the ruler on the mat with thumb and three fingers on the ruler and the pinky just off the edge of the ruler holding the ruler from slipping. Add a little pressure during an extended cutting session, and your fingers are going to be tired, creating the potential for the ruler to shift while cutting. Instead, consider forming a new habit.

Place your hand on the ruler as shown in photo 3 on the facing page, then drop your palm onto the surface of the ruler. Immediately, you'll notice the pressure on your hands and fingers is much more comfortable and the energy to hold the ruler in place comes from your shoulder rather than the muscles in your fingers and hands. You'll find that you tire less quickly and therefore can extend your cutting sessions.

CUTTING 5-INCH SQUARES

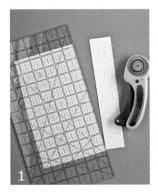

CUTTING TIPS

Cutting scraps can be a little different from cutting from yardage. For starters, the pieces are often smaller. Many scraps don't have a straight, trued-up edge. And the grain may not be as easily identified if the selvages are gone. As you cut, you'll find your own efficiencies to reduce effort and increase efficiency. Here are a few tips I find helpful when I cut my scraps:

- Try to avoid cutting fabric squares with bias edges. Hold an odd-shaped fabric in front of a light source or a window to identify the horizontal and vertical lines in the fabric weave.

- Cut multiple layers at once, but try not to cut more than six layers at a time.

- Select fabrics randomly and try not to sort by color or print at this stage.

- Sort fabrics into three stacks as they are cut, one stack for each size.

- Cut the largest size possible from each scrap. Larger scrap squares can always be cut down if needed.

CUTTING 5-IN. SQUARES

For a scrap that will become a 5-in. square, make a fresh cut a little more than 5 in. away from one raw edge. **1**

Turn the fabric 180 degrees (or use a rotating cutting mat and you won't have to disturb your newly cut fabric) and then make a parallel cut exactly 5 in. away from the first cut, using the lines on the ruler, not the lines on the cutting mat. You can see how using the orange (or purple) vinyl strips can make this step easier. **2**

Then turn the fabric (or rotating mat) a quarter turn, make the third cut perpendicular to the first two cuts and a little more than 5 in. away from the raw edge, while lining up the first two cuts with horizontal ruler lines that are 5 in. away from each other. **3**

Turn the fabric (or mat) one last 180-degree turn and make the final cut to make the 5-in. square. **4**

Cutting seems to work hand in hand with sorting, which not so coincidentally leads us to the third step.

IT'S OKAY TO THROW AWAY

What if a scrap is smaller than 2 in.? I'm here to tell you, it's okay to throw it away. Notice the careful choice of words, it's *okay* to throw away, not you *must* throw away. If you aren't convinced, get a gallon-size zipper-sealing plastic bag. Using a permanent marker, write the current month and year on the bag and place all the small pieces in the bag, starting a new one each month. Stow the bags in a specific place in your stash. In one year, if you have not used the scraps from the bags, *it's okay to throw them away!*

STEP THREE: SORT

Sort your cut fabric scraps by value or type of collection so they are ready to use and easy to find. I like to compare how I sort my scraps to how I sort laundry—darks, lights, and everything else.

For each mini cutting session, I arrange three short stacks at my cutting station. One small stack for each size. Once the cutting session is done, the stacks get placed in the scrap bins by size. But that's not all. As I cut, I also sort, not necessarily by color, but by value. Why? I try to stay mindful of the next step. When I'm cutting, I'm evaluating how I might use what I'm cutting. If it seems I have a growing pile of small scraps and I notice that as I cut, I make a mental note to make the next project heavy in the 2-in. scrap department. It's the same with values.

VALUE

What is value? Lots of quilters have difficulty determining value. For purposes of filling the scrap bins, dark generally means the scrap piece is darker than 90 percent of the rest of your scraps—dark, dark blues; deep, rich purples; blacks with just a bit of print in them. Conversely, light scraps are lighter in value than 90 percent of everything else—white-on-white prints, white with bits of print, pale yellows, pinks, and blues.

Then there's everything else. Simply put, if a scrap is not dark and not light, it falls into the "everything else" category, or medium value. Brights nearly always fall into the everything else category.

When sewing scrap fabrics next to each other in a scrap quilt, it's important that the value is different. Sometimes it's not enough that the color is different; the value also needs to contrast for the pattern to stand out.

As I place cut scraps into the bins, I have a separate bin for extreme dark scraps and extreme light fabrics; these are separate from the everything else, or the medium-value, scraps, which make up the bulk of my scrap collection. The values are determined as I cut.

A LITTLE EACH DAY

Make a little bit of cutting part of your daily sewing routine. At first, I thought I'd have bins and bins of cut-up scraps stacked to the ceiling. But you seem to reach a happy quantity and the bins wax and wane in fullness. I now have four bins of everything else scraps that I draw from. When those bins start looking a little thin, I make cutting a higher priority. I have a few other bins with themed fabrics I use a lot, like batiks, 1930s, and contemporary prints. Plus I have a bin of each size for extreme lights and darks. Once you generate a healthy stack of neatly cut and sorted scrap fabrics in a variety of values and prints, it's nearly time to start sewing!

STEP FOUR: SELECT A THEME

I've said it before, I'll say it again: I don't like scrap quilts! I don't like weird combinations of fabrics that feel forced together. Just because it's a scrappy project, doesn't mean it can't be cohesive. My solution: determine a theme for the quilt, then select the scraps according to that theme. The theme will be the common thread that pulls all the elements of the project together. Now, that's a scrap quilt I can fall in love with!

CHOOSING A THEME

When you start thinking about your next scrappy project, selecting the theme for that project usually falls into one of four broad categories.

FOLLOW YOUR HEART

See a ScrapTherapy pattern that you love? Make it happen—it's as simple as that. Follow the color scheme and value suggestions and select scraps, background fabrics, and focus prints suggested. Your quilt will be unique to you because it will have your favorite scraps and fabric pieces, but it will look similar to the photograph in the book.

USE WHAT YOU HAVE

Stand back and take a look at your scraps. What kind of fabrics do you have in excess? For example, have you been making lots of baby quilts lately, generating a ton of baby prints in your scrap bins? Consider making a kid-oriented pattern and have that baby quilt ready before the baby shower announcement! It's easy to turn scrap overkill into over-the-top quilt treasures and move those out-of-control scraps out of your scrap bins!

USE WHAT YOU WANT

I just love blue and purple! When I buy fabric, I almost always go heavy on blue and purple prints. That means many of my non-scrappy quilts are blue, which in turn means blue scraps are always at my fingertips. What to do? Make blue scrappy quilts, of course!

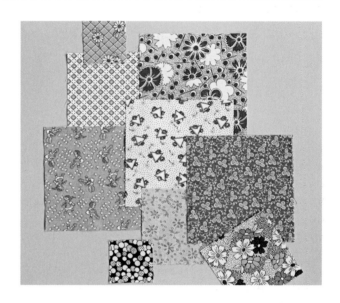

THEME BINS

You may find as you are cutting your stash that there's a recurring theme happening. Let's say every time you reach in to start a new batch to cut, you pull out some holiday-themed prints. Maybe you need separate bins, for all three sizes, for fabric themes. That way, if you decide to work on a scrappy holiday project, for example, you don't have to sort through everything just to find the holiday fabrics.

MAKE A TEST BLOCK

Once a theme is decided and scraps are selected, make a sample block. Place your test block on a design wall and stand back and take a good look at it from more than a few feet away. Does the block work? Do the mediums hold up against the lights and darks or the background fabrics? If they do, carry on and make more blocks. If they don't, the completion of one block is the best time to reconsider scrap selections.

It's so easy to get caught up in the excitement of seeing your first quilt block coming together. Try not to wait until all of the quilt blocks are done before you step back and evaluate. Often the original test block can still be included in the quilt, even though fabric selection for the remaining blocks is tweaked a little bit.

These two blocks are made entirely from scraps. One works well; the other one, not so much.

What's your favorite color? If you have a lot of one color or type of fabric print, don't worry about selecting the focus print, typically used for the border, right away. Make a few blocks within your favorite theme, then take the blocks to the stash or the quilt shop to "audition" some focus or main-player fabric selections.

LET THE FABRIC DECIDE

When using what you have and using what you want, the focus print or theme might be decided after several blocks are constructed based on what the blocks look like. Another approach starts with selecting the focus print or inspiration fabric, the fabric that is usually reserved for the border, and then selecting the scrap fabrics around the colors predominant in that print.

If you are out and about, and happen to stop into a quilt shop, do you ever see a focus print that speaks to you? The next thing you know, it's going home with you. When that happens, build a scrappy quilt around it. Why fight it? Some of the best projects can be inspired by the colors in the main-player and accent fabrics—even if you don't use the fabric in the quilt.

STEP FIVE: USE TRADITIONAL TECHNIQUES AND TRY ALTERNATIVES

All the patterns in this book can be made with basic quilting supplies. Some patterns may suggest alternatives to more traditional methods, incorporating updated processes and tools to make the construction simpler, faster, or more efficient. With so many options available to you, choose the method, tool, or gadget that works best for you. This is a hobby, after all, and it's supposed to be fun!

GOTTA LOVE GADGETS

I love gadgets and sewing notions. If a tool makes a time-honored technique more accurate or simpler, it's a winner! Scrap quilts lend themselves especially well to testing and using the latest sewing notions. Because sewing small fabric scraps can sometimes become tedious, the infusion of sewing notions change up familiar methods, refresh standard techniques, and improve results.

TRIMMING TOOLS

Trimming tools are rulers with a specific job. Most quilters have a 6-in. or 7-in. square ruler with a bias line. These lined square rulers are the most-used trimming tool in my sewing room.

Some trimming tools have a more specific, single-purpose use like trimming half-square and quarter-square triangle units, on-point square block elements, and flying geese units.

As you contemplate a trimming tool purchase, consider the added value you'll have from using that tool in multiple projects and for trimming block units in a variety of sizes.

FUSIBLES

Printed fusible interfacing and fusible web can add ease and stability to a variety of scrap sewing projects. Fusible interfacing is available with a variety of printed grids, patterns, and appliqué shapes and comes unprinted as well.

Fusible web is a favorite for machine appliquérs. However, it also makes a quick and easy stabilizer. Fusible web usually comes with protective paper on one or both sides of the actual adhesive. When applying, be sure to follow the manufacturer's instructions for the specific brand you're using.

FINISHING TECHNIQUES

When you're looking for a special border or finish, such as piping or scallops around a quilt edge, the Piping Hot Binding tool and Katie's Scallop Radial Rules™ are examples of tools that help simplify formerly elusive techniques.

THE "BEST" TECHNIQUE OF ALL

Quilting is *your* hobby. The best gadget in the world for me might be the worst gadget for you. Just because all your friends have it, you don't have to. Quilting creates an opportunity to choose from multiple methods and tools to complete almost any task. I like to try new techniques, notions, and gadgets, but sometimes the tried-and-true methods are the best.

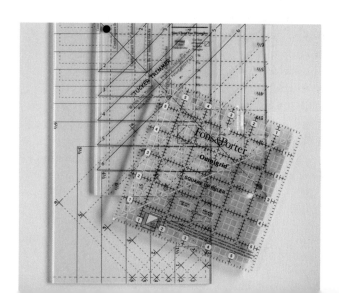

STEP SIX: PIECE AND SEW

As you sew your scraps together, keep this short list of tips in mind to help you make assembling your ScrapTherapy projects fun and problem free.

SCANT VERSUS TRUE ¼-IN. SEAMS

Most quilts are sewn together using a scant ¼-in. seam allowance, which is just one or two thread widths shy of a true ¼-in. seam allowance. Many sewing machines have a ¼-in. foot for piecing quilts. As you sew, be sure to place the fabrics right sides together with raw edges aligned. Piecing accuracy starts by aligning your fabrics properly. The machine needle should enter the aligned fabric pieces just a little bit less than ¼-in. away from the aligned raw edges for a scant ¼-in. seam allowance.

CHAIN PIECING

Chain piecing is sewing two pieces of fabric together, taking two or three stitches off the edge, then sewing the next set of fabric pieces together. Cut the stitches in between, and press the seams as needed.

Because ScrapTherapy projects work with smaller fabric pieces, not strips, chain piecing is a logical sewing strategy. Sew a test block first, so any piecing issues or light–dark value questions are worked out. Once you're satisfied with the test block, sew multiple blocks using the chain-piecing technique.

TRUING UP FINISHED BLOCKS

Simply put, I don't like to trim finished blocks. Instead, I troubleshoot the problem and make adjustments to the construction steps. The problem almost always comes down to one of three issues: cutting, seam allowance, or pressing.

Take a close look at the block, first, from the front of the block. Are block parts the correct size? Turn the block over. Are there any obvious out of shape pieces? Gently unpress some of the seams with your fingers. Measure the size of the cut pieces. Were the fabric pieces cut the correct size?

Check your seams. One seam that is too small or too big isn't really a big deal. But several seams that are off can be a real problem. Think about it. If a quilt block has seams consistently sewn too small, resulting in a block that is off by ¼ in., then it takes only four blocks sewn together in a row for the quilt to be off by a whole inch!

Finally, check the pressing. Place your fingernail right up against the seam. Does the tip of your nail disappear under an extra little flap in the seam? Are the seams stretched so piecing threads are showing?

Try making the block again, testing each unit size at each step. And, if you follow these steps, and sleuth out what's creating the inaccuracy, it won't be necessary to true up the final block. I promise!

When trimming block elements like half-square triangles, be sure to trim all four sides. Place the unit on your cutting mat, line up seams with the chosen trimming tool or ruler, and cut one or two sides, usually along the side and across the top. Then rotate the partially trimmed unit 180 degrees, line up the chosen trimming tool or ruler with the appropriate seams, and trim the remaining two sides. Work carefully when trimming across the top of the ruler.

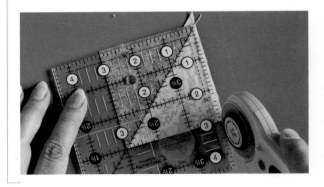

A TEST SEAM

A scant ¹/₄-in. seam accommodates the thickness of the fabric as the seam is pressed to one side. To be completely confident of your seam accuracy, try a test seam using scraps from your bin.

Align and sew two 2-in. scrap squares. Press the seam to one side. For the best results, make the extra effort to press the seam with an iron instead of finger-pressing. Place the pressed scrap two-patch on your ruler. It should be exactly 2 in. by 3¹/₂ in.

If the test two-patch is larger than 3¹/₂ in., your seam allowance is too small. Move the needle farther away from the edge of the fabric to make a larger seam allowance. If the test two-patch is less than 3¹/₂ in. wide, then your seam allowance is too big. Move the needle closer to the edge of the fabric to make a narrower seam allowance.

Continue making test two-patches until you have accurate results—or until you run out of 2-in. scrap squares!

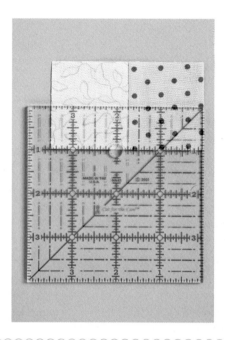

STEP SEVEN: FINISH THE QUILT

Some quilters enjoy the piecing, but not the quilting. Some prefer hand quilting or tying to hold the layers together. Choose your preference and get the job done! Consider these finishing elements as you complete your project.

BACKING

Whether you quilt your project yourself or hire someone else to do it, all quilts need backing. As you work with it, the backing should be roughly 4 in. to 6 in. larger than the quilt top in each direction.

Most of the quilts in this book require that you piece the backing with at least two sections, assuming a standard 42-in. usable fabric width. You can avoid the math and the seams by using extra-wide backing fabrics, which are between 108 in. and 110 in. wide.

Backing yardage calculations are provided for each quilt. If the backing needs to be seamed, cut the yardage length in half (4 yards becomes two 2-yard pieces), and trim the selvage off one side of each backing fabric piece. Sew a ¹/₄-in. seam along the cut lengthwise edge and press the seam open. For better wear, avoid having a seam directly in the center of the quilt back. To avoid a center seam on the backing, piece the backing in three sections: one half becomes the center, and the other half of the backing is cut in half lengthwise.

A three-piece backing.

Sew each narrow backing piece to the full-width fabric piece with the selvages removed.

LAYERING AND BASTING

The following steps assume that the quilt will be machine quilted on a standard home machine. The layering and basting process can be different, depending on the quilting method, such as hand quilting or long- or short-arm quilting on a frame.

Layering and pin-basting may seem tedious, but it's a critical step in the quilting process. With your work of art so close to being finished, it's easy to short-change these important steps; try to avoid that temptation.

SANDWICHING

Once the backing is seamed and pressed, firmly secure the flat backing, right side down, to a large work surface. Use residue-free adhesive tape, such as painter's tape, to secure the backing to the work surface.

Center the batting on the backing and smooth it with your hands from the center out until it's completely flat. Avoid the temptation to trim the batting at this stage.

Place the quilt top, right side up, on top of the batting. Starting in the center and working outward, smooth out any wrinkles, puckers, and folds. Rough-cut the batting layer 1 in. to 2 in. beyond the quilt top's edges.

PIN-BASTING

Beginning at one corner of the quilt center, place curved safety pins through all three layers of the quilt.

Place pins 2 in. to 3 in. apart. Once the quilt center is pinned, pin the borders. When the entire top is pin-basted, remove the tape from all four sides of the quilt backing. If there is enough extra backing material, fold the backing edge over the raw edges of the quilt to protect them from fraying during the quilting process. Pin the fold to the edge of the quilt through all layers with another series of curved safety pins. Don't be surprised if you use several hundred pins to baste a twin-size quilt.

QUILT AS DESIRED

For some quilters, *quilt as desired* are the three most dreaded words in pattern instructions. I say, "Bring it on!" If you have a walking foot or an integrated

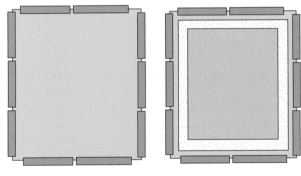

Secure the backing to the work surface.

Place the quilt top, right side up, on top of the batting.

dual-feed foot, you can easily machine quilt your own project on a standard sewing machine. With a little practice and a darning foot, you can add some free-motion quilting. Or walk away from the sewing machine and do some hand quilting.

QUILTING ON A STANDARD SEWING MACHINE

Machine quilting can be fast and fun, but sometimes intimidating. Machine quilting classes at your local quilt shop can help you hone your skills. Excellent instructional DVDs and online videos are also available. However, the best way to improve your machine quilting skills is experience. Roll up your sleeves and dive in! Look for more tips for machine quilting on p. 187.

HAND QUILTING

Hand quilting is traditional, beautiful, relaxing, and perfectly suited for scrappy quilts. Hand quilting can be done with or without hoops and frames. Seek out a local hand-quilting expert and take some classes to perfect this time-tested skill.

TIED QUILTS

Tied quilts offer another classic effect perfectly suited to scrappy projects. To tie a quilt, use yarn or heavy thread (like pearl cotton) to make the ties. The finished knots can be on the right or wrong side of the quilt, depending on your preference.

Thread a needle with the yarn or thread and insert it straight into the quilt from the side on which you want

the finished knots. Leave about a 2-in.-long tail. Take a small stitch and bring the thread back up through all the layers. Tie off in a square knot.

Ties should be no more than 3 in. to 4 in. apart across the quilt surface. After the tying is complete, clip all thread tails evenly to about $3/4$ in. long.

BINDING

When all the quilting is done, it's time to encase the raw edges of the quilt with binding.

To prepare the binding, cut the recommended number of $2^1/4$-in.-wide binding strips. All the projects in this book assume cross-grain binding cuts. Bias binding may be substituted for a different look and for a more stretchy binding, particularly nice when curved edges are involved. However, the yardage and number of cuts needed may vary slightly between cross grain and bias binding. Join the strips end to end using a diagonal seam. Fold the binding in half, wrong sides together.

Prepare the quilt for binding by trimming the batting and backing even with the quilt top's edges. Beginning along one straight side (never at the corner), sew the binding to the quilt with raw edges aligned. Miter the binding at each of the corners. Fold the binding over the quilt edge and sew the folded edge to the back of the quilt by hand. For additional instructions on binding your quilt, see p. 189.

LABEL

The label is the quilt's voice. Reach into your scrap bin for one more square of light-value fabric. Grab a

permanent fabric marking pen and a piece of fine-grain sandpaper. Place the fabric on the sandpaper for stability and jot down the important stuff!

Use the label to detail information about the quilt. Here are a few suggestions.

- The name of the quiltmaker
- The date the quilt was finished and how long it took to complete
- The pattern name, source, and designer
- City, state, country in which it was made
- Special care instructions, to accommodate batting fiber content or embellishments
- The occasion it commemorates

The label doesn't have to be complicated; all you need is a square, rectangle, or other shape and enough space to write. Jazz it up with embroidery, computer graphics, cross-stitch, or running stitches.

To sew the label to the back of the quilt, fold and press under a $1/4$-in. seam allowance around the edges, then pin the label in place with appliqué pins on a lower corner of the backing. Secure the label by hand using an appliqué stitch through the backing.

PICTURE THIS!

Only one more task needs to be completed before the quilt is officially and truly done. Before your quilt goes to the lucky recipient, take a picture of it and its label.

Why bother with a picture? One finished quilt leads to another, and you can easily forget the details associated with your quilts. A printed or digital photo is all you need to keep a record of your projects.

FINISHED SCRAP QUILTS

The beauty of scrap quilts is that no two are exactly alike. Two quilters digging into their own scrap bins to make the same exact pattern could end up making quilts that look wildly different from each other. And that's when the fun really begins!

PART TWO

Scraps Plus One Projects

Miracle Max

SCRAPS PLUS ONE WHITE-ON-WHITE PRINT

Because my inspiration for several of the projects in this book began with the American Folk Art Museum's Infinite Variety exhibit of red-and-white quilts, it seems appropriate that at least one quilt project in this collection is themed with red scraps on a white background.

Red and white fabric combinations create a very crisp, fresh-looking quilt, don't you think? I'm not sure why that is. Maybe it's the high contrast of the Turkey red (named after the place, not the bird) and stark white.

I like complicated blocks, and the blocks in this quilt incorporate lots of triangles, odd shapes, and half-square triangles that really shouldn't be trimmed after sewing. As you sew, beware of stretchy bias edges, and sew slowly and carefully. If you follow the steps and stay mindful of accurate cutting, seam allowances, and pressing, you should be in good shape.

FINISHED SIZE: **67 in. by 87 in.**
PATTERN DIFFICULTY: **Challenging**

SCRAP REQUIREMENTS:
$3^1/_2$-in. red scrap squares: 312
5-in. red scrap squares: 60
FABRIC AND NOTION REQUIREMENTS:
$4^1/_4$ yards white-on-white print for blocks and border
$^5/_8$ yard red print for binding
$5^1/_4$ yards for backing
72-in. by 92-in. batting
Half-square triangle ruler

NOTE: The half-square triangle ruler is a specialty tool used to cut half-square triangles from strips of fabric.

The quilt block features small pieces easily found within the ScrapTherapy sizes. But the bigger-size triangles in the block present a little problem. They are cut from fabric pieces that are nearly 8 in. square. But the largest ScrapTherapy size is 5 in. How do you make a small scrap bigger? Piece them together! Make nine-patches from randomly selected red $3^1/_2$-in. scraps, and then trim a little bit off. Voilà! Small scraps become bigger.

So, who is Miracle Max, and why name the quilt after him? Well, to paraphrase a line delivered by Miracle Max, the character played by Billy Crystal in the movie *The Princess Bride*, it just so happens that the scraps in this quilt are only *mostly* red. There's a big difference between *mostly* red and *all* red! *Wink, wink!*

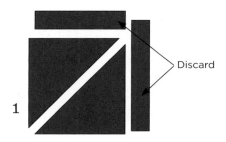

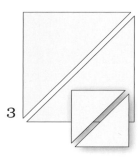

Discard

Furl

1

2

3

4

PREPARE THE SCRAPS

Select three hundred twelve $3\frac{1}{2}$-in. red scrap squares. From these scraps, select 216 for nine-patches that will become large half-square triangles (HSTs). Set aside.

Trim each of the remaining ninety-six $3\frac{1}{2}$-in. red scrap squares to $2\frac{7}{8}$-in. squares, then cut each $2\frac{7}{8}$-in. square in half diagonally to make 192 small red HSTs. **1**

Select sixty 5-in. red scrap squares. Cut each 5-in. square in half to make a total of one hundred twenty $2\frac{1}{2}$-in. by 5-in. rectangles for small red-and-white HST units. **2**

> It's not important that the red scraps match. Choose a wide range of reds, including prints that are mostly red. Light and dark value, large- and small-scale prints, and warm and cool variations of red are all acceptable.

PREPARE THE ADDITIONAL FABRICS

WHITE-ON-WHITE PRINT

Cut six $8\frac{7}{8}$-in. width-of-fabric strips; then cut twenty-four $8\frac{7}{8}$-in. squares for blocks. Cut each square in half diagonally to make 48 large HSTs. **3**

Cut eight $2\frac{7}{8}$-in. width-of-fabric strips; then cut ninety-six $2\frac{7}{8}$-in. squares for blocks. Cut each square in half diagonally to make 192 small white HSTs. **3**

Cut twelve $2\frac{1}{2}$-in. width-of-fabric strips for small red-and-white HST units.

Cut nine 4-in. width-of-fabric strips for borders.

MAKE THE BLOCKS

NINE-PATCHES

Randomly select nine $3\frac{1}{2}$-in. red scraps from the 216 you set aside for nine-patches. Arrange them in three rows of three scraps. Sew the scraps into rows. Press the seams as indicated. Sew the rows. Furl the seam intersections (shown with blue circles) so the seams rotate clockwise and counterclockwise around the seam intersection (see p. 180). **4**

> While it is not necessary to furl the seams in each nine-patch, furling reduces bulk significantly and makes the next steps in the quilt block assembly a bit more tidy.

Using a large square ruler, roughly center the middle nine-patch scrap, then trim the nine-patch to $8\frac{7}{8}$ in. square. Trim all four sides. Cut the trimmed nine-patch in half diagonally to make two large red HSTs. You should be trimming just a little more than $\frac{1}{4}$ in. off each side. **5** Repeat to make 24 scrappy nine-patches, which are cut into 48 large red HSTs. Set aside.

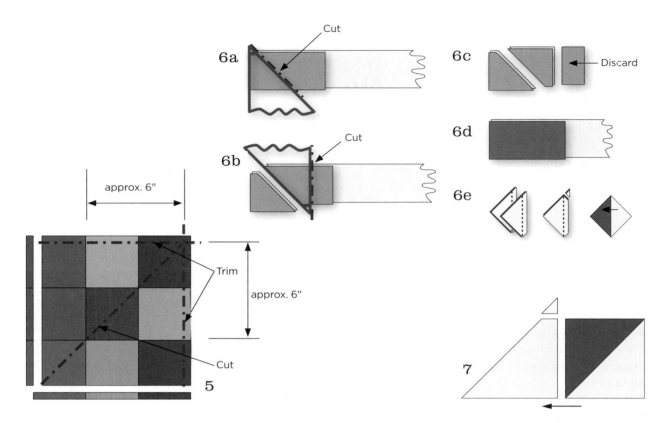

SMALL HST UNITS

Trim the selvage off one end of a white 2½-in. strip. Place the strip on the cutting mat, right side up. Randomly select one 2½-in. by 5-in. red scrap rectangle and place it right side down on top of the strip, aligning three edges. Using a HST ruler and cutting two layers at a time, cut one set of HSTs. **6a** Rotate the ruler, then cut a second set of HSTs. **6b** Discard the remainder of red scrap. **6c**

> Review the manufacturer's instructions for your HST ruler for how to cut HSTs that, once sewn into HST units, will finish to 2 in. square. Markings on these rulers vary from brand to brand.

Align a second red scrap rectangle with the cut edge of the white strip. **6d** Cut two more sets of HSTs, and discard the remainder of the red scraps. Repeat until all 120 red scrap rectangles have been cut into HSTs. Keep the layers together, and sew a scant ¼-in. seam allowance along the long edge of each triangle set. Trim the point; press the seam toward the red fabric. **6e**

Repeat to make 240 small red-and-white HST units that are 2½ in. square.

> To prevent the HST corners from jamming into the needle plate, sew the HST unit pointy end first. Then trim the little triangular dog-ear to reduce bulk before pressing the seam allowance.

TOP CORNERS

Sew one small white HST to one side of a red-and-white HST unit, as shown. Press the seam toward the white HST. Repeat to make 48 top corner units. **7** Trim the point on the white HST to reduce bulk, if desired.

> **Be careful!** Make sure you orient your scraps exactly as shown in the illustrations. It's very easy to get mixed up and have triangles turned the wrong way.

BOTTOM CORNERS

Sew one small red HST to one side of a red-and-white HST unit, as shown. Press the seam toward the red HST. Repeat to make 48 bottom corner units. **8** Trim the point on the red HST to reduce bulk, if desired.

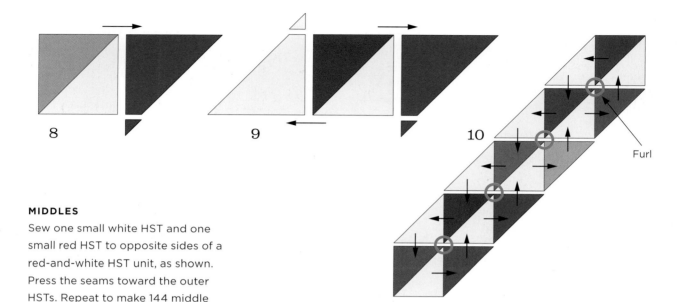

8   9   10   Furl

MIDDLES

Sew one small white HST and one small red HST to opposite sides of a red-and-white HST unit, as shown. Press the seams toward the outer HSTs. Repeat to make 144 middle units. **9**

Trim the points on the red and the white HSTs to reduce bulk, if desired.

CENTER STRIP

From your stacks of top corner units, middle units, and bottom corner units, randomly choose one of each of the top and bottom corner units and three middle units. Sew the units into a long, angled strip, as shown; match and furl the seam intersections, marked with a blue circle. Press the seams as indicated. Repeat to make 48 center strips. **10**

Once again, furling—or opening only the very center of the seam—is not necessary, but it will reduce bulk significantly. Nearby seam intersections may resist the pressing direction created by the furl. However, perseverance will pay off with a nicely formed block. Sew and press carefully. Use extra pins to keep sewing in check.

COMPLETED BLOCK

Center and sew one large pieced red HST and one large white-on-white HST to either side of the center strip, as shown. Try not to stretch the bias fabric edge, and be sure to accommodate for seam allowances at each end. Use extra pins along the seam to secure it. Press the seams toward the larger triangle after each addition. Repeat to make 48 blocks that are 10½ in. square. **11**

The last two block seams are loaded with stretchy bias edges. Use extra pins to secure the pieced units before sewing. Also, place the larger triangle with fewer seam intersections closer to the sewing machine feed dogs to keep an eye on as many seam intersections as possible as you sew.

FINISH THE CONSTRUCTION

Arrange the blocks into eight rows of six blocks, rotating adjacent blocks 90 degrees. Sew the blocks into rows. Press the block seams in one direction alternating the direction in each row, as shown. Press the row seams in one direction. **12**

Be sure to measure the quilt top before cutting the borders.

Sew five border strips together end to end, using a diagonal seam (see p. 180). Press the connecting seams open. Cut two 4-in. by 80½-in. side borders.

Sew two border strips together end to end, using a diagonal seam. Press the connecting seams open. Repeat to make two. Trim each to 4 in. by 67½ in. for the top and bottom borders.

Add the borders to the quilt, sides first, then the top and bottom. Press the seams toward the border after each addition. **12**

11

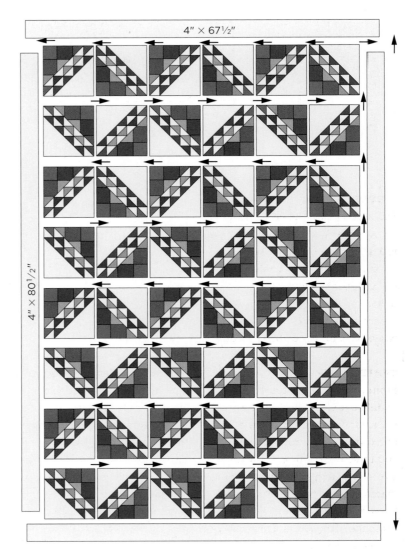

QUILT AND BIND

Layer the backing, batting, and quilt top; baste. Quilt as desired.

Cut eight $2^{1}/_{4}$-in. strips for the binding. Sew the binding strips together end to end, using a diagonal seam. Press the connecting seams open, and then press the binding in half lengthwise, wrong sides together.

Trim the batting and backing even with the quilt top. With the raw edges aligned, sew the binding to the front of the quilt using a $^{1}/_{4}$-in. seam. Miter the binding at the corners.

Turn the folded edge of the binding to the back of the quilt, and hand stitch it in place.

12

Basket Case

SCRAPS PLUS ONE SASHING AND ONE FOCUS PRINT

Okay, so I'm cheating with this one. We have two "ones" instead of one "one." Eh, well. Sometimes it's okay to bend the rules when a quilt is involved! And for this quilt, a little rule bending is absolutely worth it.

I chose a turquoise, Aboriginal-looking print for the inspiration fabric, thinking that I would pair it with dark-value scraps in cool blue hues. But laying a few of the scraps on the print yardage told me clearly that this inspiration fabric wanted nothing to do with dark scraps. Digging deep, I used just about every 5-in. light-value print from my cut-up scrap stash to make these super-size blocks. Sometimes it's best to let the fabrics decide how to proceed.

Before finishing the quilt with more of the focus print from the block, the quilt needed plain, neutral sashing strips—only 1 yard—so bending the rules came easy.

With this formula, you are only nine easy blocks away from a fabulous full-size quilt!

FINISHED SIZE: **90 in. square**
PATTERN DIFFICULTY: **Easy**

SCRAP REQUIREMENTS:
5-in. light-value scrap squares: 180
FABRIC AND NOTION REQUIREMENTS:
1 yard neutral gray solid for sashing
4 yards focus print for blocks and outer border
$3/4$ yard for binding (the sample quilt was bound with the focus print)
$8^1/4$ yards for backing
94-in.-square batting

This quilt can be easily resized to a lap version. Make four blocks instead of nine. You'll need 80 light-value 5-in. scraps, $2/3$ yard of sashing fabric, and 2 yards of focus print to complete the top.

PREPARE THE SCRAPS

Select one hundred eighty 5-in. light-value scrap squares for the blocks. Set aside 81 uncut squares for the blocks. Cut 54 of the remaining squares in half to make two $2^1/2$-in. by 5-in. rectangles each for a total of one hundred eight $2^1/2$-in. by 5-in. rectangles for the bars. Cut the remaining

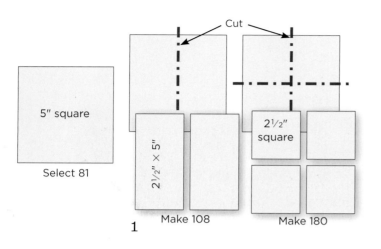

5" square

Select 81

2½" × 5"

Make 108

Cut

2½" square

Make 180

1

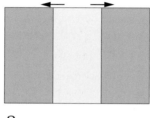

3

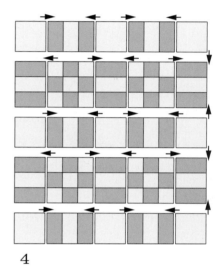

2

4

45 squares in half twice to make four 2½-in. squares each for a total of one hundred eighty 2½-in. squares for the nine-patches. **1**

PREPARE THE ADDITIONAL FABRICS

GRAY SOLID

Cut eight 1¾-in. width-of-fabric strips for the sashing.

Cut nine 2-in. width-of-fabric strips for the outer border.

FOCUS PRINT

Cut fourteen 5-in. width-of-fabric strips; then cut two hundred sixteen 2½-in. by 5-in. rectangles along the lengthwise grain for the blocks.

Cut nine 2½-in. width-of-fabric strips; then cut one hundred forty-four 2½-in. squares for the blocks.

Cut ten 4½-in. width-of-fabric strips for the outer border.

MAKE THE BLOCKS

NINE-PATCHES

Arrange five randomly selected 2½-in. light-value scrap squares and four 2½-in. focus print squares in a nine-patch that has a light center and light corners. Sew the squares into rows, then sew the rows together.

Press the seams toward the darker fabric, as indicated. **2**

Repeat to make 36 nine-patches that are 6½ in. square.

BARS

Sew a 2½-in. by 5-in. focus print rectangle to each side of one 2½-in. by 5-in. light-value scrap rectangle, as shown. Press the seams toward the darker fabric. **3**

Repeat to make 108 bar units that are 5 in. by 6½ in.

BLOCKS

Arrange nine light-value 5-in. scrap squares, 12 bar units, and four nine-patch units in rows, as shown. Sew the units into rows and press the seams as indicated. Sew the rows together and press the seams as indicated. **4**

Repeat to make nine blocks that are 26 in. square.

MAKE THE SASHING AND BORDERS

Sew all eight 1¾-in. gray solid sashing strips together, end to end, using a diagonal seam (see p. 180). From the long strip, cut six 1¾-in. by 26-in. vertical sashing strips and two 1¾-in. by 79½-in. horizontal sashing strips.

> Measure the blocks and quilt top before cutting the sashing and border strips.

Sew all nine 2-in. gray solid inner border strips together end to end, using a diagonal seam. From the long strip, cut two 2-in. by 79½-in. side inner borders, and two 2-in. by 82½-in. top/bottom inner borders.

Arrange and sew the blocks and sashing strips, as shown. Sew the shorter vertical sashing strips to the blocks first; press the seams toward the sashing. Then sew the horizontal sashing strips between the block rows; press the seams toward the sashing strips.

Sew the inner borders to the quilt center, sides first, then top and bottom. Press the seams toward the border after each addition. **5**

Sew all nine 4½-in. focus border strips together end to end, using a diagonal seam. From a long strip, cut two 4½-in. by 82½-in. side borders and two 4½-in. by 90½-in. top/bottom borders.

Sew the outer borders to the quilt center, sides first, then the top and bottom. Press the seams toward the border after each addition. **5**

QUILT AND BIND

Layer the backing, batting, and quilt top; baste. Quilt as desired.

Cut ten 2¼-in. strips for the binding. Sew the binding strips together end to end, using a diagonal seam. Press the connecting seams open, and then press the binding in half lengthwise with the wrong sides together.

Trim the batting and backing even with the quilt top. With the raw edges aligned, sew the binding to the front of the quilt using a ¼-in. seam. Miter the binding at the corners.

Turn the folded edge of the binding to the back of quilt, and hand-stitch it in place.

BACKING IT UP

When a quilt is more than 80 in. wide, it takes three width-of-fabric strips and two seams to piece the backing. More often than not, this also creates lots of leftover backing fabric. Because I have a bin of scraps, I like to improvise a simple pieced strip—a row or two of 5-in. scraps sewn together, for example—to stretch the fabric sewn in

between two width-of-fabric backing pieces. It's a nice way to increase the value of your backing and scrap fabrics. And it also makes for a pleasant surprise on the back of the quilt.

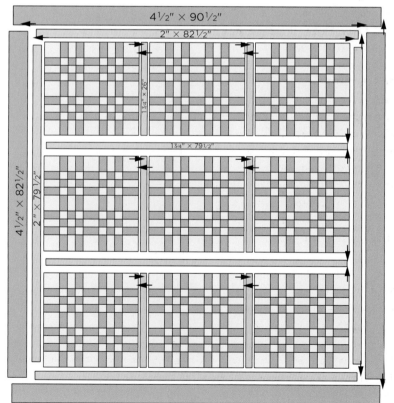

5

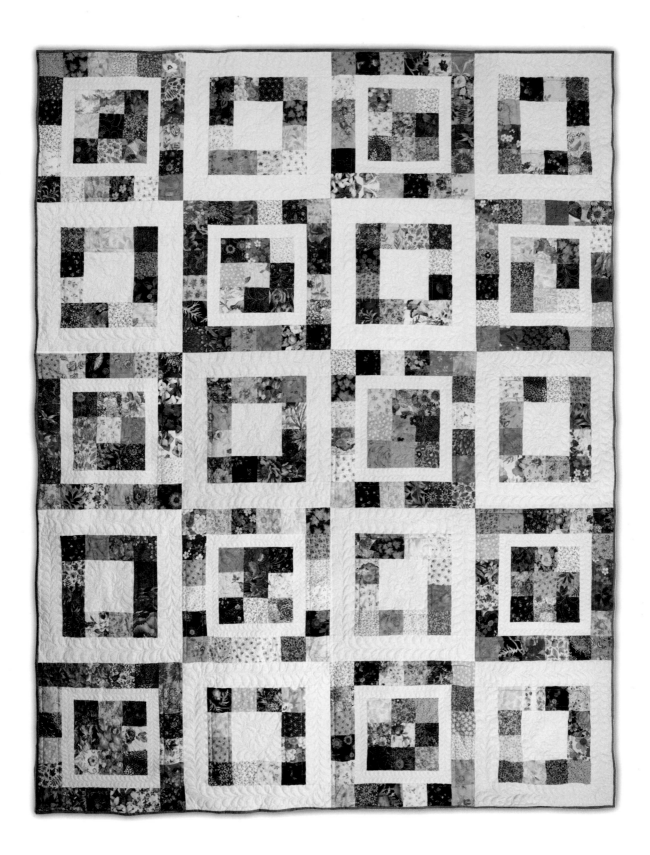

Flower Bed

SCRAPS PLUS ONE NEUTRAL

The concept for this very easy quilt came to me one Saturday morning while I was still in bed. I grabbed my digital note pad from the nightstand and started sketching and calculating and sketching some more.

Next, I needed a theme. My collection of 3½-in. scrap squares seems to be rampant with floral prints. There you go. Throw in some white, and start sewing. Hey, this quilt is practically making itself!

There went the rest of my Saturday . . . once the idea was hatched, I simply had to see it through. Make fewer blocks and you've got a smaller scrappy project. Add a border to super-size it, if you wish.

FINISHED SIZE: **72 in. by 90 in.**
PATTERN DIFFICULTY: **Easy**

SCRAP REQUIREMENTS:
3½-in. medium-value floral print scrap squares: 410
FABRIC AND NOTION REQUIREMENTS:
2¾ yards white-on-white print for blocks
²⁄₃ yard for binding
5½ yards for backing
77-in. by 95-in. batting

For this quilt, don't worry about the light and dark value or the scale of the print when selecting scraps for the block elements. Select any 3½-in. scraps that fit your theme—floral or botanical prints, in my case—then arrange the scraps randomly in the block without regard to scale or value. Just put pretty next to pretty, and the rest will take care of itself!

PREPARE THE SCRAPS
Select four hundred ten 3½-in. scrap squares for the blocks.

PREPARE THE ADDITIONAL FABRICS
WHITE-ON-WHITE PRINT
Cut two 6½-in. width-of-fabric strips; then cut ten 6½-in. squares for the solid-center blocks.

Cut one 9½-in. width-of-fabric strip; then cut twenty 2-in. by 9½-in. strips along the lengthwise grain for the scrappy-center blocks.

Cut three 12½-in. width-of-fabric strips; then cut twenty 2-in. by 12½-in. strips along the lengthwise grain for the scrappy-center blocks plus twenty 3½-in. by 12½-in. strips along the lengthwise grain for the solid-center blocks.

Cut two 18½-in. width-of-fabric strips; then cut twenty 3½-in. by 18½-in. strips along the lengthwise grain for the solid-center blocks.

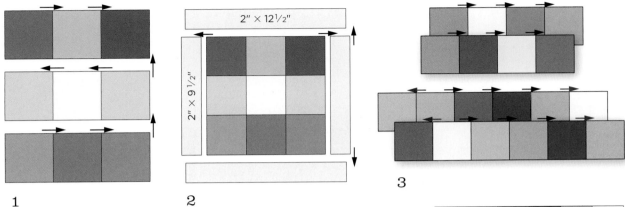

1

2" × 12½"

2" × 9½"

2

3

SCRAPPY-CENTER BLOCKS

Arrange nine randomly selected 3½-in. floral print scraps in a nine-patch. Sew the scraps into three rows of three scraps, and press the seams alternately in each row. Sew the rows together, and press the row seams in one direction. **1**

Sew one 2-in. by 9½-in. white strip to each opposite side of the nine-patch. Press the seams toward the white strips. Sew one 2-in. by 12½-in. white strip each to the top and the bottom of the nine-patch block. Press the seams toward the white strips. **2**

Sew four 3½-in. scraps in a row. Press the seams in one direction. Repeat to make two scrappy strips that are 3½ in. by 12½ in. **3**

Sew six 3½-in. scraps in a row. Press the two outer seams toward the outer edge of the strip (shown with red arrows). Press the center scrap seams in one direction. Repeat to make two scrappy strips that are 3½ in. by 18½ in. **3**

Sew one four-scrap strip to each opposite side of the scrappy-center block unit. Press the seams toward the block center. Sew one six-scrap strip each to the top and bottom of the scrappy-center block unit. Press the seams toward the block center. **4**

Repeat to make 10 scrappy-center blocks that are 18½ in. square.

SOLID-CENTER BLOCKS

Sew two 3½-in. scraps in a row. Press the seam in one direction. Repeat to make two scrappy two-patches that are 3½ in. by 6½ in. **5**

Sew four 3½-in. scraps in a row. Press the two outer seams toward the outer edge of the strip (shown with red arrows). Press the center scrap seam in either direction. Repeat to make two scrappy strips that are 3½ in. by 12½ in. **5**

Sew one two-patch strip to each opposite side of the 6½-in. white center square. Press seams toward the block center. Sew one four-scrap strip each to the top and bottom of the solid-center block unit. Press the seams toward the block center. **6**

Sew one 3½-in. by 12½-in. white strip to each opposite side of the block. Press the seams toward the outer edge of the block. Sew one 3½-in. by 18½-in. white strip each

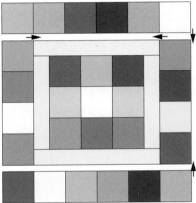

4

to the top and bottom of the block. Press the seams toward the outer edge of the block. **7**

Repeat to make 10 solid-center blocks that are 18½ in. square.

ASSEMBLE THE QUILT TOP

Arrange the blocks in five rows of four blocks, alternating the scrappy-center and solid-center blocks. Sew the blocks into rows. Press the block seams toward the solid-center blocks.

Sew the rows, and press the row seams in one direction. **8**

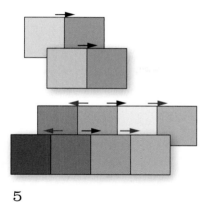

5

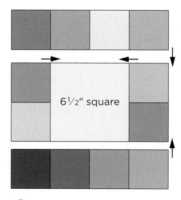

6½" square

6

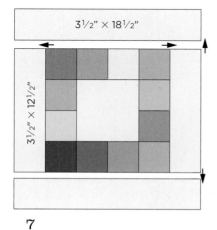

3½" × 18½"

3½" × 12½"

7

QUILT AND BIND

Layer the backing, batting, and quilt top; baste. Quilt as desired.

Cut nine 2¼-in. strips for the binding. Sew the binding strips together end to end, using a diagonal seam (see p. 180). Press the connecting seams open, and then press the binding in half lengthwise with the wrong sides together.

Trim the batting and backing even with the quilt top. With the raw edges aligned, sew the binding to the front of the quilt using a ¼-in. seam. Miter the binding at the corners.

Turn the folded edge of the binding to the back of the quilt, and hand-stitch it in place.

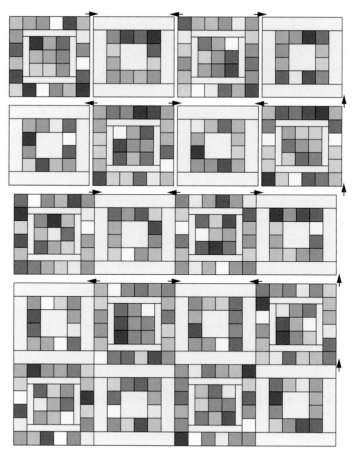

8

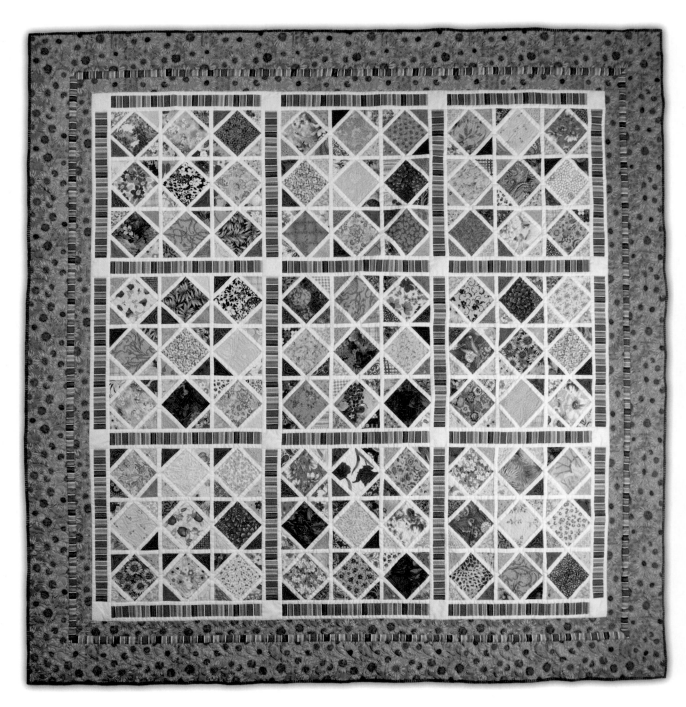

Bed quilt

Stained Glass

SCRAPS PLUS ONE BOLD STRIPE

This quilt represents a fun use of scraps that fall within a single color palette. The bold stripe used for the sashing strips, not the floral focus print, drives the scrap selection for this pattern. Once the color theme is established by the colors in the stripe, scraps in all scales and values are eligible to go into the super-size, nine-patch blocks. Because no scrap touches another, thanks to the fine lattice strips, almost anything goes.

The complicated-looking, solid-colored, skinny lattice strips are really quite easy to do. This quilt is the first time I used the technique to create thin lattice without cutting super-thin, unruly strips. The block parts look like a terrible mess until they are trimmed, tidy, and ready to sew into bigger blocks. This pattern includes two finished quilt sizes to please everyone.

FINISHED SIZE:
62 in. by 62 in. (lap size); 83 in. by 83 in. (bed size)
PATTERN DIFFICULTY: Intermediate

SCRAP REQUIREMENTS:
5-in. scrap squares: 36 (lap size); 81 (bed size)
$3^{1}/_{2}$-in. scrap squares: 72 (lap size); 162 (bed size)
FABRIC AND NOTION REQUIREMENTS:
Bold stripe (stripe must be printed along the
   lengthwise grain): $^{3}/_{4}$ yard (lap); $1^{1}/_{8}$ yards (bed)
Lattice, solid color suggested: $1^{1}/_{2}$ yards (lap);
   3 yards (bed)
Border: $1^{3}/_{4}$ yards (lap); $2^{1}/_{4}$ yards (bed)
Binding: $^{1}/_{2}$ yard (lap); $^{2}/_{3}$ yard (bed)
Backing: 4 yards (lap); $7^{1}/_{3}$ yards (bed)
Batting: 66 in. square (lap); 88 in. square (bed)

Pigma® pen or heat-erasable marker
Square ruler with a 45-degree angle line,
   at least 6 in. square (optional)

PREPARE THE SCRAPS
NOTE: Consider choosing the sashing stripe fabric first, then coordinate scraps, lattice, and borders with the stripe.

Selecting scraps for this quilt is relatively easy. In all cases, scraps are separated from one another by solid-color, narrow sashing strips. So any value, any scale print will work as long as it coordinates with your theme print, which in my case was the bold stripe fabric.

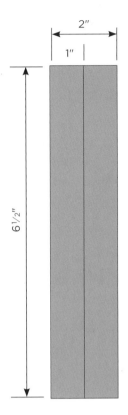

Lap quilt

LAP QUILT

Select thirty-six 5-in. scrap squares that coordinate with your stripe fabric for blocks. Trim each 5-in. scrap square to 4³⁄₄ in. square.

Select seventy-two 3¹⁄₂-in. scrap squares that coordinate with your stripe fabric for blocks. Draw a diagonal line, corner to corner, on the wrong side of each 3¹⁄₂-in. scrap square.

BED QUILT

Select eighty-one 5-in. scrap squares that coordinate with your stripe fabric for blocks. Trim each 5-in. scrap square to 4³⁄₄ in. square.

Select one hundred sixty-two 3¹⁄₂-in. scrap squares that coordinate with your stripe fabric for blocks.

Draw a diagonal line, corner to corner, on the wrong side of each 3¹⁄₂-in. scrap square.

PREPARE THE ADDITIONAL FABRICS

LAP QUILT: LATTICE FABRIC (SOLID COLOR RECOMMENDED)

Cut fourteen 2-in. width-of-fabric strips; then cut eighty-four 2-in. by 6¹⁄₂-in. rectangles. On the right side of each 2-in. by 6¹⁄₂-in. rectangle, draw a line down the center, 1 in. away from the long edge of each rectangle. **1**

Cut eight 2-in. width-of-fabric strips; then cut sixteen 2-in. by 19¹⁄₂-in. rectangles. On the right side of each 2-in. by 19¹⁄₂-in. rectangle, draw a line down the center, 1 in. away from the long edge of each rectangle.

Cut one 3-in. width-of-fabric strip; then cut nine 3-in. squares for the cornerstones.

BED QUILT: LATTICE FABRIC (SOLID COLOR RECOMMENDED)

Cut thirty-two 2-in. width-of-fabric strips; then cut one hundred eighty-nine 2-in. by 6¹⁄₂-in. rectangles. On the right side of each 2-in. by 6¹⁄₂-in. rectangle, draw a line down the center, 1 in. away from the long edge of each rectangle. **1**

Cut seventeen 2-in. width-of-fabric strips; then cut thirty-three 2-in. by 19¹⁄₂-in. rectangles. On the right side of each 2-in. by 19¹⁄₂-in. rectangle, draw a line down the center, 1 in. away from the long edge of each rectangle.

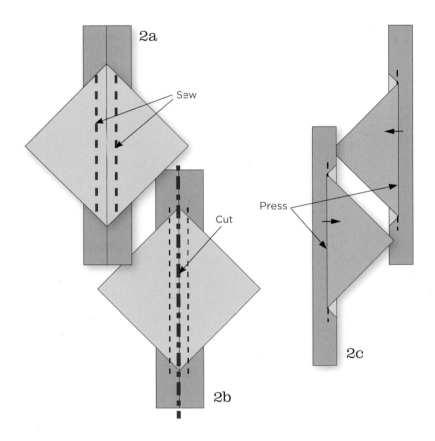

2a

Sew

Cut

Press

2b

2c

Cut two 3-in. width-of-fabric strips; then cut sixteen 3-in. squares for the cornerstones.

LAP QUILT: STRIPE FABRIC

Cut six 2-in. width-of-fabric strips; then cut twelve 2-in. by 19$\frac{1}{2}$-in. rectangles for the sashing.

Cut six 1$\frac{1}{2}$-in. width-of-fabric strips. Set aside for the border stripe.

BED QUILT: STRIPE FABRIC

Cut twelve 2-in. width-of-fabric strips; then cut twenty-four 2-in. by 19$\frac{1}{2}$-in. rectangles for the sashing.

Cut eight 1$\frac{1}{2}$-in. width-of-fabric strips. Set aside for the border stripe.

LAP QUILT: BORDER PRINT

Cut six 2$\frac{1}{2}$-in. width-of-fabric strips. Set aside for the inner border.

Cut seven 5$\frac{1}{2}$-in. width-of-fabric strips. (Cut 8 strips if you want to make a mitered border.) Set aside for the outer border.

BED QUILT: BORDER PRINT

Cut eight 2$\frac{1}{2}$-in. width-of-fabric strips. Set aside for the inner border.

Cut nine 5$\frac{1}{2}$-in. width-of-fabric strips. (Cut 10 strips if you want to make a mitered border.) Set aside for the outer border.

MAKE THE BLOCKS

Place a 3$\frac{1}{2}$-in. scrap square on a 2-in. by 6$\frac{1}{2}$-in. lattice strip, right sides together. Roughly center the scrap on the strip and align the line drawn on the wrong side of the scrap square with the one on the right side of the 2-in. by 6$\frac{1}{2}$-in. strip.

Sew $\frac{1}{4}$ in. on both sides of the drawn line. **2a**

Cut on the line. **2b** Then, press the seam toward the resulting scrap triangle to make two corner units. Don't worry about trimming them to a triangular shape. **2c**

Repeat (chain piece) to make a total of 144 corner units for the lap quilt and 324 corner units for the bed quilt.

Select a 4$\frac{3}{4}$-in. scrap square and a corner unit. Find the center of one side of the square by folding the square in half, right sides together, and pinching only the center at the very edge where the fold would be.

Likewise, find the center of the long side of the corner unit by folding the unit in half, wrong sides together and pinching the center. Match the

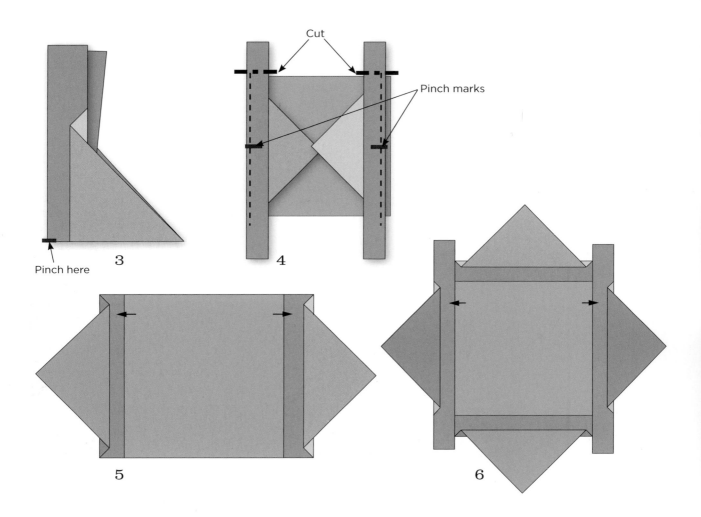

Pinch marks

3

4

Pinch here

5

6

sides of the triangle, rather than the ends of the rectangle to find the center. **3**

Using the pinch marks, center the corner unit onto one side of the 4³⁄₄-in. square, right sides together. Sew using a ¹⁄₄-in. seam allowance.

Similarly, sew a second corner unit to the opposite side of the 4³⁄₄-in. scrap square. Mix up the scrap prints! **4**

Trim the excess corner unit fabric even with the unsewn sides of the 4³⁄₄-in. scrap square, and then press the seams toward the corner unit. **5**

Center and sew two more corner units to the remaining two sides of

the 4³⁄₄-in. square. Press the seams toward the corner units. **6**

Center and trim all four sides of the block unit to a 6¹⁄₂-in. square. Try to make sure the square points are ¹⁄₄ in. away from the trimmed edge of block unit. **7**

Repeat to make 36 block units for the lap quilt and 81 block units for the bed quilt.

Arrange nine block units in three rows of three block units on the sewing table. Label each block unit with a pin and piece of scrap fabric to identify its location within the block. In between, add three 2-in. by 6¹⁄₂-in.

and one 2-in. by 19¹⁄₂-in. lattice strips, as shown. **8**

Avoid cutting and sewing very narrow lattice strips that can easily distort during the quilt construction. Instead, sew block units to the lattice strips aligned with the center of the strip, then cut them apart. To stay organized, follow the sequencing carefully, and return partially sewn blocks to your sewing table between seaming.

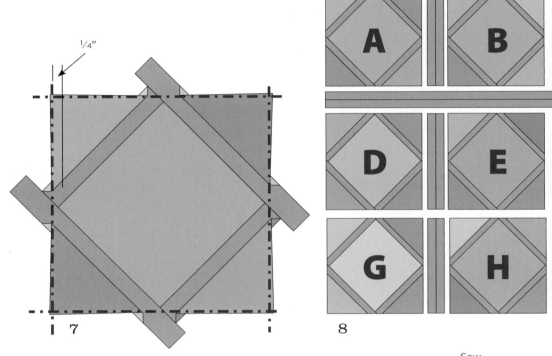

7

8

Align the inner edge of block unit A with the line drawn on the 2-in. by 6½-in. lattice strip, right sides together. Sew ¼ in. from the edge of unit A. **9**

NOTE: Use lot of pins when sewing the blocks together!

Similarly, align the inner edge of unit C with the drawn line on the opposite side of the same 2-in. by 6½-in. lattice strip, right sides together. Sew a ¼-in. seam from the edge of block unit C. **10**

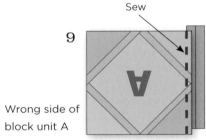

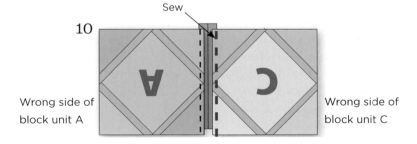

With the wrong side of the block units facing up, cut the lattice on the drawn line, exactly where the edges of units A and C meet. Press the seams toward the lattice strips. **11**

Return units A and C to the block arrangement on the sewing table. Sew unit B to unit A; then sew unit C to unit B to complete the row. Press the seams toward the lattice strips. **12**

Repeat the sequencing to make rows D-E-F and G-H-I.

Sew the rows in the same way you sewed the block units. Align the bottom edge of row A-B-C with the drawn line on the 2-in. by 19 $\frac{1}{2}$-in. lattice strip. Sew a $\frac{1}{4}$-in. seam from the edge of row A-B-C.

Align the top edge of row G-H-I with the drawn line on the opposite side of the same 2-in. by 19$\frac{1}{2}$-in. lattice strip, right sides together. Sew a $\frac{1}{4}$-in. seam from the edge of row G-H-I.

Cut the lattice on the drawn line, exactly where the edge of row A-B-C and row G-H-I meet. Press the seams toward the lattice strips. Return the rows to the block arrangement on the sewing table.

Sew row D-E-F to the lattice edge of row A-B-C; then sew the lattice edge of row G-H-I to row D-E-F to complete block. Press the seams toward the lattice. The block is 19$\frac{1}{2}$ in. square. **13**

Repeat to make four blocks for the lap quilt and nine blocks for the bed quilt, as shown at right.

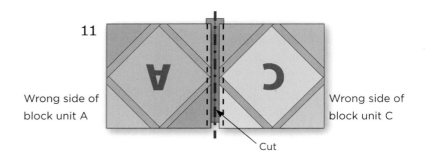

11

Wrong side of block unit A

Wrong side of block unit C

Cut

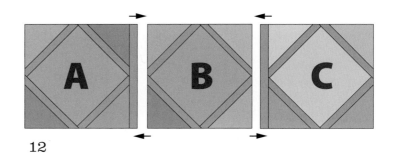

12

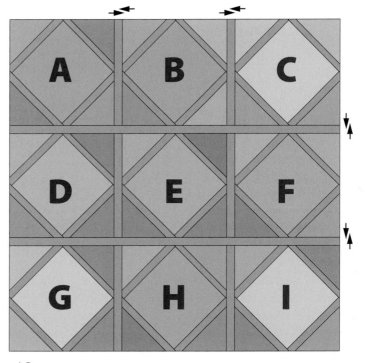

13

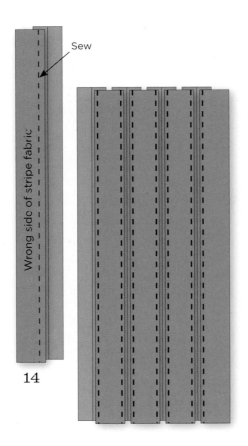

Sew

Wrong side of stripe fabric

14

15

STRIPED SASHING

Align the long edge of a 2-in. by 19$\frac{1}{2}$-in. stripe with the drawn line on a 2-in. by 19$\frac{1}{2}$-in. lattice strip, right sides together. Sew $\frac{1}{4}$ in. from the edge of the stripe.

Align the long edge of a second 2-in. by 19$\frac{1}{2}$-in. stripe with the drawn line on the opposite side of the same 2-in. by 19$\frac{1}{2}$-in. lattice strip, right sides together. Sew a $\frac{1}{4}$-in. seam from the edge of the stripe.

Always *sew* on the edge of the stripe, and *cut* through the middle of the lattice.

Continue adding 2-in. by 19$\frac{1}{2}$-in. lattice and stripe strips until all the strips have been sewn and each stripe fabric has a lattice strip sewn on each side. **14**

Chain sew, and cut the pieces apart as the width of the strip grows. Once cut apart, press the seams toward the lattice. Sashing units are 3 in. by 19$\frac{1}{2}$-in. **15**

Make 12 sashing units for the lap quilt and 24 sashing units for the bed quilt.

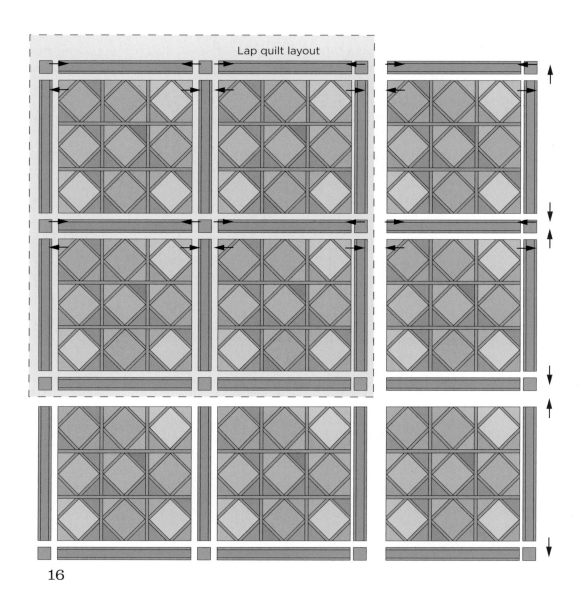

Lap quilt layout

16

ASSEMBLE THE QUILT CENTER

LAP QUILT: BLOCKS AND SASHING
Arrange 4 blocks, 12 sashing units, and nine 3-in. cornerstone squares in rows.

BED QUILT: BLOCKS AND SASHING
Arrange 9 blocks, 24 sashing units, and sixteen 3-in. cornerstone squares in rows.

BOTH SIZES
Sew the units into rows. Press the seams toward the sashing both in the cornerstone/sashing rows and in the sashing/block rows.

Sew the rows together to make the quilt center. Press the row seams toward the sashing rows.

The lap quilt center should be 46 in. square, and the bed quilt center should be 67½ in. square. **16**

NOTE: Measure the quilt top before trimming the borders to size.

BORDERS
Three borders finish this quilt. The borders may be sewn to the quilt one at a time. Or, to emphasize the stripe, all three borders may be sewn together first, then sewn to the quilt with mitered corners.

TRADITIONAL BORDERS

Use the chart below. Sew all matching width-of-fabric strips cut for the borders together end to end, using a diagonal seam (see p. 180). Cut the border strips to length as indicated.

Sew the three borders to each side of the quilt in sequence: inner border, stripe, outer border. Sew the sides first, then the top and bottom. Press the seams toward the border after each addition.

MITERED BORDERS

Use the chart below. Sew all matching width-of-fabric strips cut for the borders together end to end, using a diagonal seam (see p. 180). Cut the border strips to length as indicated.

Center and sew one border strip of each length in sequence (inner border, stripe, outer border) to make a three-border strip set. Repeat to

TRADITIONAL BORDERS

Cut two border strips from each width dimension as follows:

	Lap Quilt		Bed Quilt	
	SIDES	TOP/BOTTOM	SIDES	TOP/BOTTOM
2½-in. inner border	2½ in. × 46 in.	2½ in. × 50 in.	2½ in. × 67½ in.	2½ in. × 71½ in.
1½-in. stripe	1½ in. × 50 in.	1½ in. × 52 in.	1½ in. × 71½ in.	1½ in. × 73½ in.
5½-in. outer border	5½ in. × 52 in.	5½ in. × 62 in.	5½ in. × 73½ in.	5½ in. × 83½ in.

MITERED BORDERS

Cut four border strips from each width dimension as follows:

	Lap Quilt	Bed Quilt
2½-in. inner border	2½ in. × approximately 54 in.	2½ in. × approximately 71 in.
1½-in. stripe	1½ in. × approximately 56 in.	1½ in. × approximately 78 in.
5½-in. outer border	5½ in. × approximately 68 in.	5½ in. × approximately 88 in.

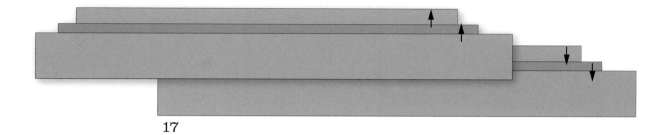

17

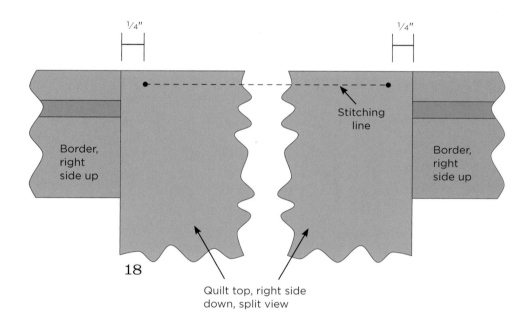

¹/₄″   ¹/₄″

Stitching
line

Border,
right
side up

Border,
right
side up

18

Quilt top, right side
down, split view

make four border strip sets. Press the seams on two border strip sets toward the inner border for the side borders.

Press the seams on the remaining two border strip sets toward the outer border for the top and bottom borders. **17**

Center and sew the side borders and top and bottom borders to the quilt, starting and stopping ¹/₄ in. from each edge of the quilt top. **18**

Miter a Corner

Choose one of the corners to miter. At the selected corner, fold the quilt top in half diagonally, right sides together. Match the outside border edges, right sides together, in a straight line. Finger-press the seam between the border and quilt top toward the quilt center and lay it flat on a work surface, as shown on the opposite page.

Place a straight ruler with a 45-degree angle line on top of the folded quilt. Place the 45-degree line even with borders' outside edges and the straight edge of the ruler even with the diagonal fold on the quilt top.

Draw a line with a pencil or quilt marking tool from the end of the border seam to the edge of the border along the edge of the ruler. **19**

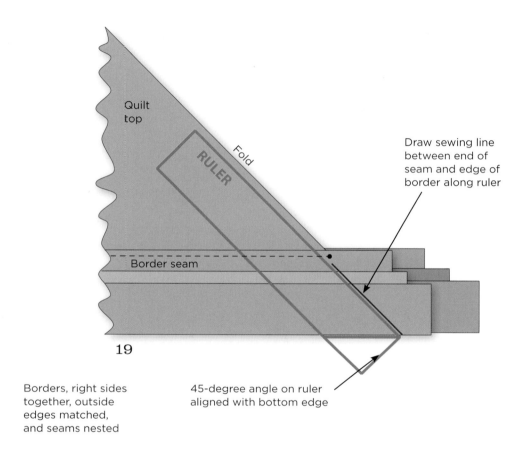

Quilt top

RULER

Fold

Draw sewing line between end of seam and edge of border along ruler

Border seam

19

Borders, right sides together, outside edges matched, and seams nested

45-degree angle on ruler aligned with bottom edge

Secure with pins along the drawn line. Carefully transfer the quilt to the sewing machine and sew directly on the drawn line, starting at the border seam intersection and sewing outward toward the quilt edge.

Return to the work table and trim the excess border fabric, leaving a ¼-in. seam allowance to the outside of the mitered seam. Repeat the mitered corner steps for the remaining three corners.

When all corners have been sewn, press from the back, pressing the mitered seams open and the quilt/border seams toward the border. Then press the entire assembly from the front.

QUILT AND BIND

Layer the backing, batting, and quilt top; baste. Quilt as desired.

Cut seven 2¼-in. strips for the lap quilt binding or nine 2¼-in. strips

for the bed quilt binding. Sew the binding strips together, end to end, using a diagonal seam. Press the connecting seams open; then press the binding in half lengthwise, wrong sides together.

Trim the batting and backing even with the quilt top. With the raw edges aligned, sew the binding to the front of the quilt using a ¼-in. seam. Miter the binding at the corners.

Turn the folded edge of the binding to the back of the quilt, and hand-stitch it in place.

From Little Acorns

SCRAPS PLUS ONE FOCUS PRINT

The Adirondack State Park in upstate New York has been compared to a patchwork quilt. Parcels of land within the park's boundaries are privately owned, and the park itself is host to many forms of year-round recreation, including quilting—a decidedly indoor sport during the winter months!

Because the Adirondacks are only a short drive from my home, I am easily enticed by the rustic colors and outdoorsy images on fabric and the quilts that they inspire.

The From Little Acorns quilt is a perfect example. The small toss print that is the single focus fabric for this quilt is fairly busy, so I had to be careful to choose scraps that held up against the print. Overall, the quilt is fairly low contrast with limited light and dark variation.

I chose to use a fusible appliqué technique to place the leaves and acorn shapes in the alternate blocks. The shapes were then secured with a tight blanket stitch on each block before piecing the blocks together. The shapes have some severe curves and turns, so a hand appliqué option is certainly doable but a little more challenging for this project.

FINISHED SIZE: **58 in. by 71 in.**
PATTERN DIFFICULTY: **Intermediate**

SCRAP REQUIREMENTS:
2-in. dark-value scrap squares: 266
3½-in. dark-value scrap squares: 64
5-in. dark-value scrap squares: at least 16

FABRIC AND NOTION REQUIREMENTS:
3½ yards focus print for blocks and outer border
½ yard dark brown for binding
4¼ yards backing
62-in. by 75-in. batting
For hand appliqué: Pigma pen or heat-erasable marker, appliqué pins, and appliqué needles
For machine appliqué: Pigma pen, 2 yards 16-in.-wide fusible web

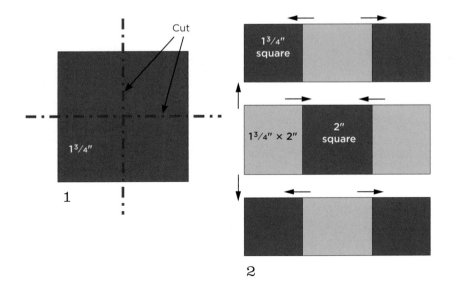

1

2

PREPARE THE SCRAPS

Select two hundred sixty-six 2-in. dark-value scrap squares. Set aside 90 for the acorn appliqué blocks. Set aside 32 for the pieced block centers. Set aside 144 for the inner borders.

Select sixty-four 3½-in. dark-value scrap squares. Cut each square in half twice, as shown, to make two hundred fifty-six 1¾-in. squares for the pieced block corners. **1** Keep the four matching squares together.

Select 16 (or more) 5-in. dark-value scrap squares for the leaf appliqué blocks.

> You need at least sixteen 5-in. scrap squares to make the leaf appliqué shapes—one for each leaf appliqué block. I doubled up the leaves on a few of the blocks, overlapping two shapes on some of the blocks to mix it up a bit. So I made three extra appliqué leaves.

PREPARE THE ADDITIONAL FABRICS

FOCUS PRINT

Cut seven 7-in. width-of-fabric strips; then cut thirty-one 7-in. squares for the appliqué block backgrounds.

Cut six 4½-in. width-of-fabric strips; then cut one hundred twenty-eight 1¾-in. by 4½-in. rectangles along the lengthwise grain for the pieced block sides.

Cut six 2-in. width-of-fabric strips; then cut one hundred twenty-eight 1¾-in. by 2-in. rectangles along the lengthwise grain for the pieced block sides.

Cut seven 5-in. width-of-fabric strips for the outer borders.

PIECED BLOCKS

Select one of the thirty-two 2-in. scrap block centers and two sets of four matching 1¾-in. scrap block corner squares. Use these selected scrap squares plus four 1¾-in. by 2-in. and four 1¾-in. by 4½-in. focus rectangles to assemble the block.

Arrange a 2-in. scrap square, one set of four 1¾-in. matching scrap corner squares, and four 1¾-in. by 2-in. focus rectangles in a nine-patch, and sew. Press the seams as indicated to make a nine-patch unit that is 4½ in. square. **2**

Arrange the nine-patch unit plus the second set of four 1¾-in. matching scrap squares and four 1¾-in. by 4½-in. focus rectangles into a second nine-patch unit and sew. Press the seams as indicated to make a pieced block that is 7 in. square. **3** Repeat to make 32 pieced blocks.

ACORN APPLIQUÉ BLOCKS

NOTE: You may use your favorite appliqué method; however, the instructions assume a machine appliqué method is used. Additional details are provided on p. 181.

Select six 2-in. scrap squares for the acorn shapes. Using your favorite appliqué method or the fusible appliqué method described on p. 181, secure six appliqué shapes to a 7-in. square background fabric, placing the bottom layers of the appliqué first, using the number sequence as a guide. Secure the appliqué with a satin, buttonhole, or zigzag stitch. Repeat to make 15 acorn appliqué blocks that are 7-in. square. **4**

LEAF APPLIQUÉ BLOCKS

Select one 5-in. scrap square for the leaf shape. Using your favorite appliqué method or the fusible appliqué method, secure one or two appliqué shapes to the center of a 7-in. square background fabric. Secure the appliqué with a satin,

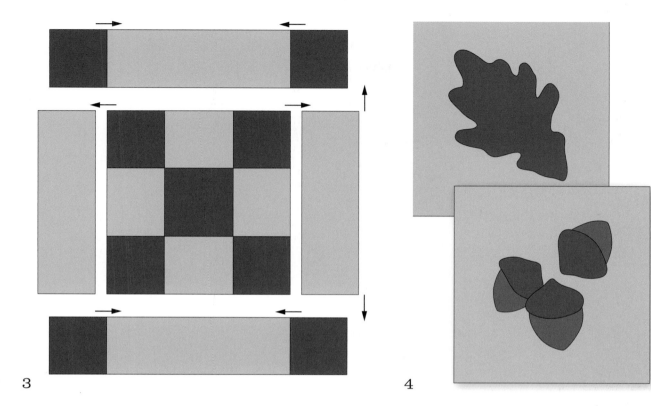

3

4

buttonhole, or zigzag stitch. Repeat to make 16 leaf appliqué blocks that are 7 in. square. **4**

ASSEMBLE THE QUILT
QUILT CENTER

Arrange nine rows of seven blocks, alternating appliqué and pieced blocks, as shown. Start and end the first and last row with a pieced block. Sew the blocks into rows, and press the seams toward the appliqué blocks within the rows. Sew the rows together, and press the seams in one direction.

BORDERS

Sew 39 of the remaining 2-in. scrap squares end to end to make a long strip that is 59 in. long. Press the connecting seams open. Repeat to make two pieced inner side borders. Attach a pieced inner border to each side of the quilt. Press the seam toward the border.

Sew 33 of the remaining 2-in. scrap squares end to end to make a long strip that is 50 in. long. Press the connecting seams open. Repeat to make two pieced inner borders for the top and the bottom. Trim each border to 2 in. by 49 in. Attach a pieced inner border to the top and bottom of the quilt. Press the seam toward the border.

Measure the quilt top before trimming the borders.

Sew two 5-in. focus strips end to end, using a diagonal seam (see p. 180). Press the connecting seams open. Repeat to make two. Trim each strip to 5 in. by 62 in. for the side borders.

Similarly, sew three 5-in. focus strips end to end, using a diagonal seam, to make one long border strip that is approximately 120 in. long. Press the connecting seams open. Cut two 5-in. by 58-in. outer borders for the top and bottom of the quilt.

Sew the outer border to the quilt. Sew the sides first, then the top and bottom. Press the seams toward the border after each addition as shown on p. 61. **5**

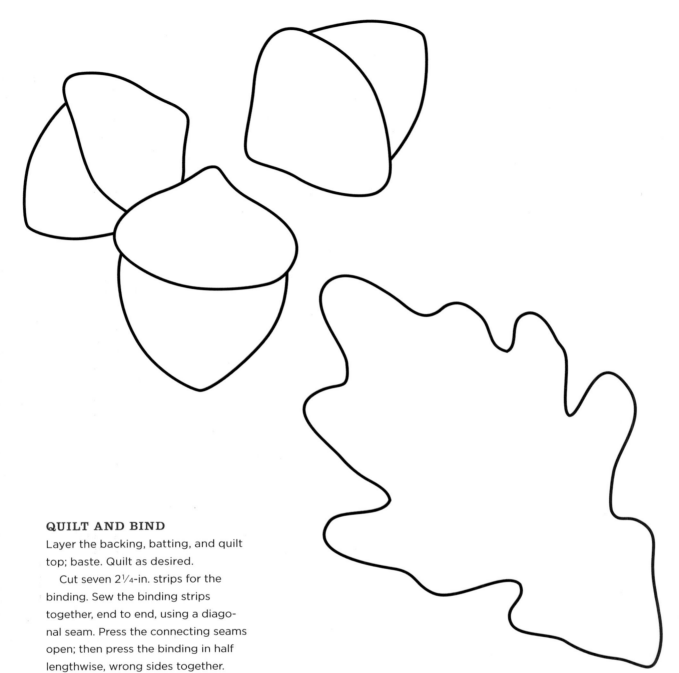

QUILT AND BIND

Layer the backing, batting, and quilt top; baste. Quilt as desired.

Cut seven 2¼-in. strips for the binding. Sew the binding strips together, end to end, using a diagonal seam. Press the connecting seams open; then press the binding in half lengthwise, wrong sides together.

Trim the batting and backing even with the quilt top. With the raw edges aligned, sew the binding to the front of the quilt using a ¼-in. seam. Miter the binding at the corners.

Turn the folded edge of the binding to the back of the quilt, and hand-stitch it in place.

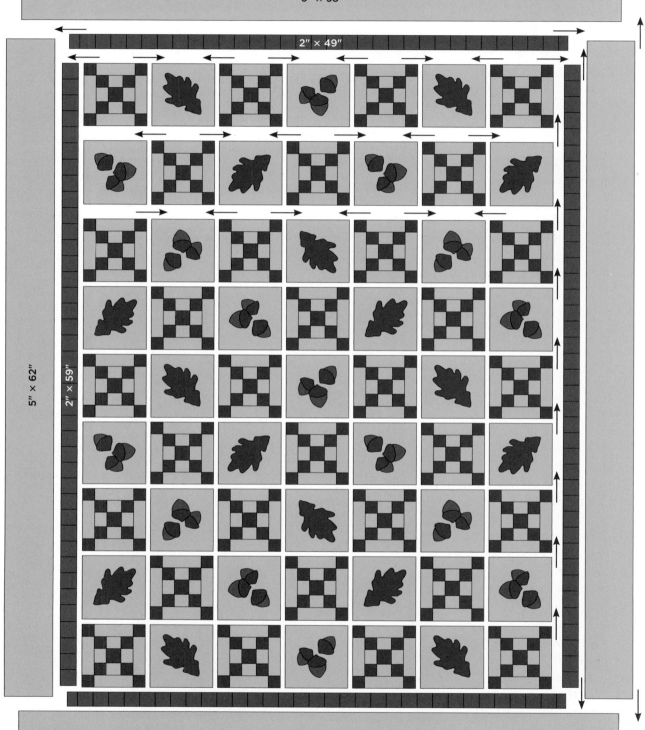

5

99 Bottles

SCRAPS PLUS ONE BLOCK

It's a strange name for a quilt, I admit. Especially one so colorful and filled with detail. But because, like the song of pop culture fame, the piecing seems to go on, and on and on the name fits.

Yes, a lot of piecing is involved. Small pieces too: 5,652 pieces of fabric, more or less. Not to worry; in the pattern, you'll find some quick piecing tips to make some of the skinny elements a little bit easier to work with and much more fun. Bottom line, this quilt will use up your scraps like crazy!

Even more good news—the blocks are based on a simple nine-patch or, shall I say, a series of nine-patches within nine-patches. It all started with a summer challenge to make one nine-patch, any size, each day over the summer. So I did. Small ones. One or two a day. And kept going. And going. And before I knew it, I had some blocks, then, eventually, a quilt. No doubt about it, this one took some time to make. But it's one of my favorites.

FINISHED SIZE: **62 in. by 78 in.**
PATTERN DIFFICULTY: **Intermediate**

SCRAP REQUIREMENTS:
2-in. scrap squares: 1,072
3 1/2-in. scrap squares: approximately 155
5-in. scrap squares: 68
FABRIC AND NOTION REQUIREMENTS:
2 3/4 yards cream for blocks, sashing, and cornerstones
5/8 yard dark blue for binding
4 2/3 yards for backing
66-in. by 82-in. batting
Pigma pen

I chose to work with batik scrap squares as my theme. But this project will work nicely with any print fabric. When using batiks, both sides of the fabric look the same, which is an added bonus, so there is no need to grab the seam ripper if a tiny scrap gets sewn pretty side down by accident!

In addition, because my background print is cream, nearly all my scraps are darker in value than it is. If you choose another color background, be careful that the scraps you select have a strong contrast for a pronounced effect.

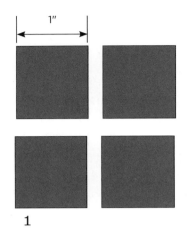

1

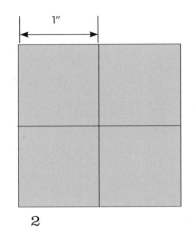

2

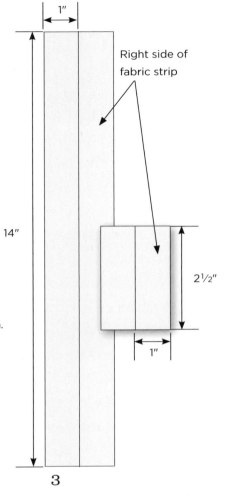

3

PREPARE THE SCRAPS

Select nine hundred seventy-two 2-in. scrap squares for the blocks. From these, set aside 480 squares for the medium nine-patches. Then cut each of the remaining 492 in half twice to make four 1-in. squares for mini nine-patches. **1** Keep matching sets of four 1-in. scraps together.

Because this quilt is likely to be a long-term project, you may prefer to cut your 1-in. squares as you progress, instead of all at once. I found it helpful to put my ready-to-sew scraps and background fabrics in a small covered box so I could take them with me if I went to a retreat or class. That way, I could sew a nine-patch or two whenever I had a spare moment—for example, while waiting for a cup of tea to brew.

Select one hundred 2-in. scrap squares for the cornerstones. From these set 80 aside for the wonky four-patches. On the remaining 20 scrap squares, using a Pigma pen (or another brand whose ink is not heat

erasable), draw two perpendicular lines 1 in. from the edges, as shown on the right side of the fabric. **2** Do not cut!

Select one hundred fifty-five $3\frac{1}{2}$-in. scrap squares for the sashing strips.

Select sixty-eight 5-in. scrap squares for the outer borders.

PREPARE THE ADDITIONAL FABRICS

CREAM

Cut sixty-two 1-in. width-of-fabric strips; then cut two thousand four hundred sixty 1-in. squares for the blocks.

Cut two 14-in. width-of-fabric strips; then cut thirty-one 2-in. by 14-in. strips for the sashing. Using a pencil or fabric marking tool, on the *right side* of each strip, draw a line down the center or 1 in. away from the long edge. **3**

Cut three 2-in. width-of-fabric strips; then cut forty 2-in. by $2\frac{1}{2}$-in. rectangles for the cornerstones. Using a pencil or fabric marking tool, on the *right side* of each rectangle, draw a line down the center or 1 in. away from the long edge. **3**

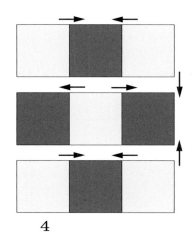

4

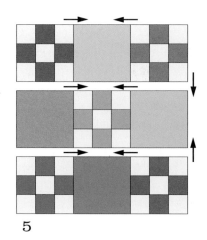

5

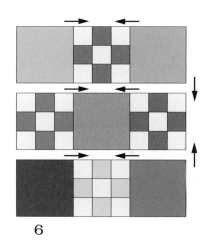

6

MAKE THE BLOCKS

A little bit of planning and discipline will make this project manageable. Try making one or two tiny nine-patch blocks each day you sit down to sew. Once you get a bunch of mini blocks, make a couple of medium blocks, and you'll see you're making progress. Once you have nine medium blocks, make the big block, and you'll really feel like you're getting somewhere.

MINI NINE-PATCHES

Arrange five 1-in. cream squares and four matching 1-in. scrap squares into a nine-patch with the cream square in the center. Sew into rows, and press the seams toward the scrap fabric. Sew the rows together, and press the seams toward the block center. Use pins and sew slowly! Each mini nine-patch will be 2 in. square. **4**

Repeat to make 492 mini nine-patches. All mini nine-patches will have cream centers.

MEDIUM NINE-PATCH

Arrange four 2-in. scrap squares and five mini nine-patches into a nine-patch, with the mini nine-patch in the center. Sew into rows. Press the seams toward the scrap fabric. Sew the rows together; press the seams toward the block center, as shown. Use pins and sew carefully! Each medium nine-patch will be 5 in. square. **5**

Repeat to make 60 medium nine-patches with mini nine-patch centers.

Arrange five 2-in. scrap squares and four mini nine-patches into a nine-patch, with the scrap square in the center. Sew into rows. Press the seams toward the scrap fabric. Sew the rows together, and press the seams toward the block edges, as shown. Use pins and sew carefully! Each medium nine-patch will be 5 in. square. **6**

Repeat to make 48 medium nine-patches with scrap centers.

SMALL SQUARE CHALLENGE

Sewing small 1-in. squares together can try your patience! However, consider this challenge: Carefully sew seams using an extra-scant ¼-in. seam allowance.

After pressing, measure each block meticulously, and trim the block down to a perfect 2-in. square. The medium-size blocks will go together much more easily, and no one will notice if a mini block or two is off just a wee bit. I promise! As an added bonus, I noticed that my piecing on the "regular-size" pieces became much more accurate after sewing mini blocks. Try it!

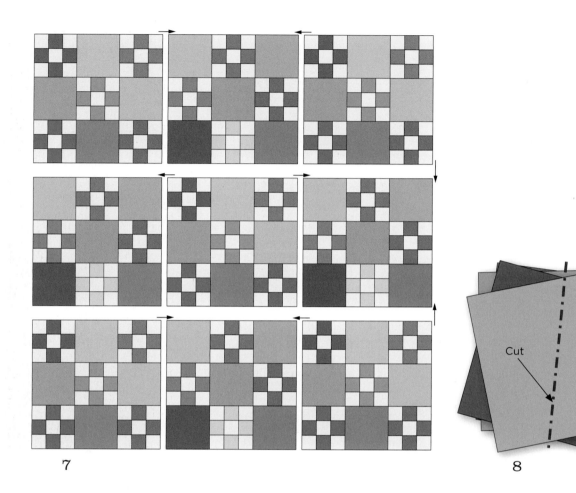

7

Cut

8

LARGE NINE-PATCH

Arrange five medium nine-patches with mini nine-patch centers, and four medium nine-patches with scrap centers into a large nine-patch, placing a nine-patch with a mini nine-patch center in the middle of the block. Sew into rows. Press the seams toward the nine-patch made with five scrap squares. Sew the rows together; press the seams toward the block center, as shown.

Each large nine-patch will be 14 in. square. **7**

Repeat to make 12 large nine-patch blocks.

MAKE THE SASHING STRIPS

Layer four or five 3½-in. scraps on your cutting mat. Stack the scraps, right side up at various angles. Place a ruler on top of the stack, at a random angle, and cut through all layers. **8** Repeat several times with

the 3½-in. scraps set aside for the sashing strips so you have a nice collection of scraps cut at different angles before you start to sew.

Sew the angle-cut scraps together in pairs, then sew the pairs together until about 10 scraps have been sewn in a row to make a wonky-angled, uneven strip that is about 3 in. wide and about 15 in. long. Offset the seams so the strip stays somewhat rectangular as you add scraps; the edges

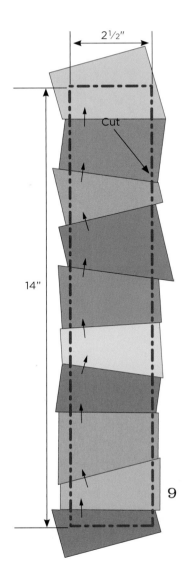

2½"

Cut

14"

9

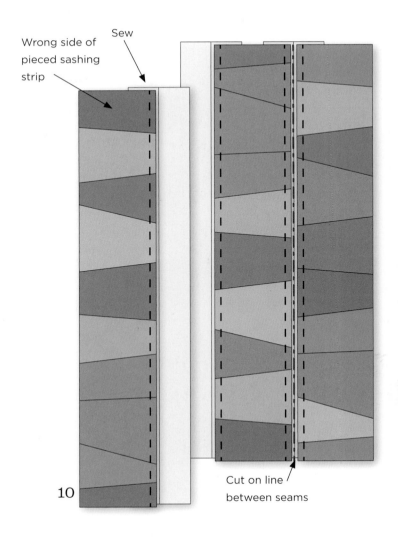

Wrong side of
pieced sashing
strip

Sew

Cut on line
between seams

10

will not align. Press the seams in one direction. Trim the strip to 2½ in. by 14 in. Repeat to make 31 pieced sashing strips. **9**

Align the 14-in. edge of 2½-in. by 14-in. pieced sashing strip with a drawn line on a 2-in. by 14-in. cream rectangle, right sides together. Pin to secure. Sew ¼ in. from the aligned edge of the pieced sashing strip. In

the same manner, add another 2-in. by 14-in. cream rectangle to the other side of the pieced sashing strip.

Align the 14-in. edge of a second 2½-in. by 14-in. pieced sashing strip on the opposite side of the drawn line on the 2-in. by 14-in. cream rectangle, right sides together. Pin to secure. Sew a ¼-in. seam along the aligned edge of the strip. **10**

Continue adding 2-in. by 14-in. cream rectangles and 2½-in. by 14-in. pieced strips until all pieced strips have been sewn to a cream rectangle and both 14-in. sides of each pieced strip are sewn.

Always *sew* along the edge of the pieced strip and *cut* through the middle of the cream rectangle.

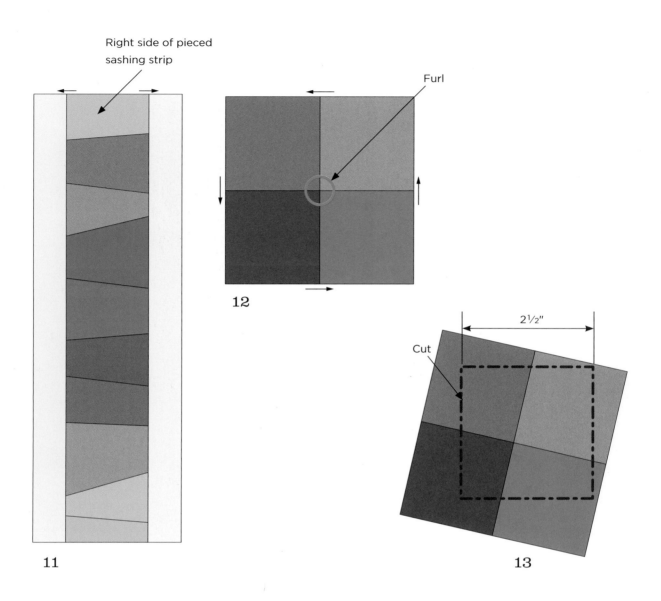

Right side of pieced sashing strip

Furl

12

2½"

Cut

11

13

Chain sew, and cut the pieces apart only after attaching both sides of the pieced sashing strip to a cream rectangle. Once cut apart, press the seams toward the cream rectangle. Make 31 sashing strips that are 3½ in. by 14 in. **11**

Sewing long narrow strips together can create disappointing results. Fabric edges don't line up, and seams can go astray. By cutting the narrow cream strips after they have been sewn, you don't have to handle strips that are only 1 in. wide.

MAKE THE CORNERSTONES

Select four 2-in. scrap cornerstone squares without lines set aside for the wonky four-patch. Sew a simple four-patch, furling the seam intersection, if desired (see p. 180). **12**

Place a small square ruler on top of the four-patch at a random angle and cut two sides of a 2½-in. square. Rotate the four-patch and cut the

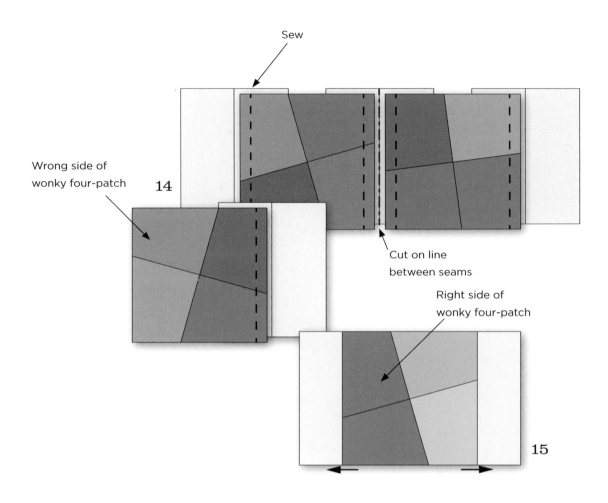

Sew

Wrong side of
wonky four-patch

14

Cut on line
between seams

Right side of
wonky four-patch

15

remaining two sides to make a 2¹/₂-in.-square wonky four-patch. Repeat to make 20 wonky four-patches. **13**

Align one edge of a wonky four-patch with a drawn line on a 2-in. by 2¹/₂-in. cream rectangle, with the right sides together. Pin to secure. Sew ¹/₄ in. from the aligned edge of the wonky four-patch. In the same manner, add another 2-in. by 2¹/₂-in. cream rectangle to the other side of the wonky four-patch.

Align the 2¹/₂-in. edge of a second wonky four-patch on the opposite side of the drawn line on a 2-in. by 2¹/₂-in. cream rectangle, with right sides together. Pin to secure. Sew a ¹/₄-in. seam from the aligned edge of the wonky four-patch. **14**

Continue adding 2-in. by 2¹/₂-in. cream rectangles and wonky four-patches until all four-patches have been sewn to a cream rectangle and

both 2¹/₂-in. sides of each wonky four-patch are sewn.

Always *sew* along the edge of the four-patch and *cut* through the middle of the cream rectangle.

You should have twenty 2-in. by 2¹/₂-in. cream rectangles left.

Chain sew, and cut the pieces apart only after attaching both sides of the wonky four-patch to a cream rectangle. Once cut apart, press

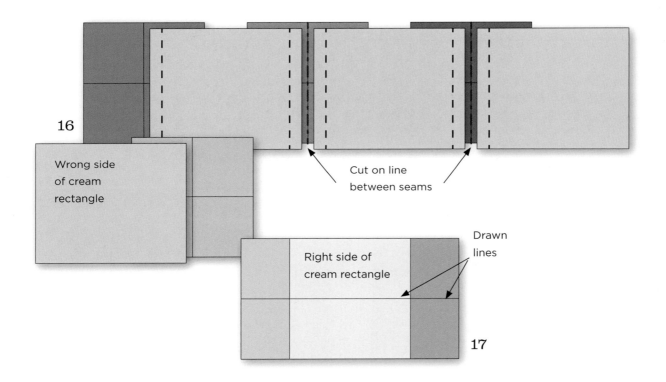

16

Wrong side
of cream
rectangle

Cut on line
between seams

Drawn
lines

Right side of
cream rectangle

17

seams toward the cream rectangle. Make 20 cornerstone center units that are 2½ in. by 3½ in. **15**

Select a 2-in. cornerstone scrap with drawn lines. Align the 2-in. edge of a 2-in. by 2½-in. cream rectangle with a drawn line on the 2-in. scrap square, right sides together. Pin to secure. Sew ¼ in. from the aligned edge of the cream rectangle. In the same manner, add another 2-in. by 2½-in. cream rectangle to the other side of the 2-in. scrap square.

Align the edge of a second 2-in. by 2½-in. cream rectangle on the opposite side of the drawn line on a 2-in. scrap square, right sides together. Pin to secure. Sew a ¼-in. seam from the aligned edge of the cream rectangle. **16**

Continue adding 2-in. scrap squares and 2-in. by 2½-in. cream rectangles until all 20 remaining cream rectangles set aside for the cornerstones have a 2-in. scrap square sewn to both 2-in. sides.

Always *sew* on the edge of the cream rectangle and *cut* through the middle of the scrap square.

Chain sew, and cut the pieces apart on the drawn line only after attaching both sides of the cream rectangle to a 2-in. scrap square. Once cut apart, press the seams toward the cream rectangle. Make 20 cornerstone outer units that are 2 in. by 3½ in. **17**

Select a cornerstone center unit. Align the 3½-in. edge of 2½-in. by 3½-in. center unit with a drawn line

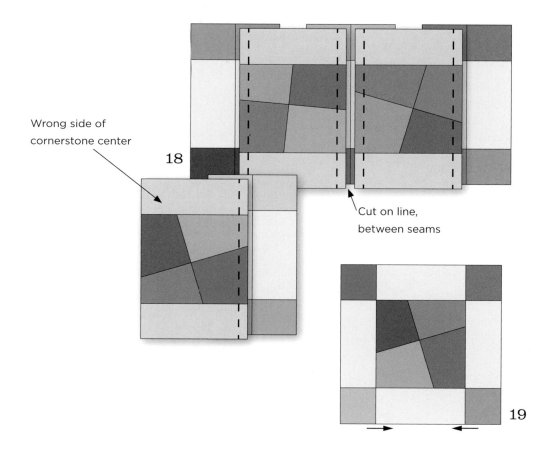

Wrong side of
cornerstone center

18

Cut on line,
between seams

19

on a 2½-in. by 3½-in. cornerstone outer unit, right sides together. Pin to secure. Sew ¼ in. from the aligned edge of the center unit. In the same manner, add another cornerstone outer unit to the other side of the center unit.

Align the edge of a second center unit with the opposite side of the drawn line on an outer unit, right sides together. Pin to secure. Sew a ¼-in. seam from the aligned edge of the center unit. **18**

Continue adding center units and outer units until all the center units have been sewn to an outer unit and both 2½-in. sides of each center unit are sewn.

For these units, always *sew* along the edge of the center unit and *cut* through the middle of the outer unit.

Chain sew, and cut the pieces apart on the drawn line only after attaching both sides of the center unit to an outer unit. Once cut apart, press the seams toward the center of the cornerstone. Make 20 corner-stones that are 3½ in. square. **19**

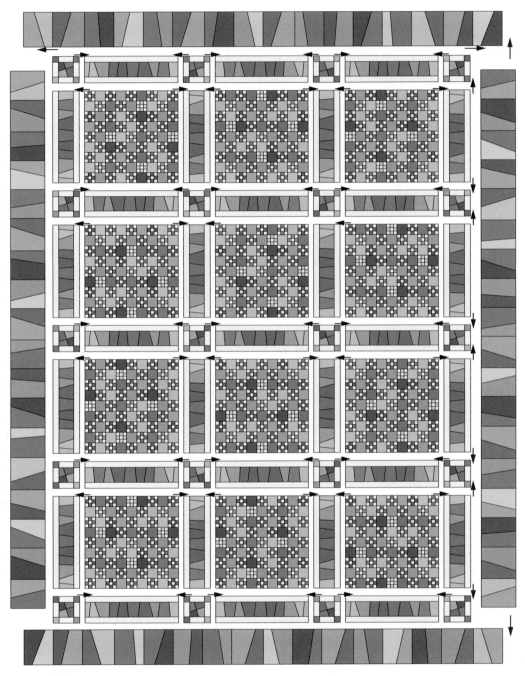

20

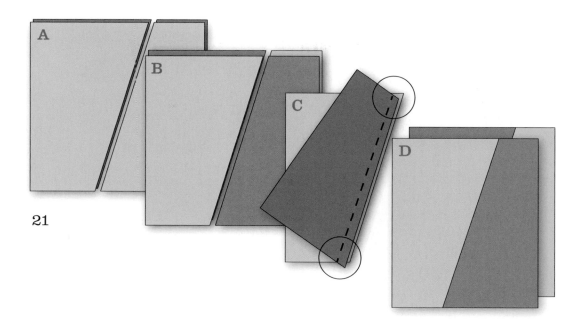

21

ASSEMBLE THE QUILT TOP

QUILT CENTER

Arrange the cornerstones, sashing units, and blocks, as shown. **20** Sew them into rows. Press the seams toward the sashing within each row. Sew the rows together, and press the seams toward the sashing/cornerstone rows.

BORDER

Randomly select two 5-in. scrap squares set aside for the borders. Stack both scrap squares on your cutting mat right side up with all the edges aligned. **21** Place a ruler on top of the scraps at a random angle, and cut through both layers. **A** Reverse the order of the top and bottom layers for the fabric pieces on the right side of the cut. **B** Then sew the pieces, first joining the top layers and then the bottom layers. **C** Be sure to offset the seams so the top and bottom edges align after sewing (circled). Press the seam in either direction. Repeat with all sixty-eight 5-in. scrap squares (34 pairs) to make 68 border rectangles with wonky seams that are each about 4½ in. by 5 in. **D**

> Measure the quilt top before trimming the borders.

Sew 18 border rectangles together along the 5-in. sides to make side borders. Repeat to make two. Trim each to 5 in. by 69½ in. for the side borders; then sew them to the quilt top. Press the seams toward the borders.

Sew 16 border rectangles together along the 5-in. sides to make the top and bottom borders. Repeat to make two. Trim each to 5 in. by 62 in.; then sew to the quilt top. Press the seams toward the borders. **20**

QUILT AND BIND

Layer the backing, batting, and quilt top; baste. Quilt as desired.

Cut eight 2¼-in. strips for the binding. Sew binding strips together end to end using a diagonal seam (see p. 180). Press the connecting seams open, and then press the binding in half lengthwise with the wrong sides together.

Trim the batting and backing even with the quilt top. With the raw edges aligned, sew the binding to the front of the quilt using a ¼-in. seam. Miter the binding at the corners.

Turn the folded edge of the binding to the back of the quilt, and hand-stitch in place.

Prairie Porcelain

SCRAPS PLUS ONE DARK BLUE FABRIC

This quilt was inspired by a quilt I saw hanging in the Infinite Variety: Three Centuries of Red and White Quilts exhibit in New York City. Quilts following a pattern similar to Prairie Porcelain appeared more than once in the display. It is interesting that, upon closer viewing, each block consisted of an appliqué shape—the curved center plus cornerstone—on a block background. I've simplified the construction and incorporated varied light-value scraps and a single solid-reading blue fabric as my theme.

Many of the quilts in that same show had minimal or no border treatments. This works particularly nicely here because the quilt can be easily increased or decreased in size by changing the number of blocks assembled.

Red or blue, the light and dark contrast in curvy and linear shape combinations to create a dramatic statement, like fine china in a rustic setting.

Find a solid color fabric that inspires you, then choose coordinating light-value scraps from your stash for your project. Easy appliqué can be done by hand or by machine.

FINISHED SIZE: **60 in. by 75 in.**
PATTERN DIFFICULTY: **Intermediate**

SCRAP REQUIREMENTS:
2-in. light-value scrap squares: 160
5-in. light-value scrap squares: 160
FABRIC REQUIREMENTS
3 yards dark blue for blocks
¹/₂ yard dark blue for binding
4¹/₂ yards for backing
64-in. by 79-in. batting

For hand appliqué: Pigma pen or heat-erasable marker, appliqué pins, and appliqué needles
For machine appliqué: Pigma pen, 2¹/₄ yards 16-in.-wide fusible web

NOTE: You may use your favorite appliqué method; however, the instructions assume the back-basting hand appliqué method is used. Additional details are provided on p. 181.

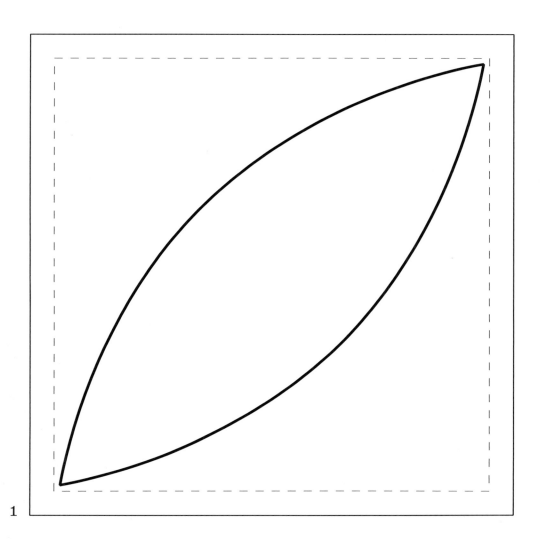

1

| 2" × 5" | 2" × 5" | Not used |

2

PREPARE THE SCRAPS

Select one hundred sixty 5-in. light-value scrap squares. From these scraps, select 40 for the appliqué shapes, 40 for the light block centers, and 80 for the light block borders. Using the 40 block centers, trace the appliqué shape, centered, on the back of each 5-in. scrap square, for back-basting appliqué. **1** From the eighty 5-in. block border squares, cut each into two 2-in. by 5-in. rectangles, as shown, to make a total of one hundred sixty 2-in. by 5-in. rectangles. **2** The leftover 1-in. by 5-in. rectangles will be unused.

Select one hundred sixty 2-in. light-value scrap squares.

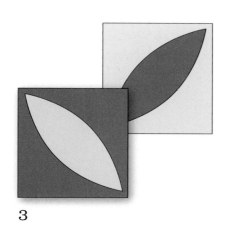

3

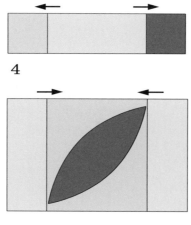

4

5

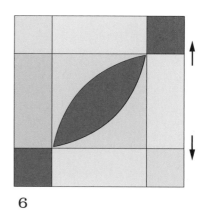

6

PREPARE THE ADDITIONAL FABRICS

DARK BLUE SOLID

Cut five 5-in. width-of-fabric strips; then cut forty 5-in. squares for the dark block centers. For the back-basting appliqué, center and trace the appliqué shape on the back of each square. **2**

Cut three 7-in. width-of-fabric strips; then cut forty 3-in. by 7-in. rectangles along the lengthwise grain for the appliqué shapes.

Cut four 5-in. width-of-fabric strips; then cut eighty 2-in. by 5-in. rectangles along the lengthwise grain.

Cut four 6½-in. width-of-fabric strips; then cut eighty 2-in. by 6½-in. rectangles along the lengthwise grain.

Cut four 2-in. width-of-fabric strips; then cut eighty 2-in. squares.

MAKE THE BLOCKS
BLOCK APPLIQUÉ

Using the forty 5-in. light scrap squares and your favorite appliqué method, or the back basting method as described on p. 181, center and secure one light appliqué shape on one of the dark blue 5-in. squares. Repeat to make forty 5-in. dark block centers with light scrap appliqué. Similarly, using the 3-in. by 7-in. blue rectangles, center and secure one dark appliqué shape on each of the light block centers. Repeat to make forty 5-in. light block centers with dark blue appliqué. **3**

The appliqué shape is sized to fit just inside the block center seam allowance so you can avoid sewing over the appliqué shape when you assemble the block.

Be sure to take advantage of the shape placement, centering it carefully within the square as shown when securing your appliqué shapes.

LIGHT BLOCKS

Sew one light-value 2-in. scrap square and one dark blue 2-in. square to either end of a light-value 2-in. by 5-in. scrap rectangle. Press the seams toward the 2-in. squares. Repeat to make 80 light block strips that are 2 in. by 8 in. **4**

Sew one light-value 2-in. by 5-in. scrap rectangle to each side of the light block center, as shown. Press the seams toward the block center. Repeat to make 40 light block centers that are 5 in. by 8 in. **5**

Sew a light block strip to the top and bottom of a light block center, as shown. Pay attention to the placement of the 2-in. blue squares as you sew pieced strips to the block center. Press the seams away from the block center. Repeat to make 40 light blocks that are 8 in. square. **6**

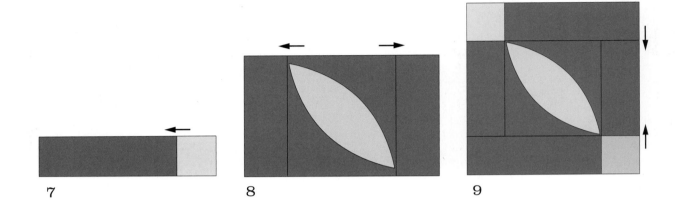

7

8

9

DARK BLOCKS

Sew one light-value 2-in. scrap square to one end of a dark blue 2-in. by 6½-in. rectangle. Press the seam toward the dark blue rectangle. Repeat to make 80 dark block strips that are 2 in. by 8 in. **7**

Sew one dark blue 2-in. by 5-in. rectangle to each side of a dark block center, as shown. Press the seams away from the block center. Repeat to make 40 dark block centers that are 5 in. by 8 in. **8**

Sew a dark block strip to the top and bottom of the dark block center, as shown. Pay attention to the placement of the 2-in. scrap squares as you sew the pieced strips to the block center. Press the seams toward the block center. Repeat to make 40 dark blocks that are 8 in. square. **9**

FINISH THE CONSTRUCTION

Arrange 10 rows of eight blocks, alternating light and dark blocks, as shown. Sew the blocks into rows; press the seams toward the dark blocks within rows. Sew the rows together, and press the seams in one direction. **10**

QUILT AND BIND

Layer the backing, batting, and quilt top; baste. Quilt as desired.

Cut seven 2¼-in. strips for the binding. Sew the binding strips together end to end, using a diagonal seam (see p. 180). Press the connecting seams open, and then press the binding in half lengthwise, wrong sides together.

Trim the batting and backing even with the quilt top. With the raw edges aligned, sew the binding to the front of the quilt using a ¼-in. seam. Miter the binding at the corners.

Turn the folded edge of the binding to the back of the quilt, and hand-stitch it in place.

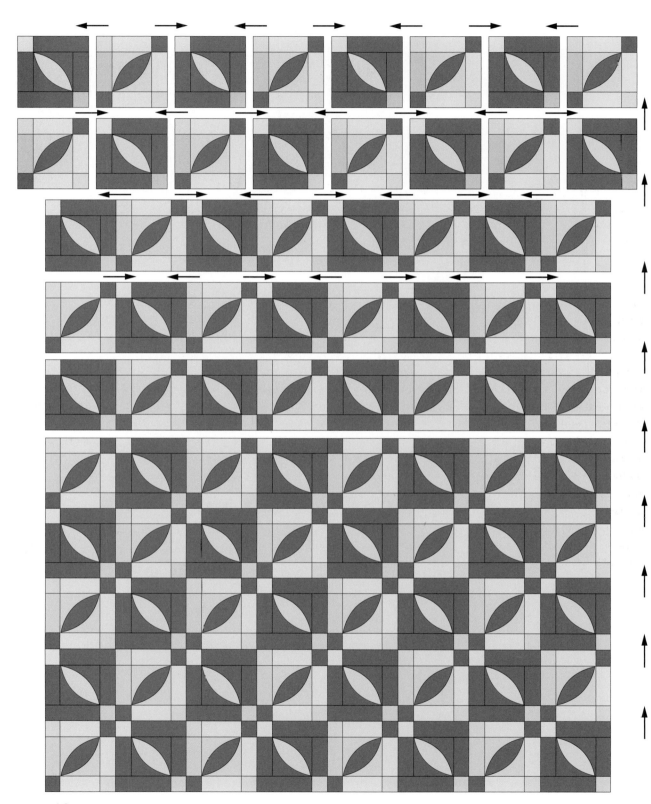

10

Scraptop Pouch and Carrier

SCRAPS PLUS ONE BOLD PRINT

The inspiration for this project started with a photo of a painted tabletop I saw somewhere on the Internet. The top of the table was painted like a quilt, but with crazy shapes next to one another—not the typical meticulously planned pieces and blocks that you might find in the design of a traditional quilt.

Two rectangular blocks, rather than square blocks, break from traditional quilting standards. The panels on both the pouch (intended for small electronics, such as an e-reader or tablet) and the larger carrier (ideal for a laptop, crafts, or just plain stuff) are intentionally made from blended, low-contrast scraps.

Somewhere in the middle of creating the sample for this pattern, I really didn't think it was working. Too many washed-out scrap fabric choices. But that was my quilters' brain insisting on putting dark values next to light values. I'm glad I didn't listen to my inner voice and persisted in putting light values next to medium-light values for the right effect.

The bold print used for the handle and lining is one of those fabrics that caught my eye in a quilt shop. It had to come home with me! I'm sure that never happens to you! *Wink, wink!*

FINISHED SIZE: 12 in. by 8 in. (pouch); 13 in. by 11 in. by 3 in. (carrier)
PATTERN DIFFICULTY: Intermediate

SCRAP REQUIREMENTS:
2-in. light- to medium-value scrap squares: 110
3½-in. light- to medium-value scrap squares: 56
5-in. light- to medium-value scrap squares: 42

FABRIC AND NOTION REQUIREMENTS:
1³/₄ yards bold print for straps and lining
16-in. by 20-in. batting scrap for pouch
20-in. by 30-in. batting scrap for carrier
Additional scrap batting strips for straps
Pigma pen or heat-erasable marker
2 decorative buttons, each about 1¼ in. to 1½ in. in diameter

NOTE: Fabric requirements are for both projects.

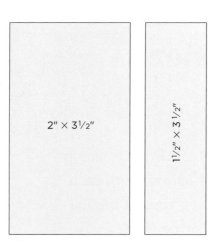

2" × 3¹⁄₂"

1¹⁄₂" × 3¹⁄₂"

1

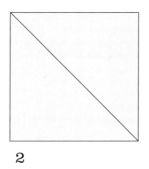

2

3

PREPARE THE SCRAPS

Select 110 light- to medium-light-value 2-in. scrap squares.

Select 56 light- to medium-light-value 3¹⁄₂-in. scrap squares.

Select 42 light- to medium-light-value 5-in. scrap squares.

PREPARE THE ADDITIONAL FABRIC

BOLD PRINT

Cut two 17¹⁄₂-in. width-of-fabric strips. From one strip cut one 17¹⁄₂-in. by 26-in. rectangle for the carrier lining. From the second strip, cut one 13¹⁄₂-in. by 17¹⁄₂-in. rectangle for the pouch lining and one 12-in. by 17¹⁄₂-in. rectangle for the carrier pocket. Trim the remainder to 13¹⁄₂ in. wide; then cut one 12-in. by 13¹⁄₂-in. rectangle for the pouch pocket.

Cut three 6-in. width-of-fabric strips for the carrier straps.

Cut one 3¹⁄₂-in. width-of-fabric strip for the pouch strap accents.

Cut one 2¹⁄₂-in. width-of-fabric strip; then cut the strip into two short strips about 10 in. long for the button loops—one for the carrier and one for the pouch.

MAKE THE FLYING GEESE BLOCKS

FLYING GEESE UNITS

Select forty 3¹⁄₂-in. scrap squares, and trim each to 2 in. by 3¹⁄₂ in. Reserve twenty 1¹⁄₂-in. by 3¹⁄₂-in. leftover rectangles for the bar units. The remaining 1¹⁄₂-in. by 3¹⁄₂-in. rectangles will not be used. **1**

Select eighty 2-in. scrap squares and sort them into pairs of matching or similar prints. Draw a diagonal line on the back of each. **2**

Select one 2-in. scrap square from a paired set and align it with one side of 2-in. by 3¹⁄₂-in. rectangle. Sew on the line, and trim the extra layers to reduce bulk, if desired. Press toward the outer corner. **3**

The two rectangular blocks for this project aren't easily identified by a traditional tag. So instead of calling them Block A and Block B, I'll identify each block by one of its more prominent elements, the flying geese block and the zigzag block.

To add to the fuss, each block is a different size. As you assemble the panels, consider rotating the blocks 180 degrees to find the most pleasing arrangement. Be aware that seam allowances may not always nest as nicely as a more predictable traditional block arrangement, so use extra pins as needed.

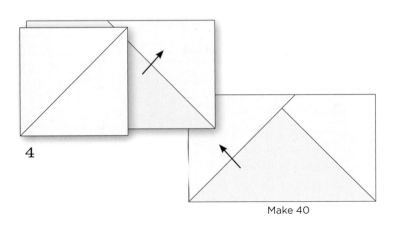

4

Make 40

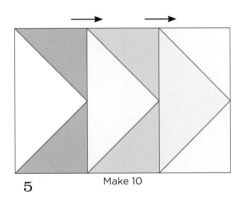

5

Make 10

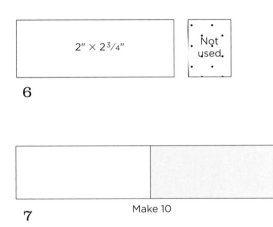

6

2" × 2³/₄"

Not used.

7

Make 10

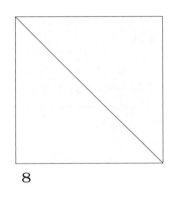

8

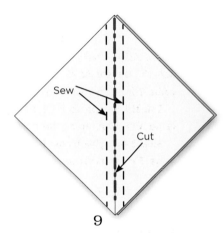

Sew

Cut

9

Align the other 2-in. scrap square from the paired set with the opposite side of the 2-in. by 3¹/₂-in. rectangle. Sew on the line, and trim the extra layers, if desired. Press toward the corner. **4**

Repeat to make forty 2-in. by 3¹/₂-in. flying geese units. Set 10 aside.

Select three flying geese units, and sew them together in a row. Press the seams as indicated. **5**

Repeat to make ten 3¹/₂-in. by 5-in. three-geese units.

BAR UNITS
Trim twenty 1¹/₂-in. by 3¹/₂-in. strips to 1¹/₂ in. by 2³/₄ in. **6**

Sew two 1¹/₂-in. by 2³/₄-in. strips together, end to end. Press the seam in either direction. **7**

Repeat to make ten 1¹/₂-in. by 5-in. bar units.

QUARTER SQUARE TRIANGLE UNITS
Select ten 5-in. scrap squares. On the back of five squares, draw a diagonal line, corner to corner. **8**

Place two 5-in. scrap squares right sides together, one with a drawn line and one without, with the drawn line on top. Sew a ¹/₄-in. seam on both sides of the line. Cut on the line, and press the seam toward the darker fabric. **9**

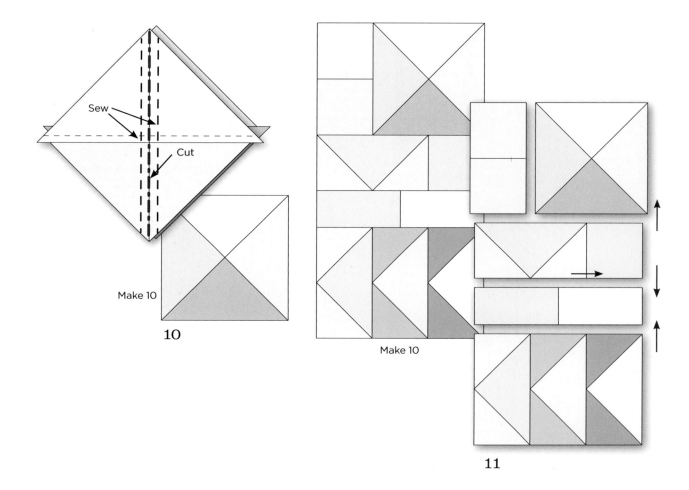

10

Make 10

Make 10

11

Repeat to make 10 half-square triangle (HST) units that are roughly 4$\frac{1}{2}$ in. square.

Draw a line on the back of five of the HST units, perpendicular to the existing seam.

Place two HST units right sides together, one with and one without lines, so the seams nest and the drawn line is on top. Sew a $\frac{1}{4}$-in. seam on both sides of the drawn line. Cut on the line, and press the seams in one direction, or furl the seam, as shown on p. 180, if desired. **10**

Repeat to make 10 quarter-square triangle (QST) units. Trim each unit to 3$\frac{1}{2}$ in. square, making sure to center the seam intersection as you trim.

FLYING GEESE BLOCKS

Arrange one three-geese unit, one bar unit, one single flying geese unit, one QST unit, and three 2-in. squares. Sew the units together, pressing the seams as shown. **11**

Make ten 5-in. by 9-in. blocks, four for the pouch and six for the carrier.

NOTE: When no pressing directions are given, seams may be pressed in either direction.

MAKE THE ZIGZAG BLOCKS
ZIGZAG UNITS

Select sixteen 5-in. scrap squares. On the back of eight squares, draw two diagonal lines from corner to corner. Place two scraps right sides together with the drawn lines on top. Sew a $\frac{1}{4}$-in. seam on both sides of the drawn lines to make a total of four stitching lines. **12**

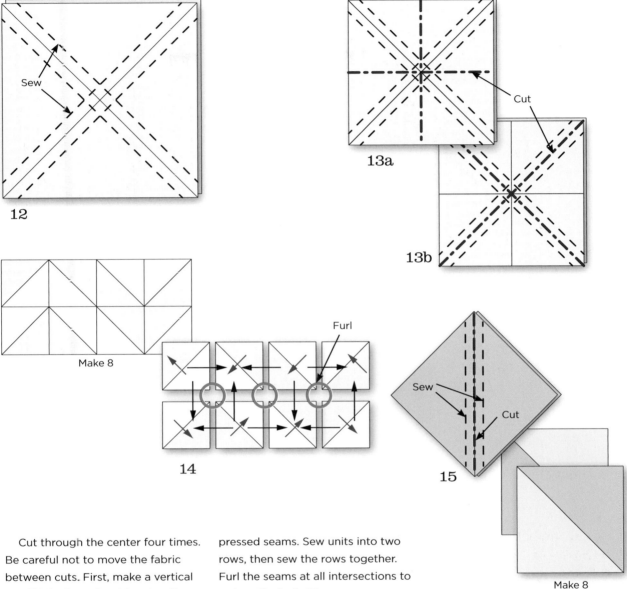

12

13a

13b

Make 8

Furl

14

Sew

Cut

15

Make 8

Cut through the center four times. Be careful not to move the fabric between cuts. First, make a vertical cut 2½ in. from the side edge; then make a horizontal cut 2½ in. from the bottom. **13a** Then cut diagonally on the drawn lines to make eight HST units. **13b**

Press half of the HST seams toward the darker fabric and half of the HST seams toward the lighter fabric. Trim each HST unit to 1½ in. square. Arrange into a zigzag unit, as shown, noting the placement of the diagonal

pressed seams. Sew units into two rows, then sew the rows together. Furl the seams at all intersections to reduce the bulk. **14**

Repeat to make eight 2½-in. by 4½-in. zigzag units.

LARGE HALF-SQUARE TRIANGLE UNITS

Select eight 3½-in. scrap squares. On the back of four squares, draw a diagonal line from corner to corner. Place two squares right sides together, one with a drawn line, and

one without, so the drawn line is on top. Sew a ¼-in. seam along both sides of the line. Cut on the line. Press the seam in one direction, and trim to 3 in. square. **15** Repeat to make eight 3-in. HST units.

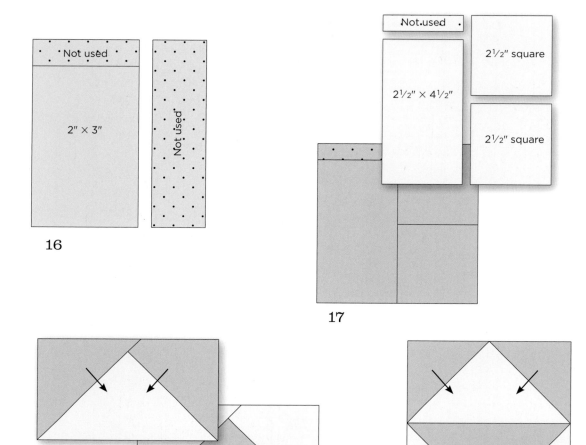

16

17

18

19   Make 8

RECTANGLES

Select eight 3½-in. scrap squares. Trim each to 2 in. by 3 in. The remaining pieces are not used. **16**

SPLIT ON-POINT SQUARE UNIT

Select sixteen 5-in. scrap squares; then choose two, and set the rest aside.

Cut one square in half to make two 2½-in. by 5-in. rectangles. Trim one rectangle to 2½ in. by 4½ in. Cut the other rectangle in half to make two 2½-in. squares. Draw a diagonal line on the back of each 2½-in. square. **17**

Pair each 2½-in. by 4½-in. rectangle with its opposite set of 2½-in. squares. Then make two 2½-in. by 4½-in. flying geese units similar to those shown in drawing **4** (p. 83) but in a slightly larger size. However, press seams toward the large triangle for one flying geese unit and press the seams away from the triangle for the other. **18**

Sew two flying geese units together to make a split on-point square unit. **19**

Repeat with the remaining fourteen 5-in. scrap squares to make a total of eight 4½-in. on-point square units.

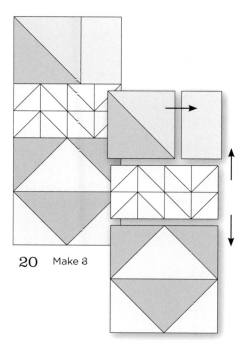

20   Make 8

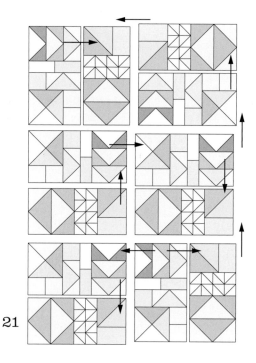
21

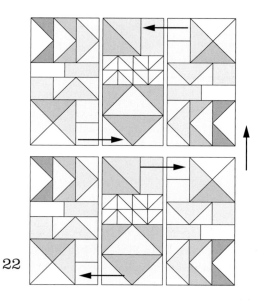
22

ZIGZAG BLOCK

Arrange one HST unit, one rectangle, one zigzag unit, and one on-point square unit. Sew the units together. Press as shown. **20**

Make eight 4$\frac{1}{2}$-in. by 9-in. blocks, two for the pouch and six for the carrier.

MAKE THE EXTERIOR PANELS

CARRIER

Arrange six flying geese blocks and six zigzag blocks, as shown. Or rotate the rectangular and square blocks into a pleasing arrangement that suits your choice of scraps.

Sew the rectangular blocks into 9-in.-square blocks; then sew the square blocks into rows. Sew the rows together. Press the seams away from the bulky intersections. Some seams may resist pressing, but hang in there! The carrier panel is 17$\frac{1}{2}$ in. by 26 in. **21**

POUCH

Arrange four flying geese blocks and two zigzag blocks, as shown. Or rotate rectangular blocks into a pleasing arrangement that suits your choice of scraps.

Sew the blocks into rows; then sew the rows together. Press the seams away from the bulky intersections. Some seams may resist pressing, but hang in there! The pouch panel is 13$\frac{1}{2}$ in. by 17$\frac{1}{2}$ in. **22**

LAYER AND QUILT

Layer the larger batting scrap and the carrier panel, right side up, on your work surface. Baste. Quilt as desired. Trim the batting even with the panel edges.

Repeat for the smaller batting scrap and pouch panel.

Set aside.

MAKE THE STRAPS
CARRIER

Sew three 6-in. bold print strips end to end, using a diagonal seam (see p. 180). Sew all the strip ends so the strip becomes a continuous loop that is about 60 in. long when folded. Be careful that the loop has no twists. Press the connecting seams open.

Drape the strip loop over one end of your ironing board and press the strip in half lengthwise, wrong sides together. Open; then fold in each raw edge so it meets the center crease. Press.

Cut scrap batting into 1½-in. strips, making enough strips to total at least 120 in. in length. Working with one short segment at a time, open one side of the strap fold and insert a 1½-in.-wide scrap strip of thin batting between a side fold and the center crease. Refold the strap on all creases to encase the batting. Pin liberally along the length of the strap to secure all layers. Continue adding 1½-in. batting strips until the entire loop has batting, is folded, and is secured with pins. **23**

Using a walking foot, edgestitch around the entire length of loop about ¼ in. away from each folded side.

Extend the strap loop to flatten it, folding the strap in half to locate the center. Mark both folded ends of the strap (center).

Place the quilted carrier panel on a large work surface, right side up, and place the strap loop on top. Align the center pins of the strap with the center (bottom) seam on the panel and 3½ in. away from the panel side edges. Pin liberally along the center section of the strap to secure it to the exterior panel.

Using a walking foot to sew through all layers, sew directly over each topstitch line on the strap, starting and ending with a tack stitch 1 in. away from the bag rim (short sides of panel). **24**

POUCH
NOTE: The strap on the pouch is decorative.

Fold the 3½-in. bold print strip in half lengthwise, wrong sides together. Open, then fold in each raw edge so it meets the center crease. Press.

Cut the scrap batting into ¾-in. strips, making enough strips to total at least 45 in. in length. Working with one short segment at a time, open one side of the fold and insert a ¾-in.-wide scrap strip of thin batting between a side fold and the center crease. Refold all creases to encase the batting and pin liberally along the length of strip to secure the layers. Continue adding ¾-in. batting strips

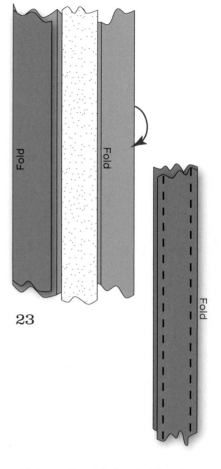

23

until the entire strip has batting, is folded, and is pinned.

Using a walking foot, edgestitch along the length of the strip about ⅛ in. away from each folded side.

Cut the strip roughly in half to make two folded and stitched strips about 20 in. long. Place the quilted pouch panel on your work surface, right side up, and place the strap on top, 3 in. away from the panel side edges. Sew directly over each topstitch line on the strap, end to end. Trim any extra strap even with edge of panel. **25**

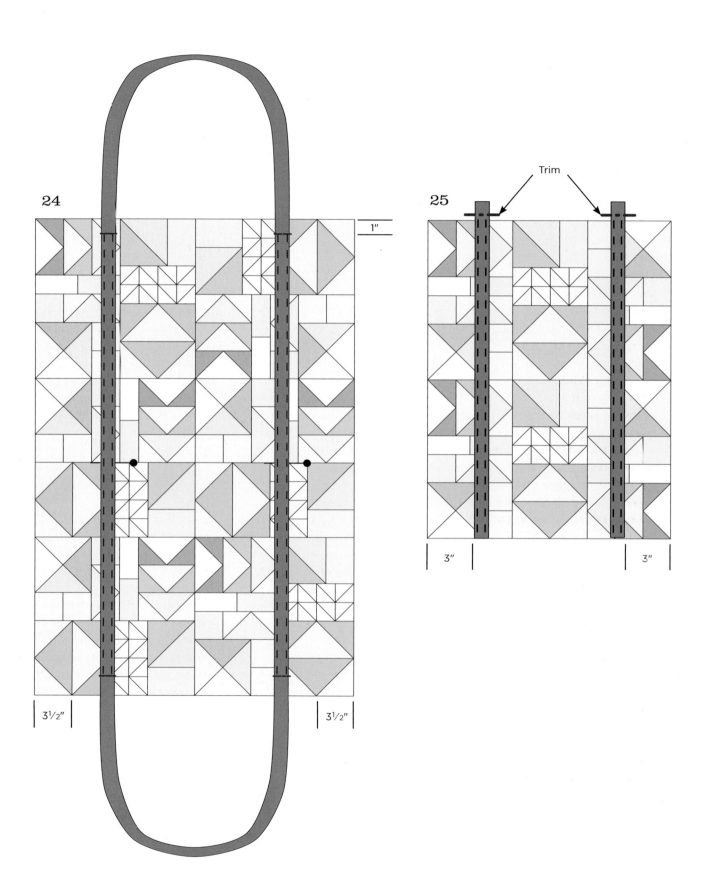

24

1"

3½"

3½"

25

Trim

3"

3"

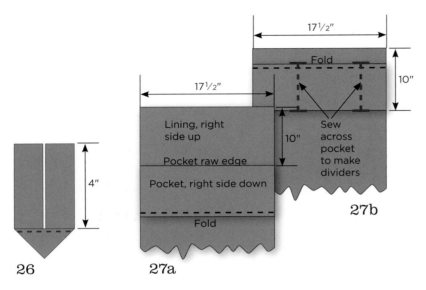

26

27a

27b

MAKE BUTTON LOOPS

Press each 2½-in. by 10-in. button loop strip in half lengthwise, wrong sides together. Open, then fold the long edges in to meet the center crease, then fold again on the original crease. Edgestitch. Fold the strip in half, aligning the raw ends, and mark the strip's center. Fold each side to form a V, as shown. **26** Pin the folds and sew horizontally across the layers, as shown. Repeat for both loops. Trim each loop 4 in. from the point. With the raw edges aligned, center one loop each on one short end of the carrier panel and the pouch panel, right sides together, and baste them into place.

MAKE THE LININGS
CARRIER

Fold the 12-in. by 17½-in. carrier pocket rectangle in half, wrong sides together, to make a 6-in. by 17½-in. pocket. Press. Topstitch along the folded edge.

Place the 17½-in. raw edge of the pocket 10 in. away from one 17½-in. side of the 17½-in. by 26-in. carrier lining. The side edges of the pocket are aligned with the 26-in. side of the lining. Sew ¼ in. along the pocket's raw edge. **27a**

Fold the pocket toward the top edge of the lining and press. Pin to secure, and baste the sides of the pocket to the lining. If desired, sew several straight lines across the pocket, perpendicular to the pocket fold, to divide the pocket into sections. **27b**

POUCH

Fold the 12-in. by 13½-in. pouch pocket rectangle in half, wrong sides together, to make a 6-in. by 13½-in. pocket. Press. Topstitch along the folded edge. Place the 13½-in. raw edge of the pocket 8 in. away from one 13½-in. side of the 13½-in. by 17½-in. pouch lining. The side edges of the pocket are aligned with the

17½-in. side of the lining. Sew ¼ in. along the pocket's raw edge. Fold the pocket toward the top edge of the lining and press. Pin to secure, and baste the sides of the pocket to the lining. If desired, sew straight lines across the pocket, perpendicular to the pocket fold, to divide the pocket into sections.

FINISH THE CONSTRUCTION

Fold the quilted carrier panel in half, right sides together. With a walking foot, sew a ¼-in. seam along each side. **28**

To make the box pleat, open the seam at the bottom corner and flatten, centering the side seam. Measure 1½ in. from the point, as shown, and draw a line perpendicular to the side seam. **29** Sew on the line, and trim the excess bulk. Repeat for the other bottom corner. Turn the carrier right side out.

Repeat for the quilted pouch panel. Fold the right sides together, sew the sides, and turn the pouch right side out.

NOTE: The pouch does not have box pleats.

Similarly, fold each lining assembly, right sides together, and sew ¼ in. along each side, leaving an 8-in. gap in the sewing on one side of the carrier lining and a 6-in. gap in the sewing on one side of the pouch lining. Add box pleats to the carrier lining, but not to the pouch lining. Do not turn the lining right side out. Place the quilted carrier assembly inside the carrier lining, with right sides facing. Pin around the rim,

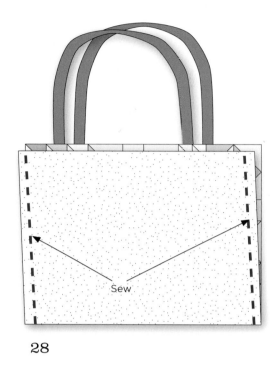

28

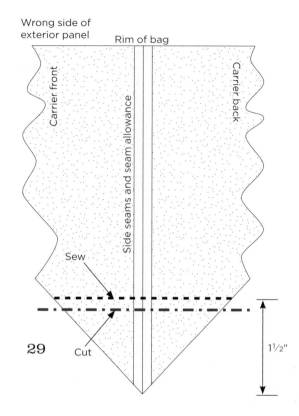

Wrong side of
exterior panel

Rim of bag

Carrier front

Carrier back

Side seams and seam allowance

Sew

Cut

$1^1/_2$"

29

making sure that the carrier handles and the button loops for the carrier are tucked in between the bag exterior and the lining. Sew a $1/_4$-in. seam around the rim of each bag. Turn the carrier inside out through the opening in the lining. Close the opening by hand or machine. Insert the lining in the bag, and edgestitch around the rim, without sewing over the handles on the carrier. **30** Repeat for the pouch and lining.

Center and secure the buttons on the front outside of the carrier and the pouch (the button loop is on the back), about 1 in. away from the bag rim.

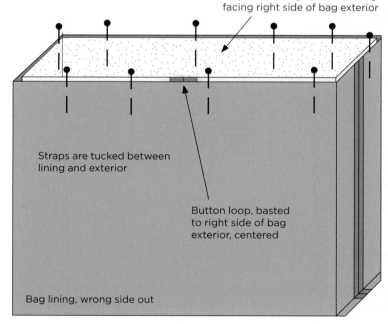

Bag exterior, right side of lining facing right side of bag exterior

Straps are tucked between lining and exterior

Button loop, basted to right side of bag exterior, centered

Bag lining, wrong side out

30

Bed quilt

Magic Carpet Table Runner and Quilt

SCRAPS PLUS ONE FAT QUARTER OR 1 YARD OR FOUR 1-YARD CUTS

When you add fabric to a scrappy quilt, isn't it nice when you can use the fabric without creating leftovers? Especially fat quarters. What quilter doesn't have a fat quarter or two (or maybe a few more) waiting in the wings to become something? The Magic Carpet table runner uses almost all of one fat quarter for the blocks, so you'll have just one extra 5-in. square to add to your scrap bin. To make the toddler quilt, use four fat quarters or 1 yard of fabric. Multiply that quantity by four and you have enough to make the bed-size quilt. Of course, you can substitute a bunch of fat quarters for the yardage to make the bed quilt, but try to coordinate color and value if you do. In any case, the rest of the quilt top is nothin' but scraps!

As you select the scraps to coordinate with your block fabric selection, consider alternating dark and light values when progressing from one pieced element to the next. In other words, if your block background is a light value, select 2-in. scraps that are medium to dark in value for the block borders. Likewise, choose dark 3½-in. scraps for the edges of the on-point square units in the middle border if the center scraps are light value, and vice versa. Printed fusible interfacing can simplify block assembly, but it is not required for the project construction.

FINISHED SIZE:

12 in. by 35 in. (runner); 36 in. by 56 in. (toddler quilt); 72 in. by 92 in. (bed quilt)
PATTERN DIFFICULTY: **Intermediate**

NOTION REQUIREMENTS:
ScrapTherapy Small Scrap Grid by Quiltsmart (optional)

One complete panel of ScrapTherapy Small Scrap Grid by Quiltsmart has two 5-square by 18-square grid sections. If you are using this, you will need a quarter panel for the runner, one panel for the toddler quilt, and four panels for the bed quilt.

PROJECT	Finished Size* (in.)	SCRAPS			FABRIC		
		2-in. squares	3½-in. squares	5-in. squares	Block background	Binding (yd.)	Backing (yd.)
Table Runner	12 × 35	48	18	—	1 fat quarter	¼	½
Toddler Quilt	36 × 56	192	54	16	4 fat quarters	³⁄₈	1²⁄₃
Bed Quilt	72 × 92	672	108	32	Four 1-yd. cuts	²⁄₃	5¼

*Add 4 in. to each finished quilt dimension for batting size.

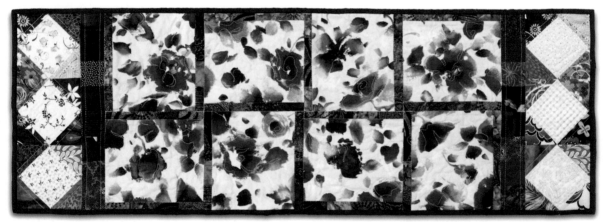

Table runner

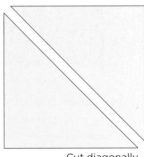

1   Cut diagonally

PREPARE THE SCRAPS

TABLE RUNNER

Select forty-eight 2-in. scrap squares in a similar color and value—32 for the blocks and 16 for the inner borders.

Select six 3½-in. scrap squares in a similar color and value for the middle border on-point square centers. Trim each center scrap to 3¼ in. square.

Select twelve 3½-in. scrap squares in a similar color and value for the middle border on-point square

corners. Cut each scrap square in half diagonally, as shown. **1**

TODDLER QUILT

Select one hundred ninety-two 2-in. scrap squares in a similar color and value—144 for the blocks and 48 for the inner borders.

Select eighteen 3½-in. scrap squares in a similar color and value for the middle border on-point square centers. Trim each center scrap to 3¼ in. square.

Select thirty-six 3½-in. scrap squares in a similar color and value for the middle border on-point square corners. Cut each scrap square in half diagonally. **1**

Select sixteen 5-in. scrap squares in a similar color and value for the outer border.

BED QUILT

Select six hundred seventy-two 2-in. scrap squares in a similar color and value—576 for the blocks and 96 for the inner borders.

Select thirty-six 3½-in. scrap squares in a similar color and value for the middle border on-point square centers. Trim each center scrap to 3¼ in. square.

Select seventy-two 3½-in. scrap squares in a similar color and value for the middle border on-point square corners. Cut each scrap square in half diagonally. **1**

Select thirty-two 5-in. scrap squares in a similar color and value for the outer border.

PREPARE THE ADDITIONAL FABRICS AND BLOCK BACKGROUND

TABLE RUNNER

Cut three 5½-in. by 21-in. strips; then cut three 5½-in. by 6½-in. rectangles from each strip to make a total of nine rectangles. One rectangle will not be used.

TODDLER QUILT

Cut three 5½-in. by 21-in. strips from each fat quarter; then cut three 5½-in. by 6½-in. rectangles from each strip to make a total of 36 rectangles.

BED QUILT

Cut six 5½-in. width-of-fabric strips from each 1-yard fabric cut; then cut six 5½-in. by 6½-in. rectangles from each strip to make a total of 36 rectangles from each fabric or a grand total of 144 rectangles.

Toddler quilt

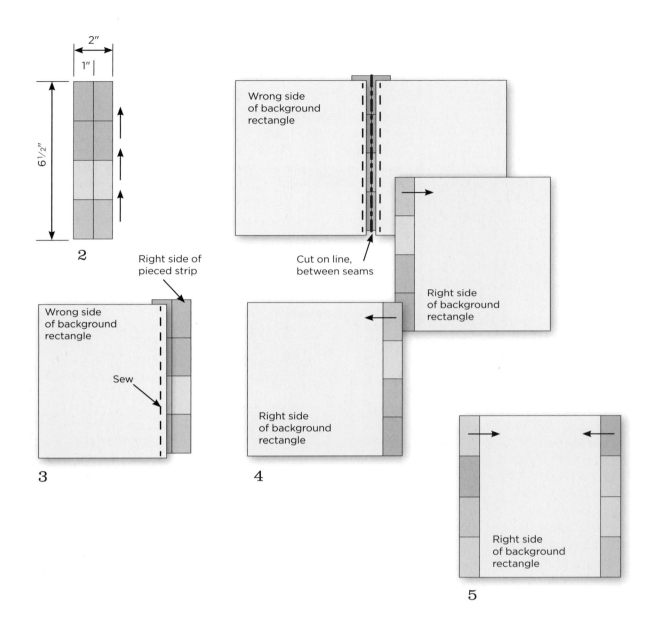

2

Right side of
pieced strip

Wrong side
of background
rectangle

Sew

3

Wrong side
of background
rectangle

Cut on line,
between seams

Right side
of background
rectangle

Right side
of background
rectangle

4

Right side
of background
rectangle

5

MAKE BLOCKS

NOTE: For tips on using printed interfacing, see the sidebar on the facing page.

Randomly sew four 2-in. scrap squares chosen for the blocks in a row. Press the seams in one direction. The pieced strip should be 2 in. by 6½ in. **2**

Repeat to make 8 strips for the table runner, 36 strips for the toddler quilt, or 144 strips for the bed quilt.

With a pencil or fabric marking tool, on the *right side* of each 2-in. by 6½-in. pieced strip, draw a line down the center, 1 in. away from the long edge.

Align the 6½-in. edge of the 5½-in. by 6½-in. block background rectangle with the drawn line on the

2-in. by 6½-in. pieced strip, right sides together. Sew ¼ in. from the aligned edge of the background fabric.

Align the 6½-in. edge of a second 5½-in. by 6½-in. background rectangle with the opposite side of the drawn line on the same 2-in. by 6½-in. pieced strip, right sides together. Sew ¼-in. from the aligned edge of the strip. **3**

PIECED STRIPS USING SCRAP THERAPY
SMALL SCRAP GRID INTERFACING

Cut each grid interfacing panel into five by four grids; 2 for the table runner, 8 for the toddler quilt, and 29 for the bed quilt.

Place one grid section on your ironing surface, with the fusible, or bumpy, side up.

Arrange 20 scrap squares randomly, right side up, on one grid section. Fuse with a hot steam iron. Be careful not to touch the iron to any exposed fusible interfacing. Plan ahead—you may have extra rows on some grid sections.

Working one row at a time, fold the interfacing on the longer seam line (across five scrap squares), with the fabric pieces right sides together. Make sure the fold is precisely on the dotted line, regardless of where the fabric edges are.

Sew a scant 1/4-in. seam allowance along the fold.

Repeat this process for each parallel row until all three rows have been sewn. Press the seams in one direction. *Important! Do not sew perpendicular seams!*

Place the panel on the cutting surface, right side down, and cut along the shorter dotted lines—the lines that have not been sewn—to make five strips of four scraps from each panel segment.

Repeat to make 8 scrap strips for the table runner, 36 scrap strips for the toddler quilt, or 144 scrap strips for the bed quilt. Sew the scraps strips to the background rectangles, as shown on the facing page, to make blocks.

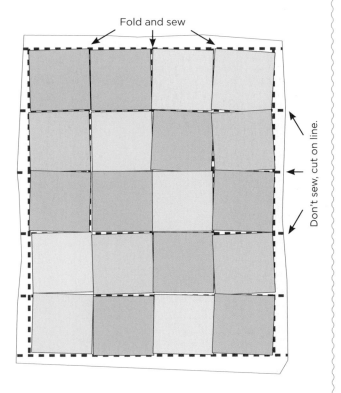

Fold and sew

Don't sew, cut on line.

Continue adding 2-in. by 6½-in. pieced strips and 5½-in. by 6½-in. background rectangles until all the strips have been sewn to a background rectangle and both 6½-in. sides of each background rectangle are sewn to a pieced strip. **4**

Always *sew* on the edge of the background rectangle and *cut* through the middle of the pieced strip.

Chain sew, and cut the pieces apart only after attaching both sides of the pieced strip to a background rectangle. Once cut apart, press the seams toward the background rectangle. Blocks are 6½ in. square. **5**

Make 8 blocks for the table runner, 36 blocks for the toddler quilt, or 144 blocks for the bed quilt.

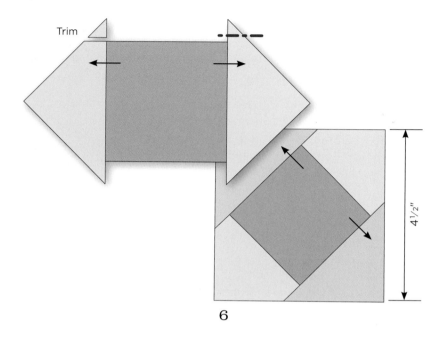

Trim

4½"

6

While a regular square ruler does the job nicely enough, the Square²™ trimming tool by Studio 180 Designs makes the scrap trimming fast and easy.

Trim the center square to the exact size on one end of the ruler, and use the markings for a 4-in. finished block on the other half of the ruler to make quick work of the on-point square trimming task. Detailed instructions come with the tool. It's one of my favorite trimming gadgets.

OUTER BORDER

Sew two sets of eight 5-in. scrap squares in a row for the toddler quilt (5 in. by 36½ in.). Sew two sets of sixteen 5-in. scrap squares in a row for the bed quilt (5 in. by 72½ in.). Press the seams open.

MAKE THE BORDERS
INNER BORDER

Randomly sew eight 2-in. scrap squares chosen for the table runner inner borders side by side in a row that is 2 in. by 12½ in. Leave the seams unpressed until quilt assembly. Repeat to make a second inner border.

Similarly, sew two inner borders for the toddler quilt using twenty-four 2-in. scrap squares (2 in. by 36½ in.), or forty-eight 2-in. scrap squares for each bed quilt inner border (2 in. by 72½ in.). Set aside.

MIDDLE PIECED BORDER

Center and sew a corner triangle to each side of a 3¼-in. center scrap square. Sew opposite sides first, trim the points, and then sew the remaining two sides.

Center and trim the on-point square unit to a 4½-in. square. **6**

Repeat to make 6 on-point square units for the table runner, 18 for the toddler quilt, or 36 for the bed quilt.

Sew 3 on-point units in a row for each end of the table runner, 9 units for each end of the toddler quilt, or 18 units for each end of the bed quilt. Press the seams open. Set aside.

ASSEMBLE THE QUILT TOP
TABLE RUNNER

Arrange the blocks in four rows of two blocks, alternating block direction, as shown. Sew the blocks into rows; press the block seams as shown. **6**

Sew the rows together; press the row seams in one direction.

Pin the inner border to each end of the quilt top. Finger-press the seams that intersect with the block seams so they nest as you pin (arrows shown in gray).

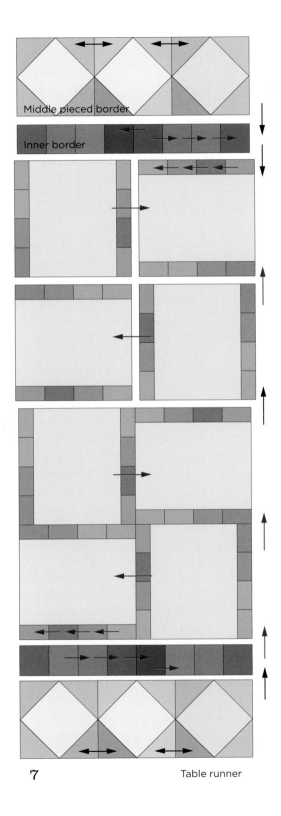

Middle pieced border

Inner border

7   Table runner

NOTE: Your results may differ from the illustrated example. Sew the inner border to each end of the quilt top, and press the seam toward the quilt center.

Sew the middle pieced border to each end of the quilt top and press the seam toward the quilt center. **7**

Why doesn't the table runner have an outer border? Without the extra outer scrap border, the table runner is just the right size for $1/2$ yard of backing fabric.

If an outer scrap border were added, the table runner would still be 12 in. wide, but it would be about 44 in. long—just a bit too long to fit on a 42-in.-wide strip of fabric. Let's not create more scraps while we're trying to use them up!

TODDLER AND BED QUILTS

Arrange the blocks in 6 rows of 6 blocks for the toddler quilt, or 12 rows of 12 blocks for a bed quilt, alternating background fabric and block direction, as shown. **8, 9** Sew blocks into rows; press the block seams as shown. Sew the rows together; press the row seams in one direction.

Pin the inner border to each end of the quilt top. Finger-press the seams that intersect with the block seams so they nest as you pin, as shown on p. 99 for the table runner. Sew; then press the seam toward the quilt center.

Sew the middle pieced border to each end of the quilt top and press the seam toward the inner border; then sew the outer border to each end. Press the outer border seam toward the outer border. **8, 9**

QUILT AND BIND

Layer the backing, batting, and quilt top; baste. Quilt as desired.

For the table runner, cut three 2¹/₄-in. strips for the binding. For the toddler quilt, cut five 2¹/₄-in. width-of-fabric strips for the binding. For the bed quilt, cut nine 2¹/₄-in. width-of-fabric strips for the binding. Sew the binding strips together end to end, using a diagonal seam (see p. 180). Press the connecting seams open; then press the binding in half lengthwise, wrong sides together.

Trim the batting and backing even with the quilt top. With the raw edges aligned, sew the binding to the front of the quilt using a ¹/₄-in. seam. Miter the binding at the corners.

Turn the folded edge of the binding to the back of the quilt, and hand-stitch it in place.

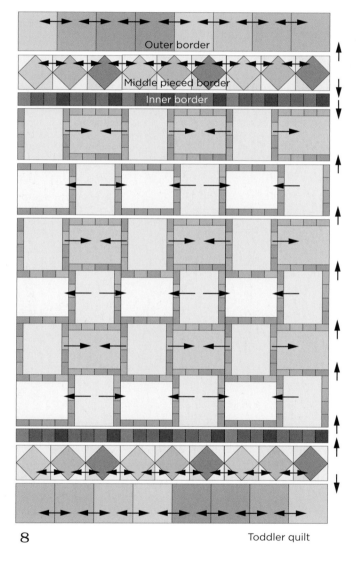

Outer border

Middle pieced border

Inner border

8 Toddler quilt

Outer border

Middle pieced border

Inner border

9

Bed quilt

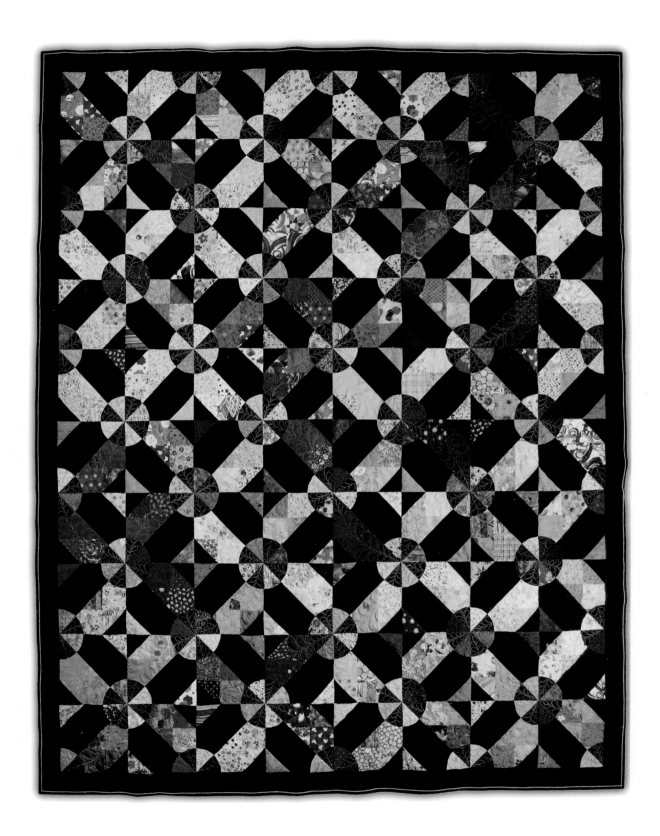

Sweet Revenge

SCRAPS PLUS ONE BLACK SOLID

It's a funny thing about scraps. Just when you think you've got them all figured out, more options surface. This quilt starts with nine-patch blocks that become half-square triangles, with stitch-and-flip snowball corners and curved piecing, a first in the ScrapTherapy family of patterns. The block cut-aways from two of the curved pieced sections find new life in Square Peg, Round Hole on p. 110 and in Friendship Bread Runner on p. 116. It's as if the scraps took on a life of their own.

Technically, the flange or piping element in Sweet Revenge makes this quilt a "scraps plus two" project. But I warned you that I cheat, and this quilt needed the pop of bright blue around the edge, regardless of the rules.

So dig out scraps in lots of colorful combinations, and roll up your sleeves! By the way, don't fret about the curves. Step-by-step instructions will help you tackle and conquer them with ease, with no special equipment or sewing machine attachments.

FINISHED SIZE: 73 in. by 90 in.
PATTERN DIFFICULTY: Intermediate

SCRAP REQUIREMENTS:
3½-in. scrap squares: 440
5-in. scrap squares: 80
FABRIC AND NOTION REQUIREMENTS
5¾ yards black for blocks and borders
¾ yard black for binding
5½ yards backing
77-in. by 94-in. batting
⅓ yard bright blue for flange (or ½ yd. for optional piping)

9½ yards 1 mm-diameter cord (for optional piping)
Template plastic (optional)
Drunkard's Path Template Set by Marti Michell
  (the set is strongly recommended for cutting the curved piecing elements)
28 mm rotary cutter for curves (optional)
Piping Hot Binding kit by Susan K. Cleveland (tool
  and instruction book; optional)

NOTE: The notions you'll need depend on whether you use the template set made by Marti Michell and whether you choose to do a flange.

1

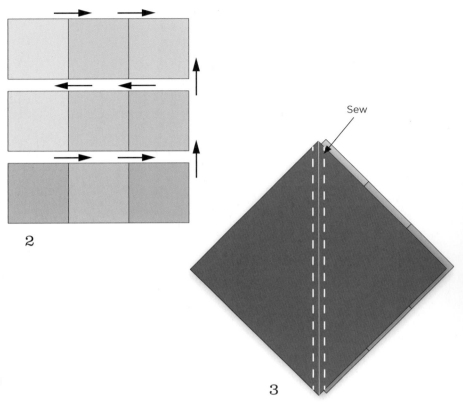

2

3

Sew

PREPARE THE SCRAPS

Select four hundred forty 3½-in. scrap squares for the blocks. From these, sort 360 scraps squares into 40 sets of nine squares. The scrap squares in each set should be of a similar color and value; however, the sets can be different colors from each other. Set aside.

With a pencil or fabric marking tool, draw a diagonal line, corner to corner, on the back of each of the remaining eighty 3½-in. scrap squares. Set aside. **1**

Select eighty 5-in. scrap squares for the blocks.

PREPARE THE ADDITIONAL FABRICS

BLACK

Cut ten 9½-in. width-of-fabric strips; then cut forty 9½-in. squares for the blocks.

Cut ten 5-in. width-of-fabric strips; then cut eighty 5-in. squares for the blocks.

Cut eight 3½-in. width-of-fabric strips; then cut eighty 3½-in. squares for the blocks.

Draw a diagonal line, corner to corner, on the back of each of the 9½-in., 5-in., and 3½-in. squares.

When you need to draw lines or details on black fabric, you'll find a variety of marking pens that can do the trick. Often lime green or pink fine line pencils show up nicely against black or dark fabrics. But the Clover White Marking Pen is one of my favorites because it erases with a touch of heat. At first, the pen line doesn't appear, but as the ink dries, it turns white. As with any other marking tool, be sure to test on a extra fabric scrap or on the selvage or seam allowance.

Cut nine 3-in. width-of-fabric strips for the borders.

MAKE THE BLOCKS

SCRAPPY NINE-PATCHES

Select one set of nine 3½-in. scrap squares and sew into a nine-patch. Press the seams in alternate directions by row; then press the row seams in one direction. Repeat to make 40 nine-patches that are 9½ in. square. **2**

LARGE HALF-SQUARE TRIANGLES

Place a nine-patch and a 9½-in. black square right sides together, with the black fabric facing up. Sew a ¼-in. seam on both sides of the drawn line. **3**

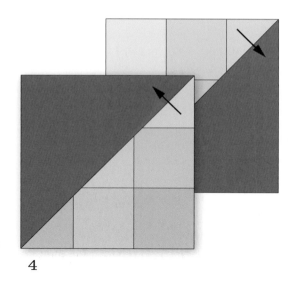

4

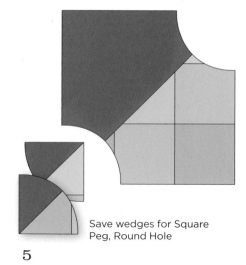

Save wedges for Square
Peg, Round Hole

5

Cut on the line, and press seam allowances toward the black fabric. Trim to a 9-in. square. **4** Repeat to make 80 large half-square triangle (HST) units.

Make a template from the 3-in. arc shape. Align the corner of the 3-in. template with a large HST corner that has a seam intersection. Trace the template and use scissors to cut a curved shape carefully on both of the two-color corners of the large HST. Save the leftover 3-in. arcs for the Square Peg, Round Hole quilt on p. 110. Set aside. **5**

If you are using Marti Michell's Drunkard's Path Template Set, use template C and a 28 mm rotary cutter to make the curved cutouts from the large HST units.

Cut slowly and with firm, even pressure around the arc. The dimensions printed on the template don't match my description; that's okay, just be sure to use template C for this step.

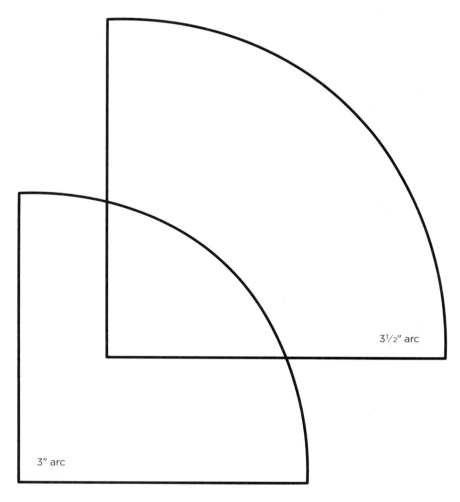

3½" arc

3" arc

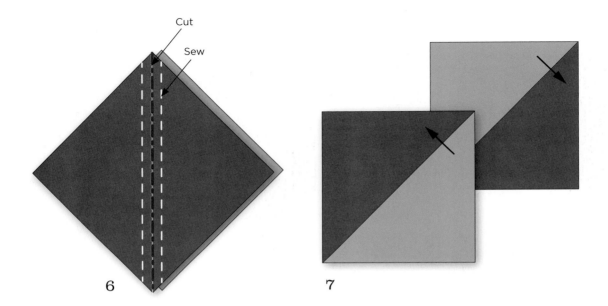

Cut

Sew

6

7

SMALL HALF-SQUARE TRIANGLES

Place a 5-in. scrap square and a 5-in black square with right sides together, with the black fabric facing up. Sew a $1/4$-in. seam on both sides of the drawn line. **6**

Cut on the line, and press the seam toward the black fabric. Trim to $4^1/2$ in. square. **7** Repeat to make 160 small HST units.

If you are using Marti Michell's Drunkard's Path Template Set, use template D and a 28 mm rotary cutter to make the curved cutouts from the small HST units.

Cut slowly and with firm, even pressure around the arc. The numbers on the template don't match my description; that's okay, just make sure you're using template D and you'll be fine.

Make a template from the $3^1/2$-in. arc shape. Arrange two small HST units on a cutting mat, both right sides up, with seams opposing and nested. The HST units do not have to be matching, but it is important that you cut two at a time and that you stack them

with scrap and background fabric in opposite-facing directions. **8**

Align the corner of the $3^1/2$-in. template with the small HST corner that has a seam intersection. Trace the template on the top layer, and place a few pins to secure the layers; then use scissors to cut the curved shape carefully on one of the two-color corners of the small HST. Cut carefully through both layers. (Reserve the leftovers for the Friendship Bread Runner on p. 116.) Make a total of 80 wedges from the HSTs. **9**

When I cut the small arcs, I threw the leftovers away and tried to carry on with my sewing. But the discarded pieces said, "Don't throw us away," in a voice audible to only me. So I retrieved them, measured, and discovered a small HST triangle unit lurked within. The scraps apparently wanted to be something else. I have found that it's important to listen when fabric talks.

COMPLETE THE BLOCKS

Secure the $3^1/2$-in. wedge unit to the 3-in. cut-away with pins, right sides together, with black fabric facing scrap fabric, and sew. Follow the detailed instructions for sewing curved pieces on p. 184. Repeat until both curve-cut corners have been sewn on all 80 large HSTs. Press the curved seams in one direction for half of the blocks. Press the curved seams in the opposite direction for the remaining blocks. **10**

Be careful when pressing curved seams!

You may find it easier first to sew all the blocks, stacking them so the scrap and black fabrics are oriented the same way throughout the pile. Then press all the blocks at the same time, pressing half in one direction and half in the other direction. Don't worry; each curved seam, if sewn carefully, should press easily in either direction.

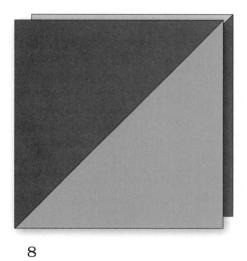

8

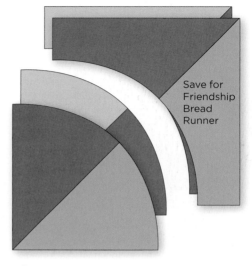

Save for Friendship Bread Runner

9

Align the 3½-in. black square on a nine-patch corner of the curved pieced block, as shown. **11** Sew on the drawn line, and press the fabric toward the corner. Align the 3½-in. scrap square on the black corner of a large HST, as shown. Trim the middle fabric layer to reduce the bulk, if desired. Repeat to make 80 blocks that are 9 in. square.

> When sewing stitch-and-flip corners, like those on the Sweet Revenge blocks, I like to trim the middle layer to reduce the bulk. Some quilters like to trim both the middle and the back layers, and some prefer to leave the layers alone. It's a matter of preference.
>
> I leave the back layer in tact so if my sewing is a little off, the integrity of the block shape is preserved, making it a little easier to sew the blocks together later. If your project will be quilted on a long-arm machine, consider reducing more bulk.

ASSEMBLE THE QUILT TOP

Arrange the blocks into 10 rows of eight blocks. Alternate the pressing direction of the curved seams carefully, as shown. **12** Sew the blocks into rows, and press the block seams toward the black HST fabric. Then sew the rows together; press the row seams in one direction.

BORDERS

> Measure the quilt top before trimming the borders.

Sew five 3-in. black strips end to end, using a diagonal seam (see p. 180), to make a strip about 200 in. long. Press the connecting seams open. Cut into two 3-in. by 85½-in. side borders.

Sew two 3-in. black strips end to end, using a diagonal seam, to make a strip about 80 in. long. Repeat to make two strips. Trim each to 3 in. by 73½ in. for the top and bottom borders. Attach the borders to the quilt, sides first, and then the top and bottom. Press the seam toward the border after each addition. **12**

QUILT AND BIND

Layer the backing, batting, and quilt top; baste. Quilt as desired.

From bright blue fabric, cut nine ¾-in. width-of-fabric strips for the flange.

Sew five ¾-in. flange strips together, end to end, using a diagonal seam. Cut in half to make two strips approximately 100 in. long, one for each side of the quilt. Next, sew two flange strips together, end to end, using a diagonal seam to make a strip approximately 80 in. long. Make two, one each for the top and bottom.

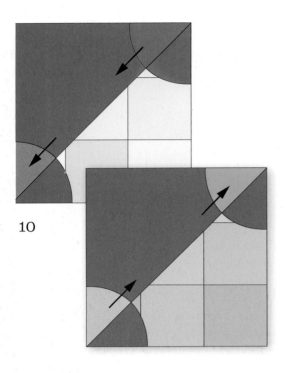

10

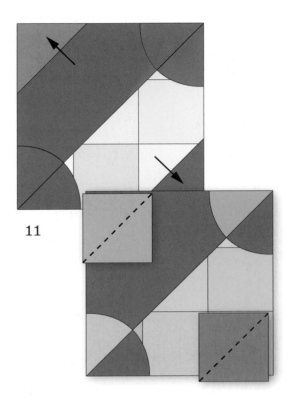

11

A flange is an easy, high-impact way to add a narrow pop of color and interest to a quilt border or binding (see p. 185). An alternative is narrow covered cord or piping. Adding covered piping to your quilt can be a bit more detailed, but the effect is well worth the effort. I have found the instructions and tool included with Susan K. Cleveland's Piping Hot Binding Kit to be very helpful when upgrading from flange to covered piping.

Press the connecting seams open; then press each flange strip lengthwise, wrong sides together.

Trim the batting and the backing even with the quilt top. Working one side at a time, pin the flange carefully to the edge of the quilt, with raw edges aligned (see p. 186). Trim the ends even with the quilt top. Baste the flange to the quilt by machine using less than a 1/4-in. seam allowance. Repeat to attach the flanges to all four sides of the quilt top.

Cut nine 2 1/4-in. strips for the binding.

Sew the binding strips together end to end, using a diagonal seam. Press the connecting seams open; then press the binding in half lengthwise, wrong sides together.

With the raw edges aligned, sew the binding to the front of the quilt using a 1/4-in. seam. Miter the binding at the corners.

Turn the folded edge of the binding to the back of the quilt, and hand-stitch it in place.

3" × 73½"

Square Peg, Round Hole

SCRAPS PLUS ONE LEFTOVER SHAPE

The ultimate scrap project is when you can take the leftovers from a scrap quilt and make another scrap quilt! And Square Peg, Round Hole is just that. If you make the Sweet Revenge quilt on p. 102, you will have leftover curved pieces that are just too beautiful to release into the great scrap stash beyond. Add one more solid-color fabric and a few more curvy cuts and you will have some modified pinwheel blocks.

When assembling this quilt, notice that half of the blocks spin in one direction, and the other half spin in the opposite direction. Placing these two types of blocks side by side creates a not-so-interesting drama where they meet. By splitting the blocks with sashing strips in a neutral print, however, you can hardly tell the two blocks oppose each other.

FINISHED SIZE: 56 in. by 61 in.
PATTERN DIFFICULTY: Intermediate

SCRAP REQUIREMENTS:
5-in. scrap squares: 72
Leftover wedge-shaped units from the Sweet Revenge
 Quilt (on p. 102): 144
FABRIC AND NOTION REQUIREMENTS
1⅓ yards blue for blocks
1¼ yards black print for sashing and borders
½ yard black for binding
3¾ yards for backing
60-in. by 65-in. batting
Pigma pen or heat-erasable marker
Template plastic (optional)

Drunkard's Path Template Set by Marti Michell (the
 set is strongly recommended for cutting the curved
 piecing elements)
28 mm rotary cutter for curves (optional)

NOTE: The notions you'll need depend on whether you use the template set made by Marti Michell.

PREPARE THE SCRAPS
Select seventy-two 5-in. scrap squares for the blocks.

Select 72 matched sets of leftover wedge-shaped units from the Sweet Revenge Quilt for a total of 144 wedges. **1** Sixteen of the leftover units will be unused.

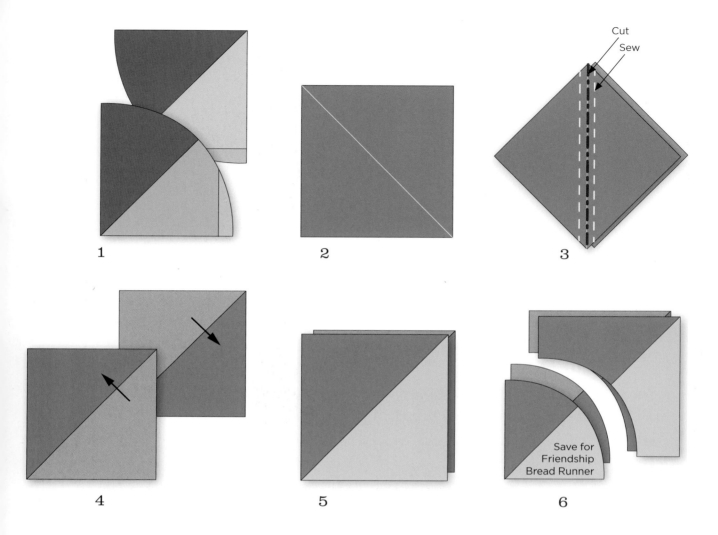

1

2

3

Cut
Sew

4

5

6

Save for
Friendship
Bread Runner

PREPARE THE ADDITIONAL FABRICS

BLUE

Cut nine 5-in. width-of-fabric strips, and then cut seventy-two 5-in. squares for blocks. Draw a diagonal line, corner to corner, on the back of each of the 5-in. squares. **2**

BLACK PRINT

Cut three 3-in. width-of-fabric strips for the sashing.

Cut six 4$\frac{1}{2}$-in. width-of-fabric strips for the borders.

MAKE THE BLOCKS

HALF-SQUARE TRIANGLES

Place a 5-in. scrap square and a 5-in. blue square with right sides together, with the blue fabric on top. Sew a $\frac{1}{4}$-in. seam on both sides of the drawn line. **3**

Cut on the line, and press the seam toward the blue fabric. Trim to a 4$\frac{1}{2}$-in. square. **4** Repeat to make 144 half-square triangle (HST) units.

Make a template from the 2$\frac{1}{2}$-in. arc shape. Arrange two HST units on the cutting mat, both right sides up, with seams opposing and nested.

The HST units do not have to be matching, but it is important that you cut two at a time and that you stack them with the scrap and background fabric in opposite directions. **5**

Align the corner of the template with the HST corner that has a seam. Trace the template on the top layer, place a few pins to secure layers, and then use scissors to cut the curved shape. Cut carefully through both layers. Make a total of 144 cut-away arcs from the HST units. **6** Reserve the leftover wedges for the Friendship Bread Runner on p. 116.

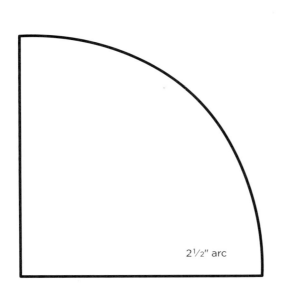

2½" arc

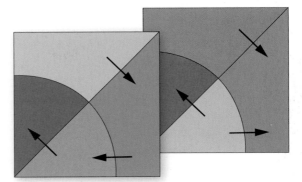

Make 36 of each variation

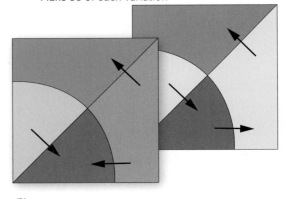

7

If you are using Marti Michell's Drunkard's Path Template Set, use template B and a 28 mm rotary cutter to make the curved cutouts from the HST units.

Cut slowly and with firm, even pressure around the arc. The numbers describing the template don't match my description; that's okay, just be sure you are using the B template.

BLOCKS

Randomly select one 3-in. wedge leftover unit and one HST unit with a 2½-in cut-away. Mix up the scraps, but be sure to sew scrap to blue and scrap to black for each unit, so the seams always nest and the blue pieces are placed on the opposite side of the black pieces. Use pins to secure the wedge to the cut-away, right sides together, and sew. Follow the detailed instructions for sewing curved pieces on p. 184. Repeat to make 144 curve-pieced HSTs.

Separate the HSTs into two stacks, 72 HSTs with the blue on one side of the block and the other 72 HSTs with the blue on the other side of the block. Keep each variation in a separate stack. For each stack, press the curved seams in one direction for half of the HSTs, and press the curved seams in the opposite direction for the remaining HSTs. **7**

It's easy to get these units muddled, so stay organized. Complete sewing all 72 units of one variation before pressing. Press the seams for 36 units toward the center of the arc, and for the other 36 units, press away from the center of the arc.

Then do the same for the second stack of 72 similar units, pressing half of the seams in one direction and half in the other direction. Don't worry; each curved seam, if sewn carefully, should press easily in either direction.

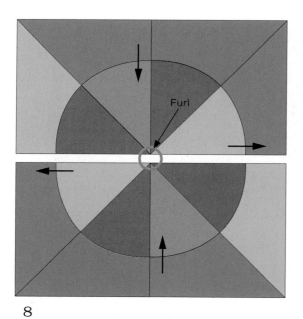

8

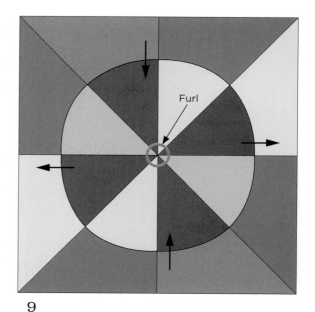

9

Working from one stack of HST block units at a time, select one HST unit with the seam pressed toward the center of the arc, and a second unit with the seam pressed away from the center of the arc.

Sew the units into a two-patch, as shown. **8** Press the seam away from the blue fabric. Repeat to make 72 two-patches.

Select two two-patches and sew them into four-patches. Furl the center seam intersection (see p. 180). Repeat to make 18 blocks that are 8$\frac{1}{2}$ in. square. **8**

For clarification, the illustrations show a limited variety in scrap selection. Your quilt will be much more scrappy.

Working from the second stack of HST block units, follow the same steps to make eighteen 8$\frac{1}{2}$-in. square

blocks that have the opposite placement of the blue and seams pressed toward the blue. **9** Continue to keep the two block variations separate.

ASSEMBLE THE QUILT TOP
QUILT CENTER

For the center section of the quilt, arrange the blocks from one variation into three rows of six blocks. Press the block seams in one direction, alternating the pressing direction in each row. Sew the rows together, and press the seams in one direction. **10a**

For the top and bottom sections of the quilt, sew six blocks from the second variation into one row. **10b** Press the seams in one direction. Sew the remaining blocks into two rows of six blocks. **10c** Press the block seams in one direction for the first row and in the opposite direction for the second row.

SASHING AND BORDERS

Measure the quilt top before trimming the borders.

Sew three 3-in. black print strips end to end, using a diagonal seam (see p. 180). Press the connecting seams open. Cut two 3-in. by 48$\frac{1}{2}$-in. strips for the sashing, and sew between sections.

Similarly, sew three 4$\frac{1}{2}$-in. black print strips end to end, using a diagonal seam to make one long border strip that is approximately 120 in. long. Press the connecting seams open. Make two.

From the first strip, cut two 4$\frac{1}{2}$-in. by 53$\frac{1}{2}$-in. side borders. From the second strip, cut two 4$\frac{1}{2}$-in. by 56$\frac{1}{2}$-in. borders for the top and bottom of the quilt.

Sew the borders to the quilt, sides first, and then the top and bottom. Press the seams toward the border after each addition. **10d**

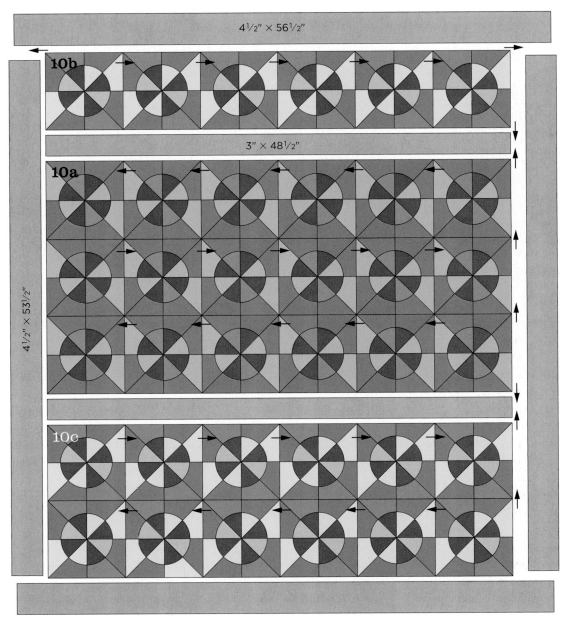

4¹⁄₂" × 56¹⁄₂"

10b

3" × 48¹⁄₂"

10a

4¹⁄₂" × 53¹⁄₂"

10c

10d

QUILT AND BIND

Layer the backing, batting, and quilt top; baste. Quilt as desired.

Cut seven 2¹⁄₄-in. strips for the binding. Sew the binding strips together end to end, using a diagonal seam. Press the connecting seams open, and then press the binding in half lengthwise, with the wrong sides together.

Trim the batting and backing even with the quilt top. With the raw edges aligned, sew the binding to the front of the quilt using a ¹⁄₄-in. seam.

Miter the binding at the corners.

Turn the folded edge of the binding to the back of the quilt, and hand-stitch it in place.

Friendship Bread Runner

SCRAPS PLUS ONE HALF DOZEN SETTING TRIANGLES

Have you ever received friendship bread dough? It's been a while since I have, but as I recall, the originator makes a batch of bread dough and takes out a cup of the batter, makes a loaf of sourdough bread from the rest, and gives the extra cup of batter to a friend. The friend adds to the batter, takes out a cup, makes bread, and passes on the extra batter to another friend. The whole process goes on and on. And on.

It's a sweet thought, but to be honest, I'm not terribly fond of the stuff. I find it troublesome that you never know how long ago the batter got its start. My gift would sit on the counter until I got the courage to toss it. Forgive me, if you've ever given me one of these dough gifts. It's the thought that counts, right? Ahem!

This table runner reminds me of the good part of that friendship bread batter. The scrappy, half-square triangle units originated with the Sweet Revenge quilt on p. 102. Add more fabrics to the leftovers from Sweet Revenge, and you can make Square Peg, Round Hole on p. 110. And you still have leftovers! So this table runner is the last attempt to use up what's left. Plus you add a half dozen triangles to bring it all together. Of course, you can always leave the leftovers on the counter, but remember how that worked out for the dough? By the way, I like this project a lot better than the bread recipe!

FINISHED SIZE: 18 in. by 50 in.
PATTERN DIFFICULTY: Intermediate

SCRAP REQUIREMENTS:
Leftover cut-away black and scrap arcs from Sweet
  Revenge (on p. 102): 144
Leftover wedge-shaped blue and scrap units from
  Square Peg, Round Hole (on p. 110): 144

FABRIC AND NOTION REQUIREMENTS:
3/8 yard focus print for setting triangles
1/2 yard black for sashing and binding
7/8 yard backing (cut on fold, then seam)
22-in. by 54-in. batting

USING LEFTOVERS TO MAKE FRIENDSHIP BREAD UNITS

If you made both quilts, Sweet Revenge and Square Peg, Round Hole, use all of your leftovers as directed in "Prepare the Scrap Half-Square Triangle Units from Leftovers," on p. 118.

If you made only the Sweet Revenge quilt, use the leftovers to prepare one hundred forty-four 1¾-in. square black/scrap half-square triangle (HST) units as directed on p. 118. But you also will need ½ yard of blue solid fabric plus eighteen 5-in. scrap squares to make 144 blue/scrap 1¾-in. square HST units, following the directions in "Make Half-Square Triangle Units," on p. 119.

If you made only the Square Peg, Round Hole quilt, use the leftovers to prepare one hundred forty-four 1¾-in. square blue/scrap HST units as directed on p. 118. But you will also need ½ yard of black solid fabric plus eighteen 5-in. scrap squares to make 144 black/scrap 1¾-in. square HST units, following the directions in "Make Half-Square Triangle Units" on p. 119.

If you made neither the Sweet Revenge quilt nor the Square Peg, Round Hole quilt, you'll need to start with ½ yard of solid black and ½ yard of solid blue fabric, plus thirty-six 5-in. scrap squares to make two hundred eighty-eight 1¾-in. square HST units, half with the solid black triangles and scraps, and half with the solid blue triangles and scraps, following the directions in "Make Half-Square Triangle Units" on p. 119.

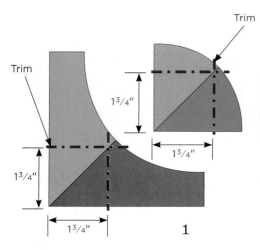

1

2

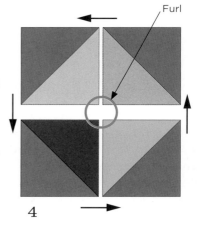

3

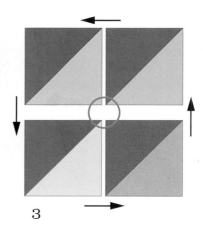

4

PREPARE THE SCRAP HALF-SQUARE TRIANGLE UNITS FROM LEFTOVERS

Select 144 leftover black/scrap cut-away arcs from the Sweet Revenge quilt. Trim each into a $1^3/_4$-in. square, as shown above. **1**

Select 144 leftover blue/scrap wedge shapes from the Square Peg, Round Hole quilt. Trim each into a $1^3/_4$-in. square, as shown above. **1**

> To make perfect half-square triangle units from odd-shaped scraps, use a small square ruler with a prominent bias line. Line up the bias line on the ruler with the seam and trim to $1^3/_4$ in. square.

PREPARE THE ADDITIONAL FABRICS

FOCUS PRINT

Cut one $11^1/_2$-in. width-of-fabric strip; then cut two $11^1/_2$-in. squares. Cut each square in half twice diagonally for the setting triangles. Two setting triangles will not be used. **2**

BLACK

Cut five $1^1/_4$-in. width-of-fabric strips; then cut two $1^1/_4$-in. by $16^1/_4$-in. strips, six $1^1/_4$-in. by $10^1/_2$-in. strips, six $1^1/_4$-in. by 10-in. strips, and two $1^1/_4$-in. by 8-in. strips for the sashing.

Reserve the remaining fabric for the binding.

BLOCKS

BLACK CENTER BLOCKS

Select 20 black/scrap half-square triangle (HST) units and 16 blue/scrap HST units.

From the 20 black/scrap HST units, select four, and arrange them with the black in the upper left position, as shown. Sew the four-patch unit, and press the seams as shown, furling the center intersection (see p. 180). Repeat to make four corner four-patch units that are 3 in. square. **3**

From the remaining four black/scrap HST units. Arrange and sew a four-patch, and press the seams as shown, furling the center intersection to make one center unit that is 3 in. square. **4**

> Because the block consists of half-square triangle units, seam intersections can get lumpy. I found it helpful to break the block into nine four-patch elements, and then sew together the complex nine-patch. To reduce bulk, each and every seam intersection within the block is furled (see p. 180). This keeps your sewing accurate, because furling won't happen if the seam intersections aren't locked in nicely. Consequently, the finished piece is flat and the pointy intersections are surprisingly successful.

From the 16 blue/scrap HST units, select four, and arrange them with the blue in the upper right position, as shown. Sew a four-patch, and press the seams, furling the center inter-section. Repeat to make four side units that are 3 in. square. **5**

Arrange the corner, center, and side four-patch units as shown. Sew, press, and furl the black center block, as shown.

Repeat to make four blocks with black centers.

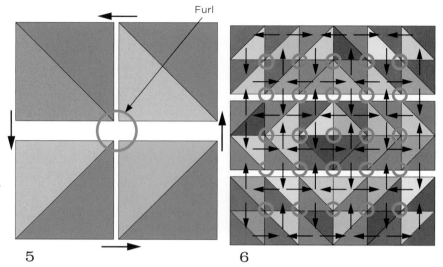

5   6

Furl

MAKE HALF-SQUARE TRIANGLE UNITS

If you need to make the half-square triangle (HST) units, you can do so by cutting each solid fabric into eighteen 5-in. squares. Then select eighteen 5-in. scrap squares from your scrap bins (see "Using Leftovers to Make Friendship Bread Units" on p. 117).

To make HST units that are about the right size for this project, use the method described for the Georgia's Garden project on p. 121.

Draw two diagonal lines on the back of each solid 5-in. square. Place one solid color square right sides together with a 5-in. scrap square, placing the solid fabric on top. Sew a ¼-in. seam on both sides of each line. Cut the sewn fabric in half four times—twice diagonally, once vertically, and once horizontally—to make eight HST units from each fabric pairing. Press each seam toward the solid fabric, and trim each HST unit to 1 ¾ in. square.

Repeat until you have the required number of solid/scrap HST units (see "Using Leftovers to Make Friendship Bread Units" on p. 117).

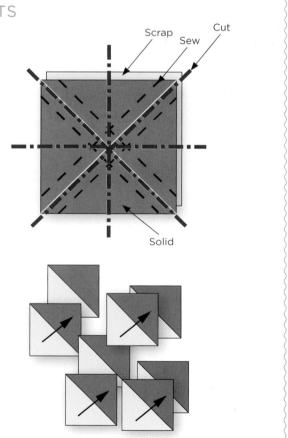

Scrap   Sew   Cut

Solid

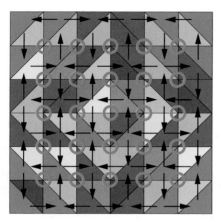

7

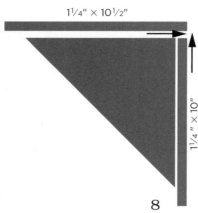

1¼" × 10½"

1¼" × 10"

8

1¼" × 16¼"

1¼" × 8"

9

BLUE CENTER BLOCKS

Select 20 blue/scrap HST units and 16 black/scrap HST units.

Follow the instructions in "Black Center Blocks" on p. 118, reversing the placement of the blue/scrap and black/scrap HST units, as shown. Make four blocks with blue centers that are 8 in. square. **7**

SETTING TRIANGLES

Sew a black 1¼-in. by 10-in. strip to one shorter, bias-cut side of each setting triangle. Press the seam toward the black strip. Sew a black 1¼-in. by 10½-in. strip to the adjacent short bias-cut side of the setting triangle. Press the seam toward the strip. Make six setting triangles with black sashing on two sides. **8**

ASSEMBLE THE QUILT TOP

Arrange the blocks, the setting triangles, and the remaining black strips in diagonal rows, as shown. **9** Sew the blocks together. Then sew

the outer border strips: the 1¼-in. by 8-in. strip first and then the 1¼-in. by 16¼-in. strip. Next sew the setting triangles and then sew the rows. Press the seams as indicated. Some seam intersections will not nest nicely. Use extra pins as needed. Trim the sashing strips even with the edge of the setting triangles before quilting, if desired. **9**

QUILT AND BIND

Layer the backing, batting, and quilt top; baste. Quilt as desired.

Cut four 2¼-in. strips for the binding. Sew the binding strips together end to end, using a diagonal seam (p. 180). Press the connecting seams open, and then press binding in half lengthwise, with the wrong sides together.

Trim the batting and the backing even with the quilt top. With the raw edges aligned, sew the binding to the front of the quilt using a ¼-in. seam. Miter the binding at the corners.

Turn the folded edge of the binding to the back of quilt, and hand-stitch it in place.

Georgia's Garden

SCRAPS PLUS ONE REALLY GOOD STORY

I'm cheating on the "one theme" again! Perhaps you'll forgive me if I tell you a really good story . . .

Georgia was a quilter. She had quite a stash of fabric when she passed away. Our mutual friend Dolly took the challenge to disburse her stash, selling much of it to benefit some of Georgia's favorite charities. I asked Dolly if she wouldn't mind snagging a piece of fabric from Georgia's stash for me to use—Dolly chose the vintage-looking print on cream and the dark purple accent fabrics used in this quilt.

Dolly and Georgia often went to quilt shows, and it nearly drove Georgia mad to see a beautiful quilt hanging with a stray thread stuck to it. So she always made an effort to get a pair of gloves from the docents so she could pick a loose thread off a quilt if she saw one, while following standard quilt show hands-off etiquette.

Dolly told this story shortly after Georgia passed away. Now, every time I see a stray thread on a quilt, I remember Georgia. Next time you see a stray thread on a quilt, who will you remember fondly?

In reality, I added only one fabric, the white fabric in the half-square triangle units, to this quilt. The others are scraps from my bins or fabrics that came to me from Georgia's stash.

FINISHED SIZE: **58 in. by 68 in.**

PATTERN DIFFICULTY: **Intermediate**

SCRAP REQUIREMENTS:

5-in. scrap squares: 113

FABRIC AND NOTION REQUIREMENTS:

2¼ yards white for pieced panel

1⅓ yards for focus print

¾ yard for accent fabric

½ yard for binding (for the quilt shown here, I used the accent fabric for the binding)

4 yards for backing

63-in. by 72-in. batting

Pigma pen or heat-erasable marker

Rotating or small cutting mat

ScrapTherapy Small Scrap Grid by Quiltsmart (optional), 5 panels

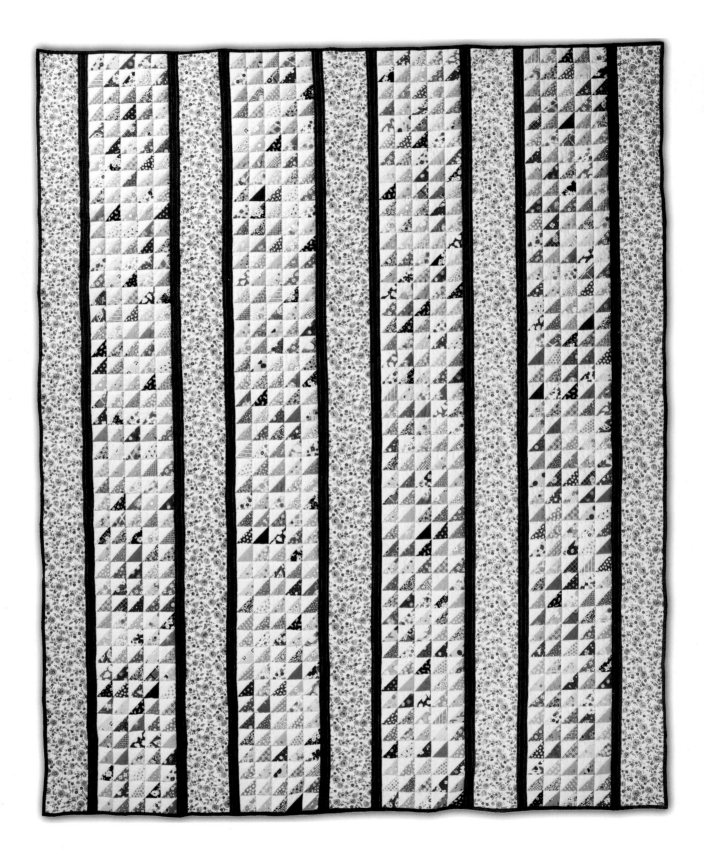

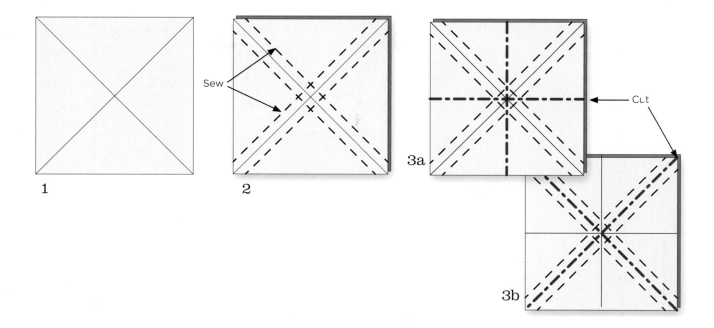

Sew

Cut

1

2

3a

3b

NOTE: Five panels of ScrapTherapy Small Scrap Grid by Quiltsmart make 10 grid sections (one complete panel has two 5-square by 18-square grid sections). See "Using the Scrap-Therapy Small Scrap Grid", on p. 126.

PREPARE THE SCRAPS
Select one hundred thirteen 5-in. scrap squares for the pieced panels.

> Because my focus print had a 1930s reproduction look, I decided to use only 1930s reproduction print scraps from my collection for the scrappy panels.

PREPARE THE ADDITIONAL FABRICS

WHITE
Cut fifteen 5-in. width-of-fabric strips; then cut one hundred thirteen 5-in. squares for the pieced panels. On the back of each white square, draw two diagonal lines. **1**

FOCUS PRINT
Cut ten 4½-in. width-of-fabric strips. Set aside.

ACCENT FABRIC
Cut sixteen 1½-in. width-of-fabric strips. Set aside.

PIECE THE PANELS
HALF-SQUARE TRIANGLE UNITS
Place a 5-in. scrap square and a 5-in. white square right sides together with the lines on the white fabric facing up. Sew a ¼-in. seam on both sides of the drawn lines to make a total of four stitching lines, as shown. **2**
Cut through the center four times. Be careful not to move the fabric

between cuts. First, make a vertical cut 2½ in. from the side edge; then make a horizontal cut 2½ in. from the bottom edge. **3a** Then cut diagonally on the drawn lines to make eight half-square triangle (HST) units. **3b**

> A rotating cutting mat, or a small cutting mat that can be turned easily, makes it much easier to cut the fabric four times without disturbing the fabric pieces.

Press the HST seams toward the darker fabric. Trim each HST unit to a 2-in. square. **4**
Repeat to make a total of 900 HST units from all one hundred thirteen 5-in. scraps and one hundred thirteen 5-in. white squares. Four HST units are unused.

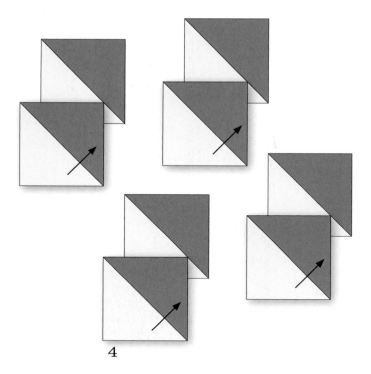

4

Sewing small HST units using this method goes pretty quickly. However, after they are cut apart, you end up with a *huge* stack of HST units to press and trim. Yikes! Roll up your sleeves, heat up the iron, and grab a small square ruler with an easy-to-see bias line. Make yourself a warm beverage and put on an old movie. Even better, find a sturdy table at your next social sewing gathering. You'll discover that it's a lot easier to keep up with the latest gossip when your sewing machine isn't running! This is a great excuse to let your mind wander a bit. But pay attention, and don't let your mind go too far astray—rotary cutters are sharp!

MAKE THE PIECED PANELS

Randomly select, arrange, and sew 45 rows of five HST units. Be careful to orient all the HST units in the same direction. Press the seams in one direction, alternating the pressing direction in each row. Sew the rows, and press the row seams in one direction. The pieced panel will be 8 in. by 68 in. **5**

Repeat to make four pieced panels.

ASSEMBLE THE QUILT TOP
ACCENT STRIPS

Sew two 1½-in. strips together end to end, using a diagonal seam (see p. 180). Press the connecting seam open. Trim the strip to 1½ in. by 68 in. Repeat to make eight accent strips.

5

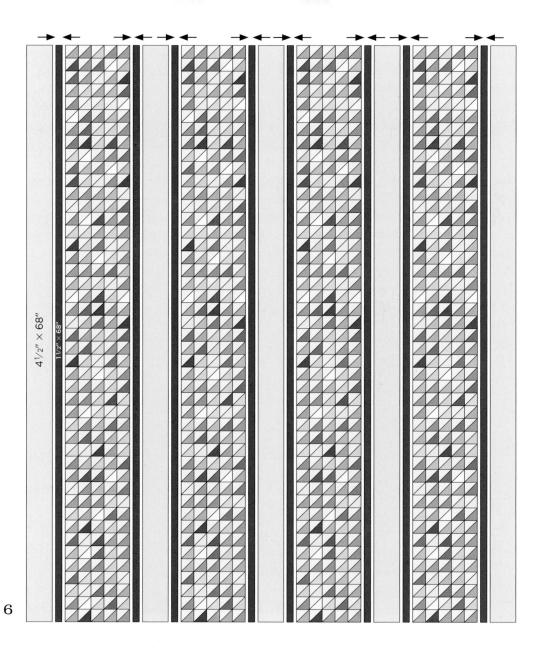

6

FOCUS FABRIC STRIPS

Sew two 4½-in. strips together
end to end, using a diagonal seam.
Press the connecting seam open as
before. Trim the strip to 4½ in. by
68 in. Repeat to make five focus
fabric strips.

MAKE THE QUILT TOP

Sew an accent strip to both sides of
each pieced panel. Then sew a focus
fabric strip alternately with a pieced
panel, starting and ending with a
focus fabric strip. Press the seams
toward the accent strip after each
addition. **6**

QUILT AND BIND

Layer the backing, batting, and quilt
top; baste. Quilt as desired.

Cut seven 2¼-in. strips for the
binding. Sew the binding strips
together end to end, using a diagonal
seam (see p. 180). Press the connecting seams open, and then press the
binding in half lengthwise, wrong
sides together.

Trim the batting and backing
even with the quilt top. With the raw
edges aligned, sew the binding to the
front of the quilt using a ¼-in. seam.
Miter the binding at the corners.

Turn the folded edge of the
binding to the back of the quilt, and
hand-stitch it in place.

USING THE SCRAP THERAPY SMALL SCRAP GRID BY QUILTSMART

The ScrapTherapy Small Scrap Grid by Quiltsmart can simplify and stabilize the scrappy panel elements with lots of seams. The preprinted interfacing allows you to arrange and position 2-in. scraps with limited risk of sloppy seam intersections. So using the grid interfacing can be a real time-saver with 2-in. scraps that have no seams.

For Georgia's Garden, each 2-in. square used for the pieced panels has one diagonal seam. When the fabric pieces don't have seams, it's okay if the scraps and the grid don't line up exactly because the grid lines, not the scrap edges, dictate where seams are sewn. With HST units, it's important to take the time and lay the HST units on the grid carefully, so the lines on the grid are aligned with the edges of the HST units before fusing.

Cut the grid roughly in half to separate the two 5-square by 18-square grid sections. Trim the extra interfacing around the grid to avoid getting fusible glue on the iron later.

Place one 5-square by 18-square grid segment on your ironing board with the fusible, or bumpy, side of the interfacing up. Place the HST units randomly, right side up, on the grid, aligned with dotted lines on the interfacing. Make sure all the HST units are aligned in the same direction. Be careful to align the edges of each HST unit with the lines on the grid. A

Trim any extra interfacing, and fuse the HST units to the interfacing with a hot steam iron.

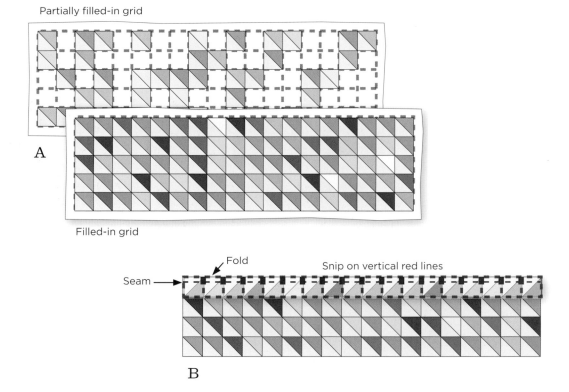

Partially filled-in grid

A

Filled-in grid

Fold

Seam

Snip on vertical red lines

B

Fold the interfacing along one long seam line, so the dotted line is precisely on the fold. Secure the fold with pins and sew a scant ¼-in. seam allowance along the folded edge, as shown by the black dotted line. Repeat for all the long seams. Don't press yet! With scissors, snip the interfacing on the dotted lines at the seam intersections, cutting through and just beyond the stitching, as shown by the short red solid line. B

Fold the short seams as before so the dotted line is directly on the fold, and flip the snipped seams so they nest at the intersec-tions. Secure each seam with pins, and sew a scant ¼-in. seam allowance. C

Repeat until all short seams are sewn, then press the short seams in one direction. D

Repeat to make eight 5-square by 18-square grids and four 5-square by 9-square grid half-panel segments.

Sew two 5-square by 18-square grids and one 5-square by 9-square grid together end to end. Press the connecting seams open to reduce bulk. Repeat to make four pieced panels that are 5 by 45 HST units, or 8 in. by 68 in. (see drawing **5** on p. 124).

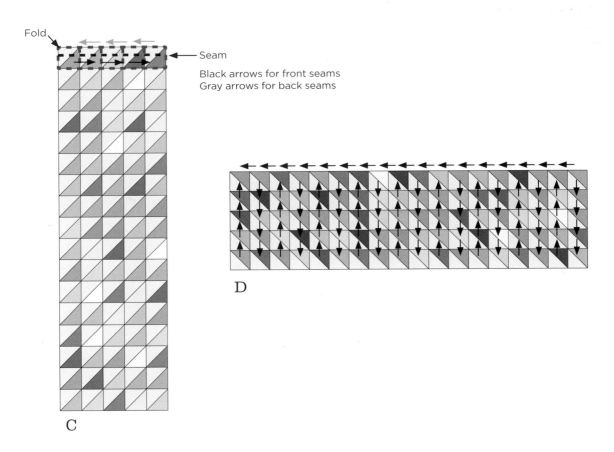

Fold

Seam

Black arrows for front seams
Gray arrows for back seams

C

D

Square Deal

SCRAPS PLUS ONE GREEN SOLID

This quilt started as leftovers from a blue and white wedding quilt, for which I definitely overbought blue fabric. I have found that the solution to just about any problem is . . . make a quilt, and Square Deal was the result.

Blue, yellow, green: the sky, the sun, and the grass. These colors seem to work together, like the earth goes with the sky. With this theme in my head, all of the sudden, my overabundance of blue scrap fabric was solved! However, my scrap bins showed me that my collection of yellow scraps was pathetic. What's a girl to do? . . . Go shopping, of course! I will shamelessly admit to buying scrap fabrics! I needed yellow, so I found some at the local quilt shop.

For your quilt, instead of using blue and yellow scraps, consider choosing them in different color or value families. Replace blue scraps with a variety of dark scraps, replace yellow with light scraps, and add a medium-value coordinate to replace the green. Maybe team colors could inspire a dorm quilt instead of the blue, yellow and green that I chose.

Now that Square Deal is done, looks like I might have overbought yellow. H-m-m. Another ScrapTherapy quilt project always seems to be right around the corner.

FINISHED SIZE: **Varies, see chart on p. 130; lap quilt: 59 in. × 71 in. (shown)**
PATTERN DIFFICULTY: **Easy**

NOTE: The fabric preparation and assembly instructions that follow are for the lap size quilt (pictured). Instructions for the additional sizes begin on p. 132.

PROJECT	Finished Size* (in.)	SCRAPS (NO.)			FABRIC (YD.)		
		2 in. Dark Value	3½ in. Light Value	5 in. Dark Value	Sashing and Border	Binding	Backing
Baby	36 × 36	4	36	36	³/₄	¹/₃	1¹/₄
Toddler	48 × 59	12	80	80	1³/₄	¹/₂	3¹/₂
Lap	59 × 71	20	120	120	2	¹/₂	4¹/₂
Twin	71 × 82	30	168	168	2⁷/₈	²/₃	5
King/Queen	94 × 94	49	256	256	4	²/₃	9

*Add 4 in. to each finished quilt dimension for batting size.

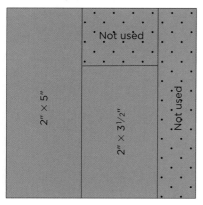

1

PREPARE THE SCRAPS

Select or cut one hundred twenty 3½-in. light-value scrap squares for the blocks.

Select or cut one hundred twenty 5-in. dark-value scrap squares for the blocks.

From each 5-in scrap square, cut one 2-in. by 5-in. rectangle and one 2-in. by 3½-in. rectangle, as shown. The remaining pieces are not used. Repeat for all one hundred twenty 5-in. squares. Keep matching 2-in. by 5-in. rectangles and 2-in. by 3½-in. rectangles together. **1**

Select or cut twenty 2-in. dark-value scrap squares for the cornerstones.

PREPARE THE ADDITIONAL FABRICS

SASHING AND BORDERS

Cut four 10½-in. width-of-fabric strips. From each of two 10½-in. strips, cut twenty 2-in. by 10½-in. strips along the lengthwise grain for the sashing. Set aside

From the third strip, cut nine 2-in. by 10½-in. strips along the lengthwise grain for a total of forty-nine 2-in. by 10½-in. strips for the sashing. Set aside. From the remainder of the third strip, cut twelve 1½-in. by 10½-in. strips along the lengthwise grain for the blocks.

From the fourth strip, cut eighteen 1½-in. by 10½-in. strips along the lengthwise grain for a total of thirty

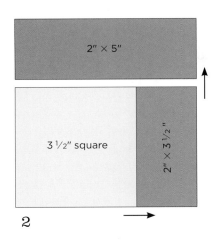

2"×5"

3½" square

2"×3½"

2

1½"×5"

1½"×10½"

3

1½-in. by 10½-in. large strips for
the blocks. From the remainder of
the fourth strip, cut two 5-in. by
approximately 12-in. strips; then cut
sixteen 1½-in. by 5-in. strips along
the lengthwise grain for the blocks.

Cut two 5-in. width-of-fabric strips.
From these strips, cut forty-four
1½-in. by 5-in. strips along the lengthwise grain for a total of sixty 1½-in.
by 5-in. small strips for the blocks.

Cut eight 2-in. width-of-fabric
strips for the borders. Set aside.

> With about 42 in. of usable fabric
> along the crosswise grain, you
> can just barely cut four 10½-in.
> rectangles from a 1½-in. or 2-in.
> width-of-fabric strip. By cutting
> the strips 10½ in. wide, you will
> easily cut 20 or more rectangles
> of each size and have the added
> benefit of less stretchy length-
> wise grain strips for your blocks
> and sashing.

MAKE THE BLOCKS

Sew one 2-in. by 3½-in. dark scrap
rectangle to the right side of a
3½-in. light scrap square. Press the
seam toward the dark rectangle.

Sew the matching 2-in. by 5-in.
dark scrap rectangle to the top of a
3½-in. by 5-in. unit. Press the seam
toward the dark rectangle. Make four
5-in.-square pieced units for each
block, for a total of 120 units. **2**

Sew four 5-in. pieced scrap units,
two 1½-in. by 5-in. small block strips,
and one 1½-in. by 10½-in. large
block strip together, as shown. Press
the seams as indicated.

Make 30 blocks. Be sure to mix up
the scrap units! Each block should
measure 10½ in. square. **3**

NOTE: Your block, made from
a variety of scrap fabrics, will be
more varied than the simplified
illustrations.

> When sewing the 1½-in. by
> 10½-in. large block strip to the
> center of the block, be careful
> to align the smaller strips across
> from each other, so the two
> shorter strips form a straight line
> across the longer center strip. It
> doesn't take much for the two
> short strips to look really out of
> whack. With the 1½-in. by
> 10½-in. block strip sewn to
> one half of the block, hold the
> remaining block half up to a light
> to align the seams. Use pins to
> secure it for sewing.

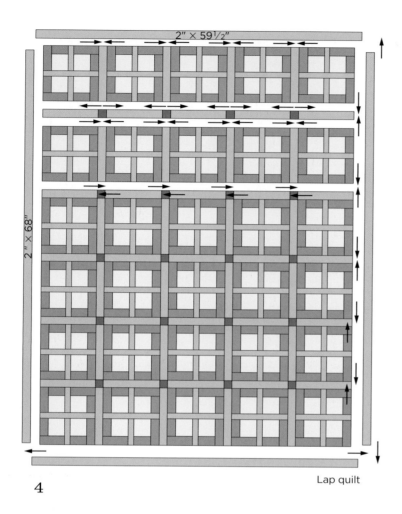

2" × 59½"

2" × 68"

4

Lap quilt

ASSEMBLE THE QUILT

Arrange the blocks into six rows of five blocks. Arrange the 2-in. by 10½-in. sashing strips and the 2-in. scrap square cornerstones between the blocks and sashing as shown.

Sew the sashing and cornerstone rows, and then the block and sashing rows. Then sew the rows together; press the seams as indicated. **4**

Using a diagonal seam (see p. 180), sew two 2-in. width-of-fabric border strips end to end to make one strip, 2 in. by approximately 80 in. long. Make two, one for each side border. Trim each to 2 in. by 68 in.

Similarly, make two 80-in. border strips from the four remaining 2-in. width-of-fabric strips. Trim each top/bottom border strip to 2 in. by 59½ in.

Sew the borders to the quilt, sides first and then top and bottom. Press the seams toward the border after each addition. **4**

> Measure the quilt center before trimming the borders to size.

QUILT AND BIND

Layer the backing, batting, and quilt top; baste. Quilt as desired.

Cut seven 2¼-in. strips for the binding. Sew the binding strips together end to end, using a diagonal seam. Press the connecting seams open, and then press the binding in half lengthwise, wrong sides together.

Trim the batting and backing even with the quilt top. With the raw edges aligned, sew the binding to the front of the quilt using a ¼-in. seam. Miter the binding at the corners.

Turn the folded edge of the binding to the back of the quilt, and hand-stitch it in place.

HOW TO MAKE THE ADDITIONAL QUILT SIZES

MAKE THE BABY QUILT

SASHING AND BORDER FABRIC

Cut one 10½-in. width-of-fabric strip; then cut twelve 2-in. by 10½-in. sashing strips and nine 1½-in. by 10½-in. large block strips.

Cut one 5-in. width-of-fabric strip; then cut eighteen 1½-in. by 5-in. small block strips.

Cut four 2-in. width-of-fabric strips for the borders.

BLOCKS

Make nine blocks from a total of 36 light-value 3½-in. scrap squares, thirty-six 5-in. scrap squares, eighteen 1½-in. by 5-in. small block strips, and nine 1½-in. by 10½-in. large block strips. Use the cutting diagram on p. 130 **(1)** to cut the 5-in. scrap squares into 2-in. by 5-in. and 2-in. by 3½-in. rectangles, keeping the matched pieces from each scrap together.

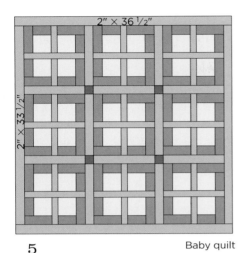

5   Baby quilt

6   Toddler quilt

QUILT TOP AND BINDING

Arrange and sew the blocks, using twelve 2-in. by 10½-in. sashing strips and four 2-in. scrap square cornerstones.

Trim the border strips into two 2-in. by 33½-in. side borders and two 2-in. by 36½-in. top and bottom borders. Sew the borders to the quilt, sides first and then the top and bottom. Press the seams toward the border after each addition. **5**

Make the binding from four 2¼-in. strips.

Refer to the Quilt and Bind instructions for the lap quilt on the facing page.

MAKE THE TODDLER QUILT

SASHING AND BORDER FABRIC

Cut three 10½-in. width-of-fabric strips; then cut thirty-one 2-in. by 10½-in. sashing rectangles and twenty 1½-in. by 10½-in. large block strips.

Cut two 5-in. width-of-fabric strips; then cut forty 1½-in. by 5-in. small block strips.

Cut six 2-in. width-of-fabric strips for the borders.

BLOCKS

Make 20 blocks from a total of 80 light-value 3½-in. scrap squares, eighty 5-in. scrap squares, forty 1½-in. by 5-in. small block strips, and twenty 1½-in. by 10½-in. large block strips. Use the cutting diagram on p. 130 **(1)** to cut the 5-in. scrap squares into 2-in. by 5-in. and 2-in by 3½-in. rectangles, keeping the matched pieces from each scrap together.

QUILT TOP AND BINDING

Arrange and sew the blocks, using thirty-one 2-in. by 10½-in. sashing strips and twelve 2-in. scrap square cornerstones.

Sew the border strips end to end, using a diagonal seam (see p. 180); then cut two 2-in. by 56½-in. side borders and two 2-in. by 48-in. top and bottom borders. Sew the borders to the quilt, sides first and then the top and bottom. Press the seams toward the border after each addition. **6**

Make the binding from six 2¼-in. strips.

Refer to the Quilt and Bind instructions for the lap quilt on the facing page.

2" × 71"

2" × 79¹/₂"

7   Twin quilt

QUILT TOP AND BINDING

Arrange and sew the blocks, using seventy-one 2-in. by 10¹/₂-in. sashing strips and thirty 2-in. scrap square cornerstones.

Sew the border strips in pairs end to end, using a diagonal seam (see p. 180), and trim to make two 2-in. by 79¹/₂-in. side borders and two 2-in. by 71-in. top and bottom borders. Sew the borders to the quilt, sides first and then the top and bottom. Press the seams toward the border after each addition. **7**

Make the binding from eight 2¹/₄-in. strips.

Refer to the Quilt and Bind instructions for the lap quilt on p. 132.

MAKE THE QUEEN/KING QUILT

SASHING AND BORDER FABRIC

Cut nine 10¹/₂-in. width-of-fabric strips; then cut one hundred twelve 2-in. by 10¹/₂-in. sashing strips and sixty-four 1¹/₂-in. by 10¹/₂-in. large block strips.

Cut five 5-in. width-of-fabric strips; then cut one hundred twenty-eight 1¹/₂-in. by 5-in. small block strips.

Cut ten 2-in. width-of-fabric strips for the borders.

BLOCKS

Make 64 blocks from a total of 256 light-value 3¹/₂-in. scrap squares, two hundred fifty-six 5-in. scrap squares, one hundred twenty-eight 1¹/₂-in. by 5-in. small block strips, and sixty-four 1¹/₂-in. by 10¹/₂-in. large block strips. Use the cutting diagram on p. 130 **(1)** to cut the 5-in. scrap squares into 2-in. by

MAKE THE TWIN QUILT
SASHING AND BORDER FABRIC

Cut six 10¹/₂-in. width-of-fabric strips; then cut seventy-one 2-in. by 10¹/₂-in. sashing strips and forty-two 1¹/₂-in. by 10¹/₂-in. large block strips.

Cut four 5-in. width-of-fabric strips; then cut eighty-four 1¹/₂-in. by 5-in. small block strips.

Cut eight 2-in. width-of-fabric strips for the borders.

BLOCKS

Make 42 blocks from a total of 168 light-value 3¹/₂-in. scrap squares, one hundred sixty-eight 5-in. scrap squares, eighty-four 1¹/₂-in. by 5-in. small block strips and forty-two 1¹/₂-in. by 10¹/₂-in. large block strips. Use the cutting diagram on p. 130 **(1)** to cut the 5-in. scrap squares into 2-in. by 5-in. and 2-in. by 3¹/₂-in. rectangles, keeping the matched pieces from each scrap together.

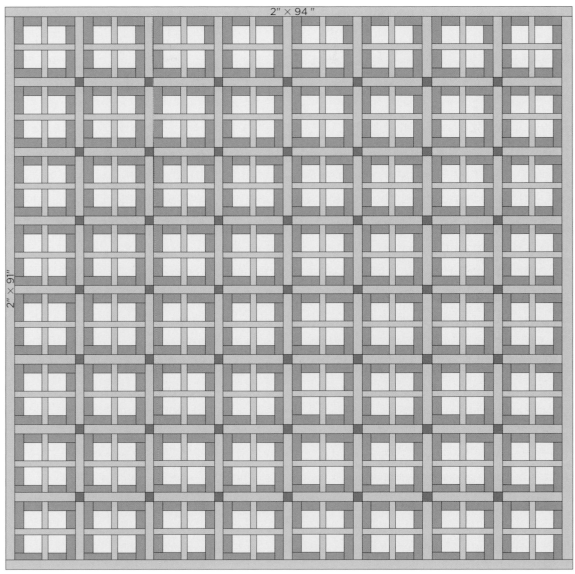

2" × 94"

2" × 91"

8   King/Queen quilt

5-in. and 2-in. by 3½-in. rectangles, keeping the matched pieces from each scrap together.

QUILT TOP AND BINDING

Arrange and sew the blocks using one hundred twelve 2-in. by 10½-in. sashing strips and forty-nine 2-in. scrap square cornerstones.

Sew five border strips end to end, using a diagonal seam (see p. 180); repeat to make two border strips. From one border strip, cut two 2-in. by 91-in. side borders, and from the second border strip cut two 2-in. by 94-in. top and bottom borders. Sew the borders to the quilt, sides first and then the top and bottom. Press the seams toward the border after each addition. **8**

Make the binding from ten 2¼-in. strips.

Refer to the Quilt and Bind instructions for the lap quilt on p. 132.

Citrus Kitchen Set: Pot Holders and Table Runner

SCRAPS PLUS ONE YARD OF A CITRUS-THEMED PRINT

Citrus. Fresh and kitchen-y. I adore anything inspired by the color, texture, or scent of citrus. Candles, fragrances, fabric, you name it—that's my weakness. I'll take lemon over chocolate any time . . . well, almost!

The fusible appliqué citrus-slice pinwheels for this project are made with scraps in a blend of similar citrusy colors—lemon yellow, breakfast orange, tart lime green, and juicy reddish pink grapefruit.

Add some bright white tone-on-tone print flowers and dark leafy green scraps, and a tropical garden kitchen delight emerges.

I'm not so sure that these pot holders are very functional—the dimensional flowers and leaves may not hold up to much of a beating. But doesn't every kitchen deserve a bright decorative touch? Besides, it's simply an excuse to eat out more! You wouldn't want to ruin your pot holders, now would you?

FINISHED SIZE: 8 in. square (potholders); 12 in. by 48 in. (table runner)

PATTERN DIFFICULTY: Intermediate

SCRAP REQUIREMENTS:

2-in. scrap squares: 40

3½-in. scrap squares: 64

5-in. scrap squares: 44

FABRIC AND NOTION REQUIREMENTS:

1⅓ yards citrus-themed print for borders and backing for table runner and pot holders (directional print not recommended)

16-in. by 52-in. batting for table runner

two 9-in. by 9-in. cotton batting scraps for pot holders

two 9-in. by 9-in. squares heat-reflective batting for pot holders

1¼ yards 20-in.-wide plain fusible interfacing

½ yard 18-in.-wide sew-through fusible web

Card stock or template plastic

Heat-erasable marker

NOTE: Fabric requirements are for both projects.

In lieu of plain fusible interfacing, substitute Quiltsmart printed circle interfacing. Quiltsmart interfacing is purchased by the panel. The number of circles on each panel may vary; you'll need enough panels to make 44 circles ranging between 2½-in. and 3½-in. finished size.

citrus kitchen set: pot holders and table runner   **137**

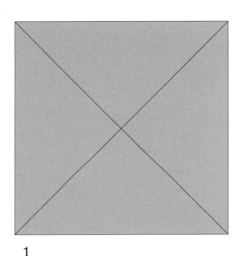

1

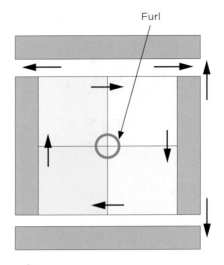

Furl

2

PREPARE THE SCRAPS

Select 8 neutral 3½-in. scrap squares for the pot holder backgrounds, and 18 neutral 3½-in. scrap squares plus 12 neutral 5-in. scrap squares for the table runner background.

Select eight orange print 5-in. squares for the orange slice centers plus eight orange solid 5-in. squares for the orange slice skins.

Select six green print 5-in. squares for the lime slice centers plus six green solid 3½-in. squares for the lime slice skins.

Select six yellow print 5-in. squares for the lemon slice centers plus six yellow solid 3½-in. squares for the lemon slice skins.

Select two reddish orange print 5-in. squares for the grapefruit centers plus two dark yellow solid 5-in. squares for the grapefruit slice skins.

Draw two diagonal lines from corner to corner on the back of four orange print, three green print, three

yellow print, and one reddish orange print 5-in. scrap squares. **1**

Select 40 bright white 2-in. scrap squares for the flowers.

Select 26 dark green 3½-in. scrap squares for the leaves.

PREPARE THE FABRICS
CITRUS-THEMED PRINT

Cut two 16-in. width-of-fabric strips from each strip, and cut one 9-in. by 16-in. rectangle for the pot holder backing. Trim both rectangles to about 9 in. square for the pot holder backing. Reserve the remaining two 16-in. by approximately 30-in. rectangles for the table runner backing.

Cut four 2-in. width-of-fabric strips; set aside for the table runner borders.

Cut two 1½-in. width-of-fabric strips. From one strip, cut four 1½-in. by 8½-in. pot holder border strips. From the second strip, cut four 1½-in. by 6½-in. pot holder border strips and two 1½-in. by 4½-in. pot holder loop strips.

MAKE THE BASE
POT HOLDER BASE

Sew four 3½-in. neutral scrap squares into a four-patch. Furl the seams (see p. 180). Add the 1½-in. by 6½-in. side borders and 1½-in. by 8½-in. top and bottom borders. Press the seam toward the border after each addition. **2**

Repeat to make two pot holder tops that are 8½ in. square.

Press each 1½-in. by 4½-in. loop strip in half lengthwise, wrong sides together. Open the fold, then press each side lengthwise, wrong sides together, so the raw edges meet along the center crease. Fold and press on the original crease so the raw edges are hidden. Topstitch along the length to secure the layers. Repeat to make two loops. Trim each strip to 4 in. long.

Layer, in order, the cotton batting square, heat-reflecting batting square, backing square (right side up), and the pot holder top

Furl

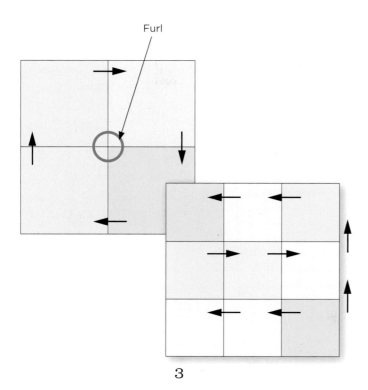

3

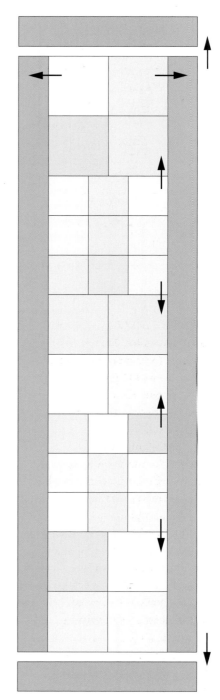

4

(right side down). Fold the loop in half and tuck under one corner in between the top and backing, with the raw edge of the loop aligned with the raw edge of the pot holder top. Secure with pins around all sides and at the loop. Using a walking foot, sew a $1/4$-in. seam around the raw edge of the pot holder top, leaving a 5-in. opening on one side for turning.

Trim all layers even with the pot holder top. Turn right side out. Close the opening by hand, then quilt in-the-ditch around the border/ four-patch seam. Repeat for both pot holders. Set aside for machine appliqué.

TABLE RUNNER BASE

Sew four 5-in. neutral scrap squares into a four-patch. Furl the seams. Repeat to make three four-patches.

Sew nine $3^1/2$-in. neutral scrap squares into a nine-patch. Press the

seams as indicated. Repeat to make two nine-patches. **3**

Sew the four-patches and nine-patches in a row, with the four-patches in the middle and on each end. Press the block seams toward the four-patch blocks. Add the 2-in. by $45^1/2$-in. side borders and 2-in. by $12^1/2$-in. end borders. Press the seam toward the border after each addition. **4**

Sew the two table runner backing pieces together along the 16-in. edge. Trim to 16 in. by 52 in. Layer, in order, the batting, backing (right side up), and table runner top (right side down). Using a walking foot, sew a $1/4$-in. seam around the raw edge of the table runner top, leaving an 8-in. opening on one side for turning.

Trim all layers even with the table runner top. Turn right side out.

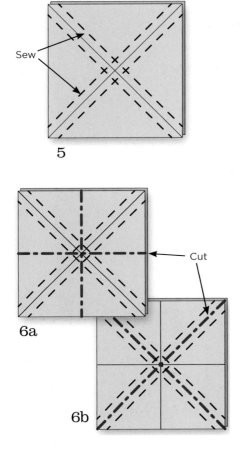

5

6a

6b

8

Furl

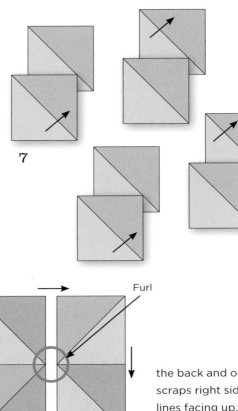

7

Once the table runner is turned right side out, instead of reaching for my hand-sewing tools, I like to close the opening by machine.

Fold the seam under at the opening, and secure with lots of pins. Then finger-press the seam flat all the way around the top—imagine you're squeezing the last bit of toothpaste out of the tube to get the folded edge nice and crisp—and secure intermittently with pins. Then sew a decorative stitch less than 1/8 in. away from the edge to close the opening and add a pretty finish.

Close the opening by hand or machine. Pin-baste all the layers; then quilt in-the-ditch around the border seam, and quilt the center and border as desired. Set aside for machine appliqué.

If your table runner curls a bit after quilting, lay it flat on your ironing surface and press with a hot steamy iron.

ADD THE MACHINE APPLIQUÉ

CITRUS PINWHEELS

Randomly select two orange print 5-in. scrap squares, one with lines on the back and one without. Place the scraps right sides together with the lines facing up. Sew a 1/4-in. seam on both sides of the drawn lines to make a total of four stitching lines. Repeat to make four stitched pairs of orange print squares. **5**

Cut through the center of each stitched pair four times. Be careful not to move the fabric between cuts. First, make a vertical cut 2 1/2 in. from the side edge; then make a horizontal cut 2 1/2 in. from the bottom edge. **6a** Then cut diagonally on the drawn lines to make eight half-square triangle (HST) units per pair, or 32 total orange print HSTs. **6b**

Press the HST seams in one direction. Trim each HST unit to 2 in. square. **7**

Randomly select four orange HST units—mix them up! Sew the HST units together as a four-patch. Furl the seam intersection to reduce bulk. **8**

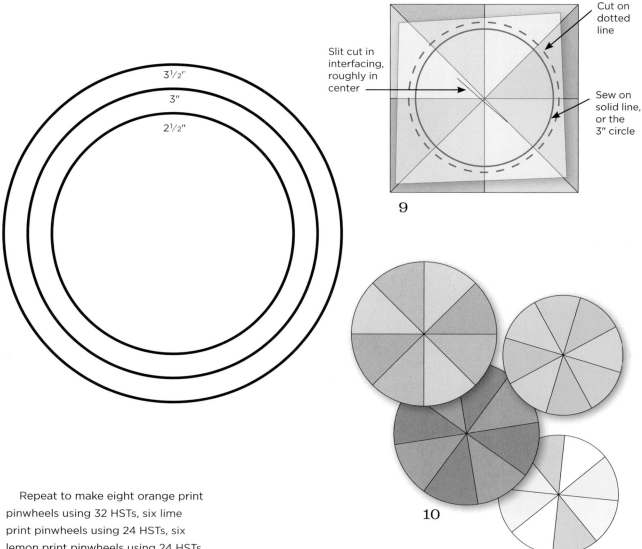

3½"

3"

2½"

Slit cut in
interfacing,
roughly in
center

Cut on
dotted
line

Sew on
solid line,
or the
3" circle

9

10

Repeat to make eight orange print pinwheels using 32 HSTs, six lime print pinwheels using 24 HSTs, six lemon print pinwheels using 24 HSTs, and two grapefruit pinwheels using 8 HSTs.

MAKE CITRUS CENTERS

Review the steps for machine appliqué using fusible interfacing on p. 182.

> Quiltsmart printed fusible interfacing saves steps! With the circles already printed on the interfacing, there is no need to trace the shape.

Trace ten 3-in.-diameter circles and twelve 2½-in.-diameter circles onto plain fusible interfacing. Cut roughly around each shape, then cut a 1½-in. slit in the center of each interfacing circle.

Select an orange pinwheel block and a 3-in.-diameter interfacing circle. Arrange the right side of the pinwheel block so it's facing the bumpy, or fusible, side of the interfacing. Center the interfacing circle over the pinwheel. Pin to secure

the interfacing to the block and sew on the line. Trim the block and interfacing ⅛ in. away from the seam (dotted line). **9**

Turn the circle right side out through the slit in the interfacing, and finger-press around the edges. Repeat to make eight orange centers and two grapefruit centers that are 3 in. in diameter and six lemon centers and six lime centers that are 2½ in. in diameter. **10**

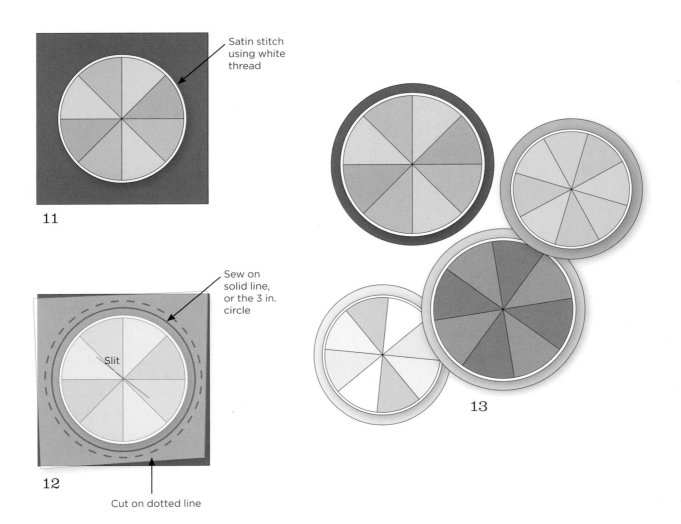

Satin stitch using white thread

11

Sew on solid line, or the 3 in. circle

Slit

12

Cut on dotted line

13

CITRUS RIND AND PITH

Fuse an orange center onto an orange solid 5-in. scrap square, roughly in the middle of the scrap square. Using white thread, secure around the edge of the appliqué with a satin stitch to simulate the white pith.

Repeat to secure each orange and grapefruit center to its corresponding orange or dark yellow 5-in. scrap square, and each lime or lemon to its corresponding green or yellow 3½-in. scrap square. **11**

Trace ten 3½-in.-diameter circles and twelve 3-in.-diameter circles onto plain fusible interfacing. Cut roughly around each shape, then cut a 1½-in. slit in the center of each interfacing circle.

Choose an orange center and a 3½-in.-diameter interfacing circle. Arrange the right side of the orange center block so it's facing the bumpy, or fusible, side of the interfacing. Center the interfacing circle over the orange pinwheel. Pin to secure the interfacing to scrap and sew

on the solid line, as before. Trim the scrap square and interfacing ⅛ in. away from the seam. Turn the circle through the slit opening in the interfacing, and finger-press around the edges. **12**

Repeat to make eight orange slices and two grapefruit slices that are 3½ in. in diameter, and make six lemon slices and six lime slices that are 3 in. in diameter. **13**

Set aside.

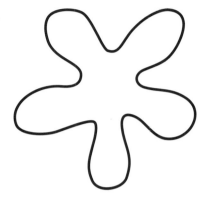

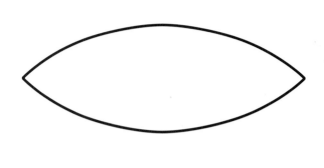

FLOWERS

Cut three 2-in. strips of fusible web, then cut twenty 2-in. squares. Fuse each fusible web square to the wrong side of 20 white 2-in. scrap squares. Remove the paper; then fuse another white 2-in. scrap square to the back of each fused scrap, making twenty 2-in. white scrap sandwiches. Trace the flower shape onto card stock or template plastic, then cut the shape. Using a heat-erasable pen, trace a flower shape onto each sandwich and cut on the line. Press to remove the tracing lines. Set aside for final assembly.

LEAVES

Similarly, cut three $1^3/_4$-in. strips of fusible web, then cut twenty-six $1^3/_4$-in. by $3^1/_2$-in. rectangles. Fuse each fusible web rectangle to the wrong side of 26 green $3^1/_2$-in. scrap squares, aligning the web along one side of the square and leaving one half of the square with fusible web and the other without. Remove the paper, then fold the green square in half along the edge of the fusible web and fuse the two halves together, making twenty-six $1^3/_4$-in. by $3^1/_2$-in. green scrap sandwiches. Trace a leaf shape onto card stock or template plastic, then cut the shape. Using a heat-erasable pen, trace a leaf shape onto each sandwich and cut on the line. Press to remove the tracing lines. Set aside for final assembly.

FINISH THE ASSEMBLY

Arrange four leaves, an orange slice, and three flowers playfully on one of the pot holders. Working with one layer at a time and using a walking foot, sew a line of quilting through the center of each leaf. Next, fuse the orange slice into place and secure the appliqué with a blanket stitch around the edge of the shape. Then tack stitch the flowers in place.

The stitching used to secure the appliqué serves a double purpose. First, it secures each appliqué shape in place, and second, it adds a little extra quilting through all of the layers.

Similarly, arrange and secure three leaves, a lemon and a lime slice, and two flowers to the second pot holder. Arrange and secure the remaining leaves, fruit slices, and flowers to the table runner.

Petal Pushers

SCRAPS PLUS ONE CHEERFUL FOCUS PRINT

The focus print I used to make this quilt really caught my attention, with its bright colors, contemporary design, and splashy look. It seemed appropriate to pair such a fun inspiration fabric with blocks and pieced sashing strips that are full of delightful, brightly colored scraps.

The border incorporates a prairie-point-type element made from scraps that have been sewn and cut into circles—don't worry, they are really easy to make! On the quilt, the petals add an extra element of play to an already lively piece. My quilt turned out very bright and colorful because of the fabrics selected—it's like a walk in a midsummer garden.

FINISHED SIZE: **68 in. by 68 in.**
PATTERN DIFFICULTY: **Intermediate**

SCRAP REQUIREMENTS:
2-in. light-value scrap squares: 48
2-in. dark-value scrap squares: 48
5-in. light-value scrap squares: 101
5-in. dark-value scrap squares: 157
FABRIC AND NOTION REQUIREMENTS:
2 yards focus print for border
1/2 yard bright pink for binding
4 yards for backing
72-in. by 72-in. batting
Pigma pen or heat-erasable marker
Square ruler with bias line, at least 6 in. square

PREPARE THE SCRAPS

Select 101 light-value 5-in. scrap squares and 157 dark-value 5-in. scrap squares.

From the light-value 5-in. scrap squares, choose 32 for the large half-square triangle (HST) units in the blocks. Draw a diagonal line from corner to corner on the back of each. **1** Then choose 13 light-value scrap squares for the small HST units to make block centers and cornerstones, and draw two diagonal lines from corner to corner on the back of each. **2**

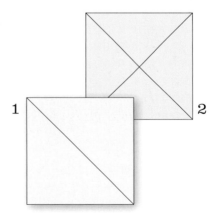

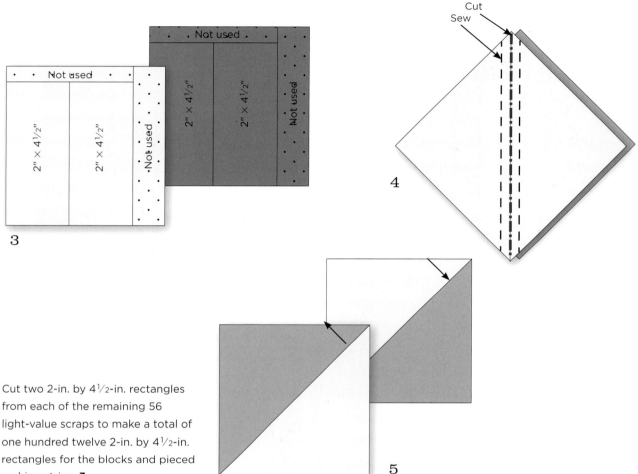

3

4

5

Cut two 2-in. by 4½-in. rectangles from each of the remaining 56 light-value scraps to make a total of one hundred twelve 2-in. by 4½-in. rectangles for the blocks and pieced sashing strips. **3**

From the dark-value 5-in. scrap squares, choose 56 for the petals in the border, 32 for the large HSTs in the blocks, and 13 for the small HSTs; set aside. Then from each of the remaining 56 dark-value scraps, cut two 2-in. by 4½-in. rectangles to make a total of one hundred twelve 2-in. by 4½-in. rectangles for the blocks and pieced sashing strips. **3**

For the petals, select bold, solid-reading scraps that will hold up against your focus fabric.

Select 48 light-value 2-in. scrap squares and 48 dark-value 2-in. scrap squares for the pieced sashing strips.

PREPARE THE ADDITIONAL FABRICS

FOCUS PRINT

Cut four 2-in. strips along the length-wise grain. Set aside for the inner borders.

Cut four 6½-in. strips along the lengthwise grain. Set aside for the outer borders.

PIECE THE TOP

LARGE HALF-SQUARE TRIANGLE UNITS

Randomly select a light-value 5-in. scrap square and a dark-value scrap square from the ones set aside earlier for the large half-square triangle

(HST) units. Place the scraps right sides together with the marked light-value scrap on top. Sew a ¼-in. seam on both sides of the drawn line. **4** Cut on the line; then press the seam toward the dark-value fabric. Repeat with all 32 light-value and dark-value scraps set aside for large HSTs to make a total of 64 large HST units. Trim each unit to 4½ in. square. **5**

SMALL HALF-SQUARE TRIANGLE UNITS

Randomly select a light-value 5-in. scrap square and a dark-value scrap square from those set aside earlier

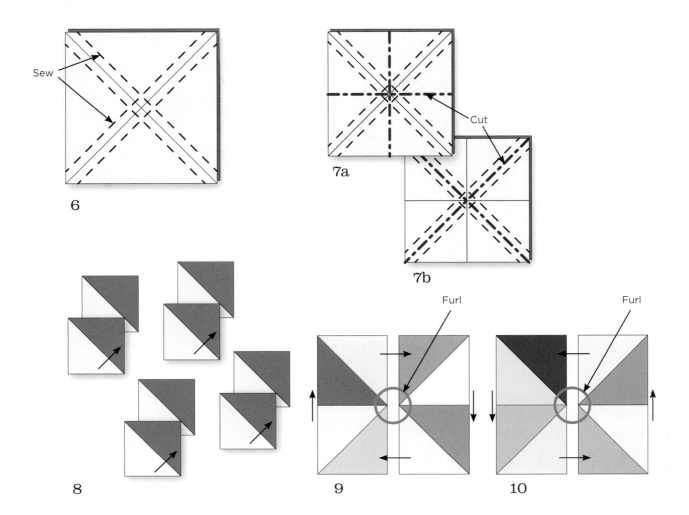

6

7a

Cut

7b

8

Furl

9

Furl

10

for the small HST units. Place the scraps right sides together with the marked light-value scrap on top. Sew a 1/4-in. seam on both sides of the drawn lines to make a total of four stitching lines, as shown. **6**

Cut through the center four times. Be careful not to move the fabric between cuts. First, make a vertical cut 2 1/2 in. from the side edge; then make a horizontal cut 2 1/2 in. from the bottom edge. **7a** Then cut diagonally on the drawn lines to make eight HST units. **7b**

Press the HST seams toward the darker fabric. Trim each HST unit to 2 in. square. **8**

Repeat to make a total of 104 HST units. Four will be unused.

PINWHEELS

Randomly select four small HST units, and sew them together as a four-patch, as shown, noticing the placement of the dark-value scraps. Furl the seam intersection to reduce the bulk (see p. 180). Be sure to feed each two-patch into the sewing

machine in the same way, so all four-patch seams furl in the same direction. Repeat to make 16 block pinwheel units that are 3 1/2 in. square. **9**

Randomly select four small HST units, and sew them together as a four-patch, as shown, noticing the placement of the dark-value scraps. Furl the seam intersection to reduce bulk. Repeat to make nine cornerstone pinwheel units that are 3 1/2 in. square. **10**

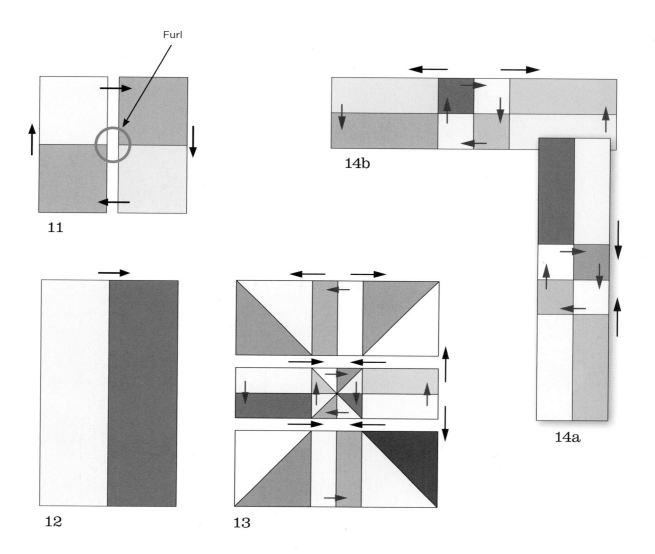

Furl

11

12

13

14a

14b

NOTE: It's important to notice that the pinwheel units for the block centers and cornerstones are different. They look very similar, but the placement of the dark-value scraps and the direction of the furled seams are different, so be careful.

FOUR-PATCHES

Randomly select and sew two light-value and two dark-value 2-in. scrap squares into a four-patch, as shown. Furl the seam intersection to reduce the bulk. Repeat to make 24 four-patches that are $3\frac{1}{2}$ in. square. **11**

PIECED RECTANGLES

Randomly select and sew a light-value 2-in. by $4\frac{1}{2}$-in. rectangle to a dark-value 2-in. by $4\frac{1}{2}$-in. rectangle, as shown. Press the seam toward the darker fabric. Repeat to make 112 pieced rectangles that are $3\frac{1}{2}$ in. by $4\frac{1}{2}$ in. **12**

MAKE THE BLOCKS

Randomly select four large HST units, four pieced rectangles, and one block pinwheel and arrange as shown, noticing the placement of the dark-value scraps. Sew as for

a nine-patch. Press the seams as indicated. Repeat to make 16 blocks that are $11\frac{1}{2}$ in. square. **13**

PIECED SASHING

Randomly select two pieced rectangles and one four-patch and arrange as shown, noticing the placement of the dark-value scraps. Sew. Repeat to make 24 pieced sashing strips: 12 with seams pressed toward the four-patch for the vertical sashing **14a** and 12 with seams pressed away from the four-patch for the horizontal sashing. **14b** Each strip is $3\frac{1}{2}$ in. by $11\frac{1}{2}$ in.

15

QUILT CENTER

Arrange the blocks, sashing, and cornerstones as shown. Sew the block and vertical sashing rows; press the seams toward the sashing strips. Sew the horizontal sashing and pinwheel cornerstone rows; press the seams toward the sashing strips. Then sew the rows together. Press the row seams toward the block rows. The quilt center should be 53½ in. square. **15**

A few of the seam intersections, particularly where the sashing strips meet the cornerstones, may not nest nicely. Rather than generate a whole lot of confusing repressing logic, use extra pins where needed. Relatively speaking, only a few intersections will need a little extra attention.

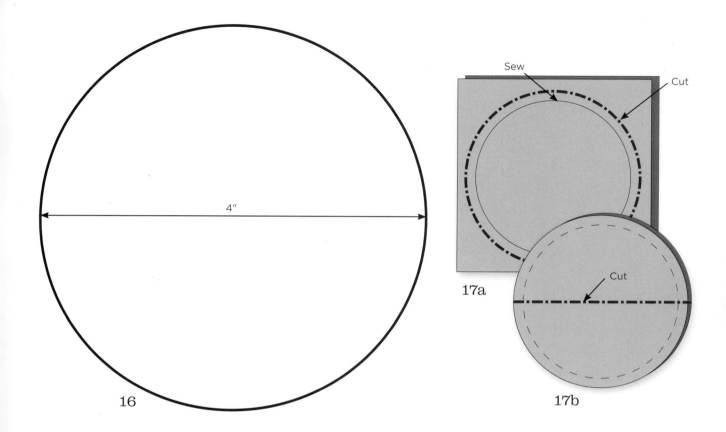

4"

16

Sew

Cut

17a

Cut

17b

MAKE THE BORDERS

INNER BORDER

Trim two inner border strips to 2 in. by 53$\frac{1}{2}$ in. Sew to the sides of the quilt. Press the seams toward the border.

Trim the two inner border strips to 2 in. by 56$\frac{1}{2}$ in. Sew to the top and bottom of the quilt. Press the seams toward the border.

Measure the quilt before trimming the borders.

PETALS

Roughly center and trace a 4-in.-diameter circle onto the wrong side of 28 of the 56 remaining 5-in. scrap squares set aside for the petals. **16** Pair each scrap that has a drawn circle with a similar scrap without a

drawn circle, right sides together, with the drawn-circle scrap on top. Sew on the line. With scissors, trim $\frac{1}{4}$ in. away from the seam. **17a** Cut the circle in half, then turn each half circle right side out. **17b** Edgestitch around the curved edge, if desired. Repeat to make 56 half-circle petals with one raw, open, straight edge.

OUTER BORDER

Starting and ending about $\frac{1}{2}$ in. from the corner, with raw edges aligned, place 14 petals evenly spaced along each side of the inner border. Petals may overlap a bit. Pin liberally to hold the petals in place. Trim the two outer side borders to 6$\frac{1}{2}$ in. by 56$\frac{1}{2}$ in. each. With raw edges aligned and right sides together, pin the outer side border

on top of the side edge, sandwiching the petals in between the layers, similar to the flange technique shown on p. 185. Sew a $\frac{1}{4}$-in. seam through all layers. Press the seam toward the inner border, allowing the curved edges of the petals to flip outward toward the quilt edge. Repeat for both sides of the quilt.

Similarly, with raw edges aligned, place 14 petals evenly spaced along the top inner border. Keep the petals in between the side outer border seams (red arrows), as shown. The petals may overlap a bit. Pin liberally to hold the petals in place. Trim the top and bottom outer borders to 6$\frac{1}{2}$ in. by 68$\frac{1}{2}$ in. each. With the raw edges aligned and right sides together, pin the top outer border to the top edge of the quilt, sandwich-

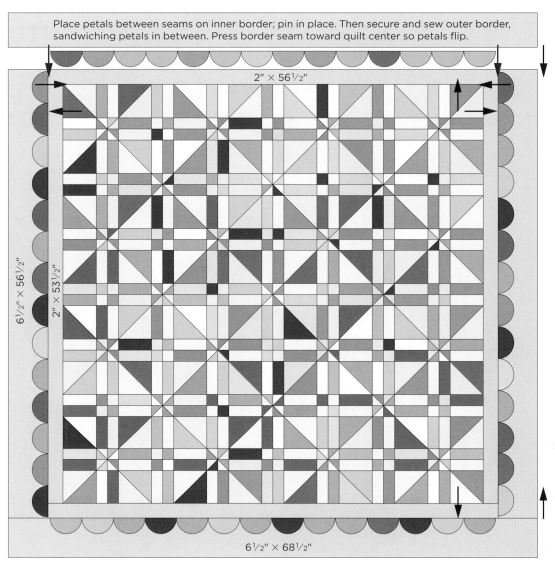

Place petals between seams on inner border; pin in place. Then secure and sew outer border, sandwiching petals in between. Press border seam toward quilt center so petals flip.

2" × 56¹⁄₂"

6¹⁄₂" × 56¹⁄₂"

2" × 53¹⁄₂"

6¹⁄₂" × 68¹⁄₂"

18

ing the petals in between the layers, as for the side borders. Sew a ¹⁄₄-in. seam through all the layers. Press the seam toward the inner border, allowing the curved edges of the petals to flip outward toward the quilt edge. Repeat for the bottom outer border. **18**

QUILT AND BIND

Layer the backing, batting, and quilt top; baste. Quilt as desired. Cut seven 2¹⁄₄-in. strips for the binding.

Sew the binding strips together end to end, using a diagonal seam (p. 180). Press the connecting seams open; then press the binding in half lengthwise, wrong sides together.

Trim the batting and backing even with the quilt top. With the raw edges aligned, sew the binding to the front of the quilt, using a ¹⁄₄-in. seam. Miter the binding at the corners.

Turn the folded edge of the binding to the back of the quilt, and hand-stitch it in place.

Confetti Pillow

SCRAPS PLUS ONE PILLOW FORM

Sometimes simple is best. But even an easy project can contain a secret for success. And this pillow is no exception. You'll find a little tip to make your pillow form fit perfectly inside its scrappy exterior.

This is also a great opportunity to show off some decorative stitching. Quilters, myself included, tend to shy away from those extra stitches on your sewing machine, focusing on the straight stitch most of the time for piecing and quilting.

With all the raw-edged scraps decorating the front, this project is not likely to be an heirloom classic. But this pillow is just the ticket for a fun, contemporary home decorating detail. And it's a fast and easy way to use your scraps.

For my pillow, I had a mini-stack of extra border fabric leftover from the Petal Pushers quilt on p. 144. So they became somewhat of my inspiration for the rest of the coordinating scraps.

FINISHED SIZE: **18 in. by 18 in.**
PATTERN DIFFICULTY: **Easy**

SCRAP REQUIREMENTS:
2-in. medium-value scrap squares: up to 150
   (24–30 for each raw-edged scrappy row)
3¹/₂-in. light/neutral-value scrap squares: 36
FABRIC AND NOTION REQUIREMENTS:
³/₈ yard backing
¹/₄ yard, 16-in.-wide sew-through fusible web
18-in. pillow form
20-in. or longer straightedge ruler
Heat-erasable marker

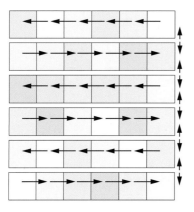

1

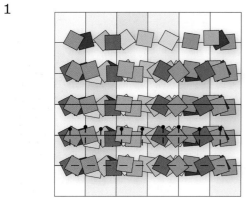

Scraps

More scraps

Draw line

Pin

Sew

2

1/2"

4³/₄"

Wrong side of
pillow front

3

PREPARE THE SCRAPS

Select one hundred fifty 2-in. medium-value scrap squares. Coordinate them into a color theme or just go scrappy.

Select thirty-six 3¹/₂-in. light/ neutral scrap squares.

PREPARE THE BACKING PRINT

Cut one 12-in. width-of-fabric strip; then cut two 12-in. by 18¹/₂-in. rectangles for the backing.

PREPARE THE PILLOW FRONT

Sew 3¹/₂-in. scraps into six rows of six scraps. Press the seams alternately by row. Sew the rows together; press the row seams open. The pillow background is 18¹/₂ in. square. **1**

Place the pillow background on your work table, right side up. Starting and ending about ¹/₂ in. away from the edge, arrange twenty-four to thirty 2-in. scraps over each row seam. Place the scraps one at a time, right side up and wonky. Without disturbing the scrap arrangement, place a long straightedge ruler over the 2-in. scraps, aligned with the visible seam at either end of the row. With a heat-erasable marker, draw a straight line over the 2-in. scraps. Remove the ruler carefully, and pin through all the layers to secure.

Sew a decorative stitch over the straight line. Repeat with all five seam lines. **2**

Place the pillow front right side down on your work table. Make a mark ¹/₂ in. from the corner, as shown. Then make a second mark on each adjacent side 4³/₄ in. from the corner. Draw a line connecting the marks. Repeat for all four corners. Set aside. **3**

This little corner marking trick will help your pillow cover fit perfectly over the pillow form with no extra fabric bulk. When assembling the pillow, you'll sew around the edges following these marked lines. It's a minor adjustment that can make a big difference.

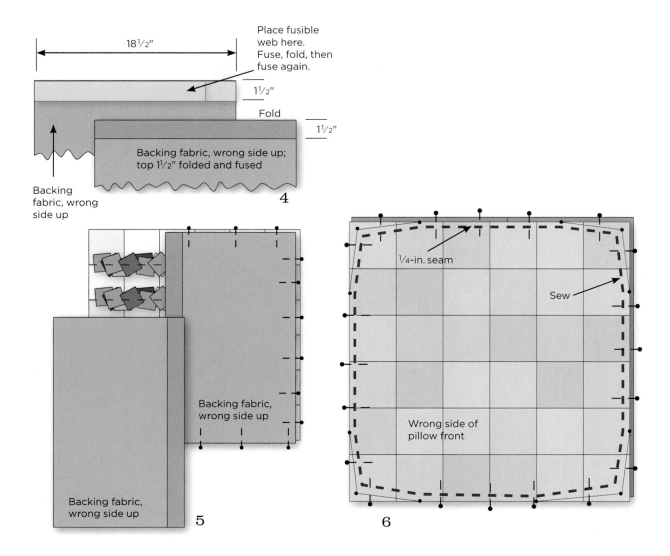

18½"

Place fusible web here. Fuse, fold, then fuse again.

1½"

Fold

1½"

Backing fabric, wrong side up; top 1½" folded and fused

Backing fabric, wrong side up

4

Backing fabric, wrong side up

Backing fabric, wrong side up

5

¼-in. seam

Sew

Wrong side of pillow front

6

PILLOW BACK

Cut three 1½-in. by 16-in. strips from fusible web. Place the fusible side of the fusible web strip on the wrong side of one 12-in. by 18½-in. backing rectangle, aligning it with an 18½-in. edge of the fabric. Abut a partial strip next to the 16-in. strip to cover the fabric edge across the entire 18½-in. length. Fuse with a hot iron. Remove the paper, fold the fabric 1½ in. from the edge (along edge of the fusible web), and fuse again to encase the fusible material. Repeat with the second 12-in. by 18½-in. backing piece. **4**

ASSEMBLE THE PILLOW

Place the pillow front, right side up, on a large work surface. Make sure it is flat.

Place one backing piece, right side down, on the pillow top, with right sides facing and raw edges aligned.

Place the second backing piece, right side down, on the pillow assembly, aligning the raw edges on the opposite side of the pillow top.

Pin liberally around the entire pillow assembly to secure the edges. **5**

Flip the entire assembly so the wrong (marked corner) side of the pillow front is facing up. Sew a ¼-in. seam allowance around the entire outside edge and along the corner markings. Remove the pins as you sew. Trim on the lines. **6**

Turn the pillow assembly right side out through the opening in the back. Insert an 18-in. by 18-in. pillow form.

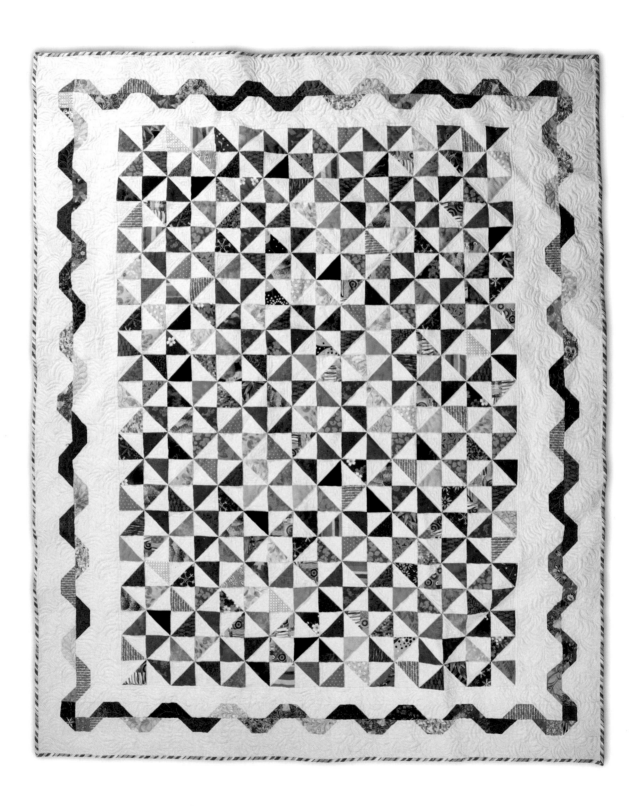

Twirly Whirly

SCRAPS PLUS ONE CREAM PRINT

What is it about the pinwheel block that makes a quilt so much fun? The block is straightforward—half-square triangle units made into four-patches. Blocks can be monochromatic or scrappy. On point or straight set. They just work. When sewn into simple rows, the block itself disappears into a mosaic of secondary shapes and colors.

For this quilt, I selected scraps in yellows, blues, and greens—the colors of nature for a summery combination sure to lift your spirits any time of year. A ribbon of scrappy color in the border adds a little extra to bring it all together.

FINISHED SIZE: 58 in. by 70 in.
PATTERN DIFFICULTY: Intermediate

SCRAP REQUIREMENTS:

2-in. scrap squares: 20
3$\frac{1}{2}$-in. scrap squares: 176
5-in. scrap squares: 34

FABRIC AND NOTION REQUIREMENTS:

3$\frac{1}{2}$ yards cream print for blocks and border
$\frac{1}{2}$ yard striped print for binding
4 yards for backing
62-in. by 74-in. batting
Pigma pen or heat-erasable marker
Square ruler with bias line for trimming,
    at least 6 in. square

PREPARE THE SCRAPS

Select one hundred seventy-six 3$\frac{1}{2}$-in. scrap squares for blocks.

Select thirty-four 5-in. scrap squares for the border. Cut each 5-in. scrap square into two 2-in. by 5-in. rectangles, as shown, to make a total of sixty-eight 2-in. by 5-in. rectangles. The remaining pieces are not used. **1**

Select twenty 2-in. scrap squares for the border cornerstones.

1

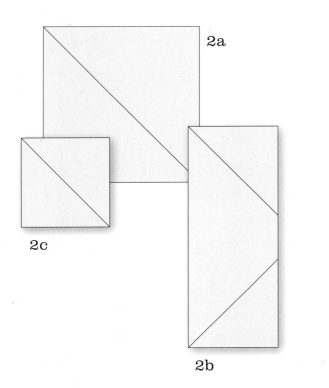

2a

2c

2b

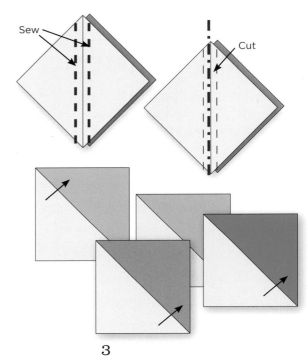

Sew

Cut

3

PREPARE THE ADDITIONAL FABRICS

CREAM PRINT

Cut sixteen 3$\frac{1}{2}$-in. width-of-fabric strips; then cut one hundred seventy-six 3$\frac{1}{2}$-in. squares for the blocks. Using a fabric marking tool, draw a diagonal line from corner to corner on the back of each cream square for the pinwheel blocks. **2a**

Cut four 5-in. width-of-fabric strips; then cut sixty-eight 2-in. by 5-in. rectangles along the lengthwise grain for the pieced border. On the back of each rectangle, draw a 45-degree line from two corners, as shown. **2b**

Cut one 2-in. width-of-fabric strip; then cut sixteen 2-in. squares for the pieced border. On the back of 12 of the squares, draw a diagonal line from corner to corner. **2c**

Cut three 2$\frac{1}{4}$-in. width-of-fabric strips for the inner borders.

Cut three 3$\frac{3}{4}$-in. width-of-fabric strips for the inner borders.

Cut seven 3-in. width-of-fabric strips for the outer border.

MAKE THE BLOCKS

HALF-SQUARE TRIANGLE UNITS

Place one 3$\frac{1}{2}$-in. scrap square and one 3$\frac{1}{2}$-in. cream square right sides together, with the cream fabric on top. Sew a $\frac{1}{4}$-in. seam on both sides of the drawn line. Cut on the drawn line. Press the seam toward the scrap fabric. Using a small square ruler with a bias line, trim each half-square triangle (HST) unit to 3 in. square. **3**

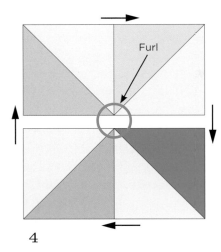

4

5

Repeat to make 352 HST units that are 3 in. square.

Randomly select and sew HST units into two-patches; then press the seam toward the scrap fabric. Sew two two-patch units together to make a pinwheel block. Furl the seams, as shown on p. 180. **4**

Repeat to make 88 pinwheel blocks that are 5½ in. square.

> Although it is not necessary to furl the seams in each four-patch, furling, or opening only the very center of the seam so the adjacent seams can rotate around the intersection, reduces the bulk in the center of the block and makes assembling the rows easier because, no matter how many times you rotate a block, the seams in adjoining blocks will nest.

QUILT CENTER
Arrange the blocks into 11 rows of eight blocks. Sew the blocks into rows; press the seams in one direction in alternate rows. Sew the rows together, then press the seams in one direction. **5**

MAKE THE BORDERS
INNER BORDER
Sew three 3¾-in. strips together end to end, using a diagonal seam (see p. 180) to make a strip approximately 120 in. long. Press the connecting seams open. Cut two 3¾-in. by 55½-in. side inner borders.

Similarly, sew three 2¼-in. strips together, end to end, using a diagonal seam, and cut two 2¼-in. by 47-in. inner borders for the top and bottom.

Sew the inner borders to the quilt, the sides first, then the top and bottom; press the seams toward the border after each addition.

Although it's always important to measure the quilt top before cutting borders, for quilts that have a pieced element in the border, it's even more critical that measurements are accurate.

Your quilt center should be pretty close to 40½ in. by 55½ in.; if not, it might be worth doing some troubleshooting. Check for accurate seam allowances, meticulous pressing technique, and proper cutting. Otherwise, you may need to do some math to make sure the quilt top is 47 in. by 59 in. after adding the inner border, so you can add the pieced border successfully.

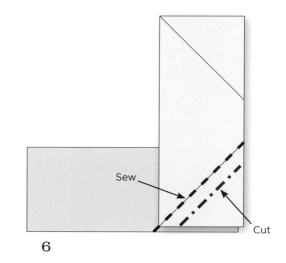

6

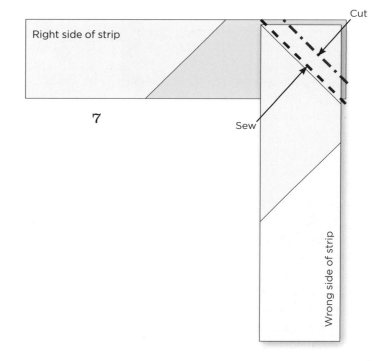

7

PIECED SIDE INNER BORDER

The ribbon-like pieced border is easy to make, but many of the parts look similar, so the steps can get confusing if you aren't careful. Each pieced border is assembled in two parts: an inner and an outer pieced border.

Select ten 2-in. by 5-in. scrap strips and nine 2-in. by 5-in. cream strips.

Complete each pieced border unit before moving on to the next.

Select a 2-in. by 5-in. scrap strip and place it horizontally, right side up, on your work table. Place a cream strip vertically on top of the right end of the strip so the bottom end of the cream strip is aligned with the right end of the scrap strip. Be sure the drawn line on the cream strip is facing up and crosses from lower left to upper right. **6**

Sew on the line and trim the corner triangle. Chain piece pairs of cream and scrap fabrics until all nine cream strips are sewn to a scrap strip. There will be one extra scrap strip. Press the seams toward the scrap fabric.

Place a sewn strip on your work table horizontally, right side up, so the scrap strip is on the right. Place the next sewn strip vertically on top of the first sewn strip, so the top end of the cream strip is aligned with the right end of the scrap strip, as shown. Be sure the drawn line on the cream strip is facing up and crosses from upper left to lower right. **7**

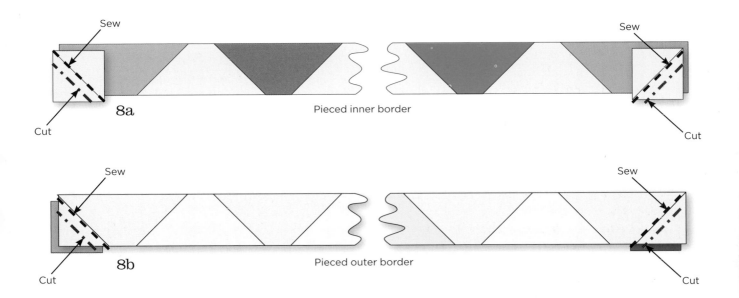

Sew

8a

Cut

Pieced inner border

Sew

Cut

Sew

8b

Cut

Pieced outer border

Sew

Cut

Sew on the line. Trim the corner triangle. Chain piece all nine sewn pairs; then, in the same manner, sew the remaining scrap piece to the end cream strip.

Place a cream 2-in. square aligned with each end, right sides together, so the drawn line is positioned at the correct angle for that end of the strip, as shown. **8a**

Sew on the line. Trim the corner triangle. Repeat for both ends. Press the seams toward the scrap fabric. The strip should be 2 in. by 59 in. Make two pieced side inner borders.

PIECED SIDE OUTER BORDER

Select ten 2-in. by 5-in. cream strips and nine 2-in. by 5-in. scrap strips.

Sew the cream strips and scrap strips together as for the inner

border, until two cream strip ends are unsewn. Align a 2-in. scrap square with a cream strip end, right sides together. **8b** Sew on the line marked on the wrong side of the cream strip; trim the corner triangle as before. Make two 2-in. by 59-in. pieced outer borders.

PIECED SIDE BORDER ASSEMBLY

Sew each pieced side inner border strip to a pieced side outer border strip, so the wide base of the scrap fabrics meet at the seam, creating the wavy ribbon appearance; press the seam toward the inner border. The pieced side border is 3½ in. by 59 in. Make two pieced side borders, sew onto the quilt, and press the seam toward the inner cream border (see **11** on p. 163).

PIECED TOP/BOTTOM BORDERS

For each pieced top/bottom inner border, select eight 2-in. by 5-in. scrap strips and seven 2-in. by 5-in. cream strips. For each pieced top/bottom outer border, select eight 2-in. by 5-in. cream strips and seven 2-in. by 5-in. scrap strips.

Construct the top and bottom borders following the same steps for the side borders. Each border strip will be 2 in. by 47 in. Sew each top/bottom inner border strip to an outer border strip. Press the seam toward the inner pieced border. The border is 3½ in. by 47 in. before adding the cornerstones. Make two.

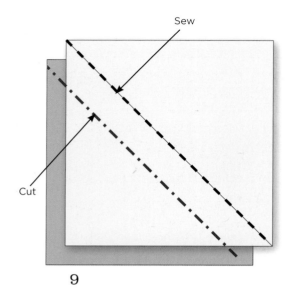

Sew

Cut

9

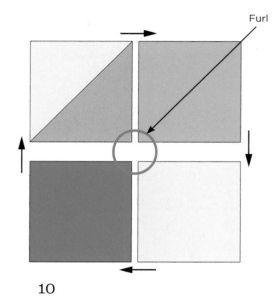

Furl

10

PIECED CORNERSTONES

Select three 2-in. scrap squares and two 2-in. cream squares, one with a line drawn diagonally on the back of the square. Place a scrap square with the cream square (with the line) right sides together. Sew on the drawn line. Cut 1/4 in. from the seam and discard the smaller triangle. **9**

Press the seam toward the scrap fabric to make a small HST that is 2 in. square.

Arrange and sew the HST, two scrap squares, and one cream square into a four-patch. Furl the seam. The four-patch is 3½ in. square. Make four. **10**

Sew one cornerstone to each end of the top and bottom pieced border.

Be careful! Watch the placement of the scrap and cream squares. Note that every other cornerstone seam will nest with the center pieced border seam. Use extra pins when needed. **11**

OUTER BORDER

Sew all seven strips together end to end, using a diagonal seam. Press the connecting seams open. From the long strip, cut two 3-in. by 65-in. side borders and two 3-in. by 58-in. top/bottom borders. Sew each border to the quilt, the sides first, and then the top and bottom. Press the seam toward the outer border after each addition. **11**

QUILT AND BIND

Layer the backing, batting, and the quilt top; baste. Quilt as desired.

Cut seven 2¼-in. strips for the binding. Sew the binding strips together end to end, using a diagonal seam. Press the connecting seams open, then press the binding in half lengthwise, wrong sides together.

Trim the batting and backing even with the quilt top. With the raw edges aligned, sew the binding to the front of the quilt using a ¼-in. seam. Miter the binding at the corners.

Turn the folded edge of the binding to the back of the quilt, and hand-stitch it in place.

3" × 58"

2" × 47"

2" × 47"

2¼" × 47"

3" × 65"

2" × 59"

2" × 59"

3¾" × 55½"

11

Chruściki Tote

SCRAPS PLUS ONE PRETTY COOL COOKIE TECHNIQUE

All four of my grandparents emigrated to the United States from Poland in the late 1800s. With them came many family traditions and Old World recipes.

Any time of year, but especially at Christmastime, my family celebrations always seem to include a big tray of cookies. Chruściki (pronounced *cruise-CHEEK-ee*), a fried cookie dusted with powdered sugar, is an annual favorite of mine. Each crispy cookie has a twist in the middle that perplexed me as a child. How in the world did that twist get there? It was a magical, tasty mystery.

And so, the cookie technique has found its way into a quilty project. The twisty strap for this spacious tote bag carries on the secret.

Add a casual closure for a less-than-full load with a hook and D-ring inserted on each side of the bag's rim.

Whether you take this satchel to your next quilt retreat or to the market, you've got plenty of space for a big load, including a few ScrapTherapy bins filled with cut-up scraps.

FINISHED SIZE: **19 in. by 16 in. by 9 in.**
PATTERN DIFFICULTY: **Intermediate**

SCRAP REQUIREMENTS:

3½-in. medium blue scrap squares: 64
3½-in. medium brown scrap squares: 15
3½-in. dark brown scrap squares: 56

FABRIC AND NOTION REQUIREMENTS:

⅞ yard neutral print for base
2¼ yards neutral solid for lining and straps
30-in. by 36-in. batting, two pieces, each the same size
Pigma or heat-erasable marker
Hook and D-ring hardware (optional)
ScrapTherapy Scrap Sack Support (optional)

NOTE: The Chruściki Tote was designed so it would hold a ScrapTherapy Scrap Sack Support, which shapes and strengthens the bottom of the bag.

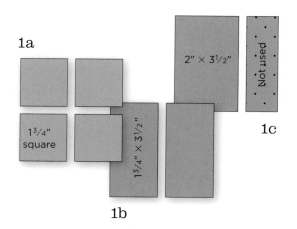

1a

1¾"
square

1¾" × 3½"

1b

2" × 3½"

Not used

1c

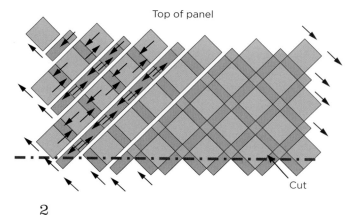

Top of panel

Cut

2

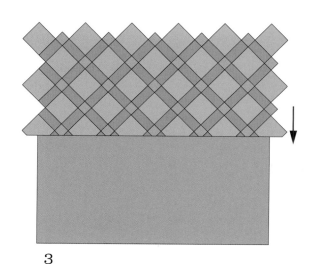

3

PREPARE THE SCRAPS

Select 64 medium blue 3½-in. scrap squares for piecing.

Select 15 medium brown 3½-in. scrap squares for piecing. Cut each scrap in half twice to make a total of sixty 1¾-in. squares for the cornerstones. **1a** Three squares will be unused.

Select 56 dark brown 3½-in. scrap squares. Cut 54 scraps in half to make a total of one hundred eight 1¾-in. by 3½-in. rectangles for the sashing **1b**. Trim two scraps to 2 in. by 3½ in. for the loops. **1c**

PREPARE THE ADDITIONAL FABRICS

BASE PRINT

Cut one 28-in. width-of-fabric strip; then cut two 14-in. by 28-in. rectangles for the base.

LINING AND STRAPS

Cut one 48½-in. width-of-fabric strip; then cut a 48½-in. by 26-in. rectangle for the lining. From the remainder, cut one 8-in. by 11-in. rectangle for the pocket lining.

Cut eight 3½-in. width-of-fabric strips for the straps.

MAKE THE BAG EXTERIOR

Arrange 28 blue 3½-in. scrap squares, 50 dark brown 1¾-in. by 3½-in. rectangles, and 25 light brown 1¾-in. squares, as shown. Using a ¼-in. seam, sew them into diagonal rows; then sew the rows together. Press the blue and light brown scrap seams toward the dark brown sashing strips within the rows; press the row seams toward the outer edge of panel. **2**

Trim the pieced panel evenly across the bottom, as shown.

Place a ruler so the long edge aligns with the bottom points on the light brown scraps and cut directly through the points.

Center and sew the trimmed edge of the pieced panel to the long edge of the base. Press the seam toward the base fabric. **3** Repeat to make two exterior panels. The panels will look strange, but don't worry, they'll be trimmed later, after quilting.

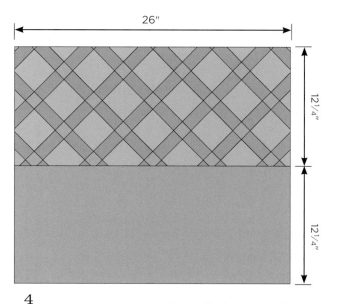

26"

12¼"

12¼"

4

5

2"

3"

2"

3"

2"

1½"
1½"

2"

3"

2"

3"

2"

Center

Drawn lines
¾ in. from edge

6

2"

3"

2"

3"

2"

3"

2"

3"

2"

3"

2"

Center

Sew

center: 1½ in., 2 in., 3 in., 2 in., 3 in., and 2 in. Repeat on the other side of the strip, starting at the center and working out the same way. Repeat to make the same markings on a second 3½-in. strip. **5**

Place a strip with markings and a strip without markings right sides together, with the markings facing up. Sew along one lengthwise line, stopping at the first crosswise mark; then backstitch to secure. Start again at the next mark: Begin with a back-stitch, sew 3 in. to the next crosswise mark, and then backstitch to secure. Repeat, backstitching at each start and stop, until all 3-in. segments (five total) are sewn and all 2-in. segments (six total) have gaps in the sewing. At the last mark, finish sewing along the line to the end of the strap. Repeat for the second lengthwise line on the same strip. **6**

Repeat for the second strap.

To reduce the bulk for turning, trim so the seam is ⅜ in. seam on the long sewn sections of strap, tapering the trimmed seam as you approach the first gap on each side. Turn the strap right side out carefully through one end. Press the strap flat, so the seam is in the center of the strap along the entire length. **7**

NOTE: To the extent possible, press the seam allowance inside the tube open, particularly at each gap.

Topstitch along the entire length of the strap about ⅟₁₆ in. away from both sides of the seam to secure the seam allowance inside the strap. Pay particular attention to the seam allowance along the gaps, making sure they stay inside the strap. **7**

Layer the batting and exterior panel, right side up, on large work surface; baste. Quilt as desired through the two layers.

Once quilted, trim each exterior panel. First trim the top and bottom of panel 12¼ in. away from the seam. Next trim the sides so the panel is 24½ in. by 26 in. Repeat to trim the second panel. **4**

Trim the sides of the panel so that the piecing is centered across the 26-in. width.

MAKE THE STRAPS

Sew two 3½-in. lining strips end to end, using a diagonal seam (see p. 180). Repeat to make four strap strips, each approximately 80 in. long. Leave the selvages on the ends for now.

With a fabric marking tool, on the wrong side of one fabric strip strap, draw a line ¾ in. from each edge along the entire length of the strip. Then fold the strip in half, end to end, to find the center. Mark the center with a pin or drawn line. Measure and mark perpendicular lines across the width of the strip, starting from the

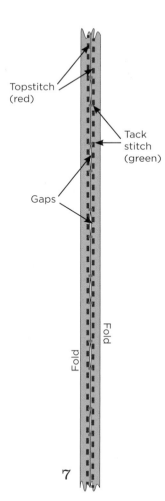

Topstitch
(red)

Tack
stitch
(green)

Gaps

Fold

Fold

7

Trimming the seam allowance seems wasteful. However, the middle part of the strap needs the extra bulk, but the ends of the strap do not. If you prefer, leave the full length of the strap seam allowance untrimmed, but turning the strap right side out will be a bit more difficult.

NOTE: Tack stitch—by making a securing zigzag stitch set to 0 stitch length—across the seam at each gap end.

TWISTING THE STRAP

Hold the strap to the left side of the first gap.

Insert the right side tail end of the strap into the opening of the first gap.

Pull the right tail end of the strap all the way up through the gap.

Hold the strap to the left side of the first gap. From underneath, insert the right side tail end of the strap into the opening of the first gap. Pull the right tail end of the strap all the way up through the gap and to the right, forming a twisty shape at the gap. Flatten the twisty shape, but don't press. Repeat for each gap, each time, holding the left side of the strap and pulling the right side of the strap up through the gap and back out the top and to the right. Repeat to make two straps.

Layer the straps on a cutting surface, and trim the selvage ends off while making both straps the same length. Each should be approximately 80 in. long.

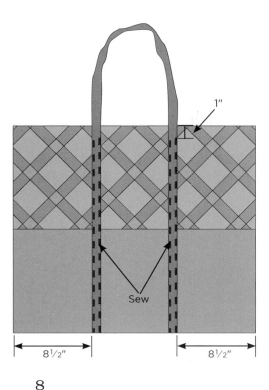

1"

Sew

8½" 8½"

8

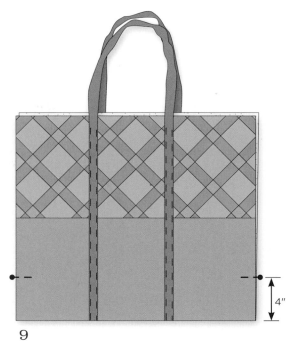

4"

9

4"

Sew   Sew

10

ASSEMBLE THE BAG EXTERIOR

Position and securely pin the straps onto the right side of the exterior bag panel, as shown, 8½ in. away from each side and aligning the strap's raw edges with the bottom edge of the base fabric. Be careful not to twist the straps. **8**

Using a walking foot, sew the strap to the bag, starting at the bottom edge of the bag, and continuing about ⅛ in. along one side. Pivot 1 in. from the rim of the bag, continue across the strap, pivot again, and proceed ⅛ in. along the other side of the strap, sewing back down to the

bottom edge. Repeat to secure both straps, one on each panel.

Place the exterior panels, right sides together, with bottom edges aligned. Using ⅜-in. seam allowance, sew the bottom seam. Open the seam allowance, secure with pins, and topstitch through all the layers on both sides of the seam to secure the seam allowances and flatten the bag's bottom.

Fold the bag panel in half, wrong sides together. Mark each side edge with a pin, 4 in. away from the bottom seam. **9**

Fold each panel side onto itself at the pins, right sides together. With a walking foot and a ⅜-in. seam, sew the sides through all layers. **10** Use lots of pins to secure the side edges for sewing. Turn the bag exterior right side out.

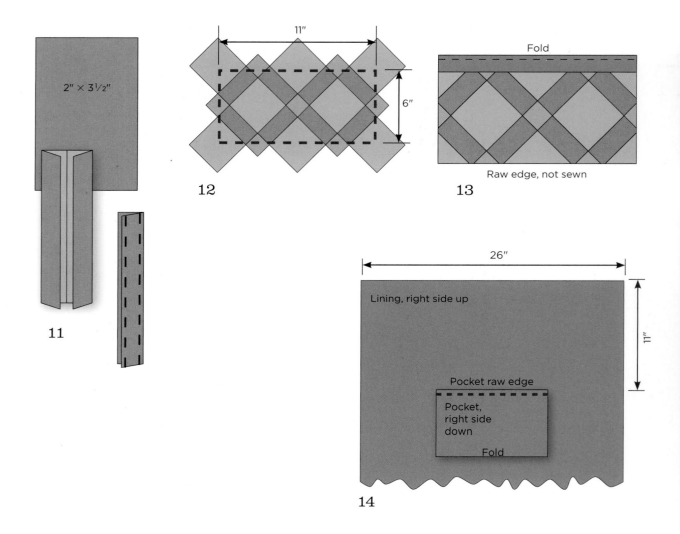

2" × 3½"

11

11"

6"

12

Fold

Raw edge, not sewn

13

26"

Lining, right side up

11"

Pocket raw edge

Pocket,
right side
down

Fold

14

MAKE THE LOOPS

Press one 2-in. by 3½-in. dark brown rectangle in half lengthwise, wrong sides together. Open the fold, and press each side edge toward the center crease. Re-press in half, right sides together. Pin or baste to secure the layers and trim the loop to 3 in. long. Make two. **11**

Fold the loops in half and pin to the right side of the exterior panel, one at each side seam, aligning the raw edges with the rim of the bag.

Set the bag exterior aside while making the lining.

MAKE THE LINING
POCKET

Pick eight blue 3½-in. squares, eight dark brown 1¾-in. by 3½-in. rectangles, and seven light brown 1¾-in. squares. Using a ¼-in. seam, make a small pieced panel for the pocket similar to the exterior bag panels. Center and trim to 6 in. by 11 in. **12**

Use a ¼-in. seam to sew the 11-in. side of the pieced pocket panel to the 8-in. by 11-in. pocket lining. Press in half, right sides together. Align the raw edges of the pocket panel to the lining. Sew a ¼-in. seam along

the sides, leaving the bottom open for turning. Turn the pocket right side out, press, and topstitch along the pocket rim. Use decorative stitching, if desired. **13**

LINING

Place the 48½-in. by 26-in. lining on a work table, right side up. Place the pocket, right side down, centered, with the raw edge 11 in. from the top edge (the 26-in. side of the lining rectangle). Sew a ¼-in. seam along the bottom edge of the pocket to secure. **14**

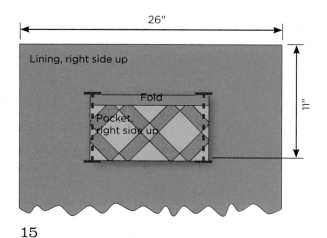

26"

Lining, right side up

11"

Fold

Pocket, right side up

15

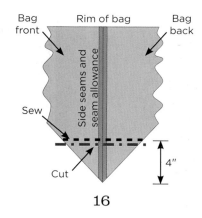

Bag front

Rim of bag

Bag back

Side seams and seam allowance

Sew

Cut

4"

16

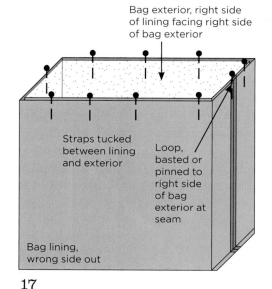

Bag exterior, right side of lining facing right side of bag exterior

Straps tucked between lining and exterior

Loop, basted or pinned to right side of bag exterior at seam

Bag lining, wrong side out

17

Fold the pocket, right side up, toward the top of the bag lining. Pin to secure, and topstitch along the sides, backstitching at each stop, to secure the pocket. **15**

Fold the lining in half, right sides together. Sew a ¼-in. seam along one side, leaving an 8-in. opening, and starting about 4 in. from the rim of the lining for turning. Sew the second side seam complete.

Open the bottom corner of the lining and flatten, centering the seam, as shown. Measure 4 in. from the corner, and draw a line perpendicular to the side seam. Sew on the line to

make a box pleat. Trim the corner fabric to reduce the bulk. Repeat for both bag bottom corners. Leave the lining wrong side out. **16**

FINISH THE CONSTRUCTION

Place the bag exterior, right side out, inside the lining. Align the side seams, and pin around the entire rim of the bag. Be sure that the handles are tucked in completely between the bag exterior and the lining and that only the raw edges of the loops

are exposed. Sew a ¼-in. seam around the bag rim. **17**

Turn the bag right side out through the lining opening. Sew the lining closed by hand or machine. Edgestitch around the rim, this time stitching over the straps where they cross the bag rim.

Add the hook on one loop and the D-ring on the second loop for the side-to-side closure. Insert the Scrap Sack Support in the bottom of bag to maintain the shape, if desired.

Beach Blanket Bingo

SCRAPS PLUS ONE SQUARE SHAPE

Fabric selection is always a challenge when making a scrap quilt. Or at least I think it is. If you are a follower of the ScrapTherapy process, then you know that I like to choose a theme for my scrappy quilts, rather than let the scraps take over the design.

That statement is particularly true for this themed quilt. The top consists of nothing but scraps, chosen to follow a graded color and value scheme to represent a feeling of transitioning from the deep blue ocean, to the shallows, onto the sandy beach, and to the plants along the shore. The quilt could just as easily represent the warm hues of a summer sunset or the bright color wheel elements of a rainbow.

And the key to success? Organization. The sewing is easy—the quilt consists of nine-patches and four-patches. Staying organized is a little tricky. As you select scraps within each prescribed color category, be prepared for a fair amount of trial and error. Some scraps, once set in place, will fit naturally. Others won't. Go with the flow. Pay close attention to the tips in the pattern. You'll be dreaming of your next picnic at the shore in no time!

FINISHED SIZE: 45 in. by 63 in.
PATTERN DIFFICULTY: Intermediate

SCRAP REQUIREMENTS:
2-in. scrap squares: 204
3$\frac{1}{2}$-in. scrap squares: 174
5-in. scrap squares: 40

NOTE: For colors and values see the chart on p. 174.

FABRIC AND NOTION REQUIREMENTS:
$\frac{1}{2}$ yard dark blue for binding
4 yards for backing
50-in. by 68-in. batting

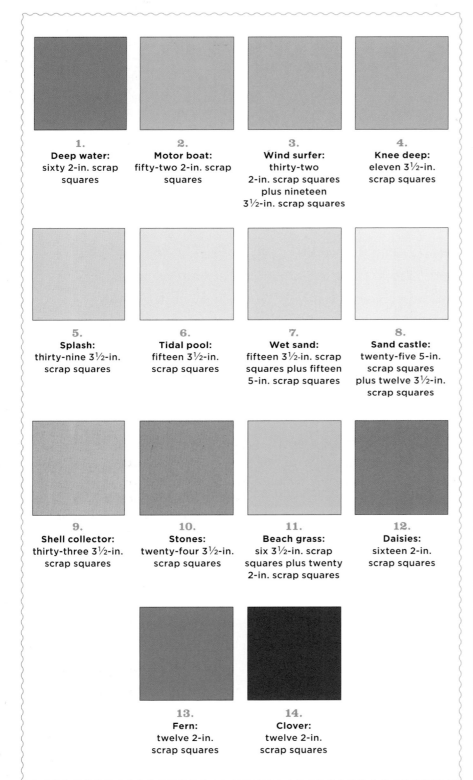

1.
Deep water:
sixty 2-in. scrap
squares

2.
Motor boat:
fifty-two 2-in. scrap
squares

3.
Wind surfer:
thirty-two
2-in. scrap squares
plus nineteen
3½-in. scrap squares

4.
Knee deep:
eleven 3½-in.
scrap squares

5.
Splash:
thirty-nine 3½-in.
scrap squares

6.
Tidal pool:
fifteen 3½-in.
scrap squares

7.
Wet sand:
fifteen 3½-in. scrap
squares plus fifteen
5-in. scrap squares

8.
Sand castle:
twenty-five 5-in.
scrap squares
plus twelve 3½-in.
scrap squares

9.
Shell collector:
thirty-three 3½-in.
scrap squares

10.
Stones:
twenty-four 3½-in.
scrap squares

11.
Beach grass:
six 3½-in. scrap
squares plus twenty
2-in. scrap squares

12.
Daisies:
sixteen 2-in.
scrap squares

13.
Fern:
twelve 2-in.
scrap squares

14.
Clover:
twelve 2-in.
scrap squares

PREPARE THE SCRAPS

Select two hundred four 2-in. scrap squares, one hundred seventy-four 3½-in. scrap squares, and forty 5-in. scrap squares for the blocks. Choose scraps in colors that fall into the 14 categories described at left.

To select and organize the scraps to make this quilt, create 14 separate stacks of fabric on a large work table.

Use clear resealable plastic bags, marked with the identifying number (according to the scrap list at left), color description, and quantity of scraps and sizes needed on each bag. Sort through your cut-up fabrics and place the appropriate amount of scraps in each bag by color.

Some scraps may cross over between neighboring color groups. However, while selecting scraps for each category, keep the color transitions from one stack to the next distinct but gradual.

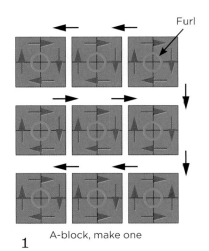

Furl

1 A-block, make one

Sew

2

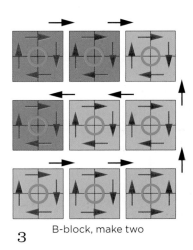

3 B-block, make two

MAKE THE BLOCKS

With the many gradual color changes in this project, it is important to arrange the pieces within each block before sewing them together. That way, adjustments can be made easily before the blocks are sewn. Don't worry about matching each scrap in a color group exactly. Variety will add interest to your quilt. Remove and replace the scraps with colors that are too severe for their category.

Closely follow the quilting diagram on p. 178. Working in diagonal rows, arrange the scraps for the first three blocks (one A-Block and two B-Blocks). Once satisfied, sew the A-Block, but keep the two B-Blocks unsewn. Then arrange scraps for all three of the C-blocks and set them in their place in the emerging quilt layout. Then sew the B-blocks. Continue in this manner until all blocks are sewn. Then sew the blocks into rows to make the quilt. Each block measures 9½ in. once sewn and pressed.

A-BLOCK

Arrange thirty-six 2-in. deep water scraps into six rows of six scraps. Sew the scraps into nine four-patches. Furl the four-patch seams, as shown (see p. 180). Arrange the resulting four-patches into a nine-patch. Sew and press, as shown. **1** Make one A-Block.

While furling the seams within the four-patch units isn't required, it surely simplifies the pressing when all block elements are pressed the same. Be sure to sew two-patches into four-patches with the seam allowance on top pressed toward you as it is sewn. **2** That way, the seams will rotate in the same direction on all four-patch units throughout the quilt.

With lots of similar blocks, pressing direction can get confusing. If you find the seams aren't nesting properly when you sew the blocks together, you have two choices. Re-press or use extra pins to secure seams that aren't intersecting nicely. Then call it good.

B-BLOCK

Arrange twelve 2-in. deep water scraps, twenty 2-in. motor boat scraps, and four 2-in. wind surfer scraps into nine four-patches. Sew, press, and furl the seams as shown.

Don't let block similarities deceive you. The pressing configuration varies from block to block.

Arrange the resulting four-patches into a nine-patch. Sew and press, as shown. **3** Make two B-Blocks.

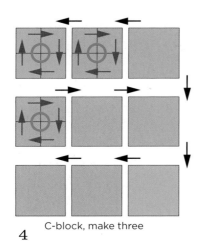

C-block, make three

4

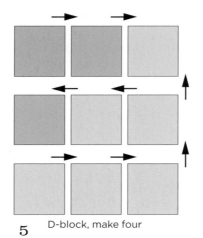

D-block, make four

5

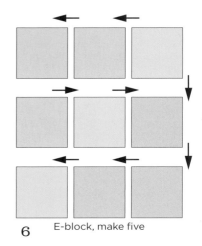

E-block, make five

6

C-BLOCK

Arrange four 2-in. motor boat scraps, eight 2-in. wind surfer scraps, five 3½-in. wind surfer scraps, and one 3½-in. knee deep scraps into a nine-patch, as shown. Sew, press, and furl the four-patch seams as before.

Sew the four-patches and scraps into three rows of three units. Press the seams as shown. Sew the rows together; then press the row seams. **4** Make three C-Blocks.

D-BLOCK

Arrange one 3½-in. wind surfer scrap, two 3½-in. knee deep scraps, and six 3½-in. splash scraps into a nine-patch, as shown.

Sew the scrap units into three rows of three scraps. Press the seams as shown. Sew the rows together, and then press row seams. **5** Make four D-Blocks.

E-BLOCK

Arrange three 3½-in. splash scraps, three 3½-in. tidal pool scraps, and three 3½-in. wet sand scraps into a nine-patch, as shown.

Sew the block scraps into three rows of three scraps. Press the seams as shown. Sew the rows together, and then press the row seams. **6** Make five E-Blocks.

F-BLOCK

Arrange three 5-in. wet sand scraps and one 5-in. sand castle scrap into a four-patch. Sew, press, and furl the seams. **7** Make five F-Blocks.

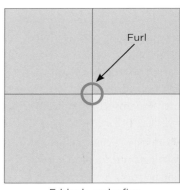

Furl

7 F-block, make five

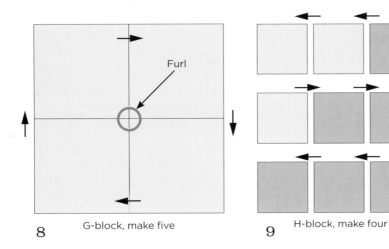

8 G-block, make five

Furl

9 H-block, make four

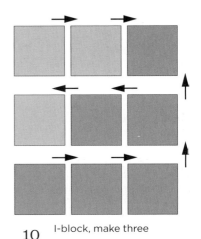

10 I-block, make three

G-BLOCK

Arrange four 5-in. sand castle scraps into a four-patch. Sew, press, and furl the seams. **8** Make five G-Blocks.

H-BLOCK

Arrange three $3^{1}/_{2}$-in. sand castle scraps and six $3^{1}/_{2}$-in. shell collector scraps into a nine-patch. Sew, press, and furl the seams. **9** Make four H-Blocks.

I-BLOCK

Arrange three $3^{1}/_{2}$-in. shell collector scraps and six $3^{1}/_{2}$-in. stones scraps into a nine-patch. Sew, press, and furl the seams. **10** Make three I-Blocks.

J-BLOCK

Arrange three $3^{1}/_{2}$-in. stones scraps, three $3^{1}/_{2}$-in. beach grass scraps, eight 2-in. beach grass scraps, and four 2-in. daisies scraps into a nine-patch, as shown. Sew, press, and furl the seams. **11** Make two J-Blocks.

K-BLOCK

Arrange four 2-in. beach grass scraps, eight 2-in. daisies scraps, twelve 2-in. fern scraps, and twelve 2-in. clover scraps into nine four-patches. Sew, press, and furl the seams. Arrange the resulting four-patches into a nine-patch. Sew and press, as shown. **12** Make one K-Block.

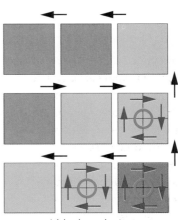

11 J-block, make two

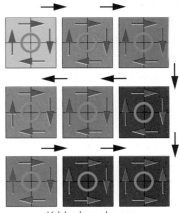

12 K-block, make one

ASSEMBLE THE QUILT TOP

Arrange the blocks in seven rows of five blocks as shown. Sew the blocks into rows, and press the block seams in one direction, alternating the seam direction in each row. Sew the rows together. Press the row seams in one direction. **13**

QUILT AND BIND

Layer the backing, batting, and quilt top; baste. Quilt as desired.

Cut six 2¼-in. strips for the binding. Sew the binding strips together end to end, using a diagonal seam (p. 180). Press the connecting seams open, and then press the binding in half lengthwise, wrong sides together.

Trim the batting and backing even with the quilt top. With the raw edges aligned, sew the binding to the front of the quilt using a ¼-in. seam. Miter the binding at the corners.

Turn the folded edge of the binding to the back of the quilt, and hand-stitch it in place.

13

APPENDIX I: QUILTMAKING BASICS

I've made a few assumptions in the process of preparing the quilt patterns and instructions for this book. Perhaps you've made a few quilts and already have a good grasp of the basics of quilt construction. In that light, you may view this section as a collection of a few hints that might be of interest as you create the projects specific to this book.

Many quilters know that almost every quilting technique can be done differently with the same or similar end results. For example, some quilters would rather cut fabric into mathematically correct sizes before sewing, for, let's say, half-square triangle units. Some prefer to sew pieces slightly larger than needed, then trim after sewing and pressing. Some might argue that only one way is correct. Some may say that one way is better than the other. And they'd all be right, depending on the circumstances!

My advice: As a hobbyist, find the technique that makes the most sense for you. The more you quilt, the more you'll generate some favorite best practices.

So in the following pages of basic quilting tips, I'm not going to say that my way is the best way. I prefer to think that my way is . . . well, my way.

FABRICS

If you have fabric, thread, and batting, you have pretty much everything you need to make a quilt.

By and large, the quilts in this book are designed for cotton quilting fabrics. Can other fabrics work? Sure. But for the purposes of this book, I'd recommend 100 percent quilting-quality cotton. Use the best stuff you can afford. When you purchase high-quality quilting fabrics for your quilts, it stands to reason that you'll be using that same quality in your scrap fabrics.

THREAD

Along with that, I like to use 100 percent cotton thread, for the basic reason that cotton thread will age at the same rate as the cotton fabric used to make the quilt. Other options include polyester, rayon, and cotton/poly blends.

BATTING

Cotton batting, too, right? Well . . . I cannot tell a lie. My favorite batting is 100 percent washable wool. Why? It doesn't retain folds like cotton batting does. It's lighter and fluffier than cotton batting, so quilting patterns seem more dramatic. It's a dream to quilt by hand or machine. On a bed, it transitions easily from season to season, and it really is washable and dryable on light settings.

For a project that I know might get a lot of use and get washed a lot, I'll use cotton—usually an 80/20 cotton/poly blend.

ACCURACY

Accuracy in a pieced quilt top always comes down to three things: cutting, piecing, and pressing. Throughout the instructions in this collection, I have tried to provide unfinished sizes of in-process elements, so you can check to make sure your sewing is staying on track. If something is off, check that the pieces are cut accurately, that seams are not too big or too small, and that the pressing didn't create a stretched-out shape or extra folds near the seam allowance.

SEWING MACHINE

For your hobby, invest in the best sewing machine you can afford. Visit several dealers and test drive a variety of models. When you are shopping for a new sewing machine, be sure to ask about servicing. Whether you sew a little or a lot, your machine will need regular maintenance. Your relationship with the service department at your dealer can make a huge difference in the enjoyment of your hobby.

Features to look for in a quilting machine:

- Even straight stitches, with balanced, adjustable tension
- 1/4-in. foot
- Needle up, needle down capability
- Adjustable needle position so you can move the needle to the left or to the right
- Decorative stitch options, particularly zigzag and buttonhole stitches for use in machine appliqué
- If you're going to do your own quilting, an attachable or integrated walking foot, and a free-motion darning foot, plus the ability to drop the feed dogs for free-motion quilting
- A large throat
- Hand controls that override the foot pedal for free-motion quilting

SELECT BLOCK AND QUILT CONSTRUCTION TECHNIQUES

FURLING

Furling seams, so that the seam allowance is opened only where the seams meet in the center, is a technique borrowed from hand-piecing. Once the center seam intersection is opened, all four seams rotate in one direction around the center. This technique is particularly nice on blocks in which several seams come together in the center like pinwheel blocks. The blue circle in the patterns indicates furled seams.

TO MAKE FOUR-PATCH BLOCKS WITH FURLED CENTER SEAMS

Sew two-patch units and press the seams consistently to one side, usually toward the darker fabric. Sew pairs of two-patches with opposing fabric facing and seams nested.

Be sure to feed the four-patches into the sewing machine exactly the same each time—that is, the light fabric first or dark fabric first.

Using a seam ripper, remove the last two or three stitches from the two-patch seam on each side of the four-patch unit. Stop removing stitches at the intersection with the longer four-patch seam.

Press from the back so the seams rotate and the center intersection is furled. Note that only the center of the block seam section is open; the rest of the seams are pressed to one side, each rotating around the center. Press from the front.

Seams can furl clockwise or counterclockwise. Also notice that a clockwise seam rotation from the back is counterclockwise from the front. The secret isn't that the seams furl one way or another; it's that they all furl in the same direction for the quilt construction.

If blocks don't nest as you want them to, just use some extra pins to secure the "errant" seam intersection and sew as normal. The seams are on the inside of the quilt. No one will ever know!

CONNECTING STRIPS FOR BORDERS, BINDING, BAG HANDLES, AND OTHER APPLICATIONS

When connecting cross-grain strips end to end, I prefer to use a diagonal seam. A diagonal seam is stronger and less noticeable than a straight one. An exception: When connecting seams for a cross-grain border using striped fabric, I try to match the stripes using a vertical seam.

To Sew a Diagonal Seam

1. Align the cut strips, right sides together, with the ends perpendicular.
2. With a pencil, draw a line across the diagonal intersection.
3. Pin to secure, and sew directly on the line.
4. Trim ends 1/4 in. away from the seam.
5. Trim the point extensions.
6. Press the seams open. This is one of the few times I press seams open.

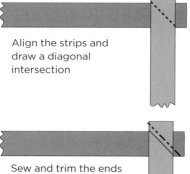

Align the strips and draw a diagonal intersection

Sew and trim the ends about 1/4 in. away from the line of stitching

APPLIQUÉ

Beginner quilters often shy away from appliqué quilts. They're so beautiful and have so many pieces, and beginners think they must be complicated. But like anything else in quilting and in life, once you break down the steps and find the method and technique that suits you, it's all really pretty easy and can be very satisfying.

With so many appliqué methods to choose from, it's sometimes difficult to decide which appliqué method to use. Because I really enjoy handwork, I often choose hand appliqué and the back-basting method when the shapes are simple with only a few deep curves or points, like **Prairie Porcelain**, on p. 74. Often I'll choose machine appliqué using fusible web if the shapes are more complex, as in **From Little Acorns**, on p. 56. If I want to secure appliqué pieces to the quilt after it is quilted, such as for **Citrus Kitchen Set**, on p. 136, I'll either choose machine appliqué using fusible web or machine appliqué using fusible interfacing.

HAND APPLIQUÉ

If I had to pick only one, back-basting would be my favorite method. It's extremely accurate, and very relaxing. Once you draw the motif on the back of the background fabric, no further prep is required for the fabric used for the appliqué shapes. So this method lends itself very nicely to travel or a summer day relaxing comfortably in a favorite Adirondack chair.

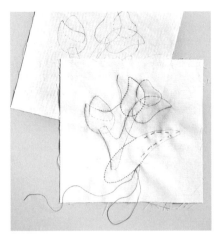

Trace the appliqué shape in reverse onto the back of the base fabric.

From the front, trim the appliqué fabric about 1/8 in. from the running stitch.

Bend the appliqué seam allowance under and secure the fold to the background fabric.

1. Trace the appliqué shape in reverse onto the back of the base fabric.
2. Cut the appliqué fabric piece slightly larger than the appliqué shape.
3. Pin the shape to the right side of the fabric, right side up, so that the appliqué fabric covers the lines plus at least a 1/8-in. seam allowance, preferably a little more. Hold the fabrics to a light source to be sure all lines plus seam allowances are adequately planned.
4. From the wrong side of the background fabric, pin-baste roughly around the shape using appliqué pins.
5. From the wrong side of the background fabric, using a heavy thread (like YLI Hand Quilting Thread) in a high contrast color, a thicker needle (I use a size 7 sharp), and a thimble if you wear one, sew a tight running stitch (about 10 stitches to the inch) directly on the line to secure the appliqué shape to the block. Don't knot the thread at the beginning or end of the running stitch, and stitch all the way around the shape.
6. From the front, trim the appliqué fabric about 1/8 in. from the running stitch. Leave the running stitch in place for at least an hour or overnight.
7. Working from the front, and using an appliqué needle (I like Clover Black Gold Appliqué Needles, size 10 or 11), a very fine cotton thread (I like YLI Soft Touch) in a color that

Continue adding appliqué pieces, one layer at a time, until the block is complete.

matches the appliqué, and a thimble if you wear one, pull out a few of the running stitches. Bend the appliqué seam allowance under, and secure the fold to the background fabric with short appliqué stitches that just catch the fold of the shape. The heavier needle and thread will have left a perforation in the appliqué fabric that will allow the seam allowance to turn under exactly where you want it. And the running stitch will also have left marks in the base fabric so you can just barely see the outline of the shape.

8. Proceed around the appliqué shape, pulling out the running stitches about 1/2 in. ahead of where you are securing the appliqué.

9. Continue adding the appliqué pieces, one layer at a time, until the block is complete.

MACHINE APPLIQUÉ USING FUSIBLE INTERFACING

Fusible interfacing is a very lightweight nonwoven fabric that is smooth on one side and has heat-sensitive glue, or fusible material, on the other side. The fusible material becomes part of the quilt's construction.

I'm a big fan of using fusible interfacing for appliqué! For one thing, the interfacing can help stabilize elements that have been pieced. For example, the citrus centers used to make **Citrus Kitchen Set**, on p. 136, are scraps pieced into common pinwheel blocks. Once the circular interfacing is sewn and turned and the citrus slices are fused into place, it looks like it took hours and hours to cut and sew complex shapes that are pointy on one end and curved on the other.

I also like using printed fusible interfacing because it allows me to skip the tracing step. This puts me one step closer to sewing, and because the sewing is my favorite part, that's always a good thing. Plus the raw edges of the appliqué shape are turned under, so the project won't be as apt to fray over time as would machine appliqué using fusible web.

On the downside, appliqué using fusible interfacing gets a little tricky if the appliqué shape has lots of points or is very complex.

1. Using a permanent Pigma pen, trace the appliqué shape onto the smooth side of the interfacing. The traced shape should be drawn as it will appear in the quilt, not reversed. If you are using printed fusible interfacing, move on to the next step.

2. Cut a slit in the center of the shape to be used for turning later.

3. Roughly trim the interfacing around the shape, and place the right side of the fabric selected for the appliqué shape facing the bumpy, or fusible, side of the interfacing. Secure the interfacing to the shape with a few pins.

4. With the interfacing facing up, sew directly on the traced line all the way around the shape (see below).

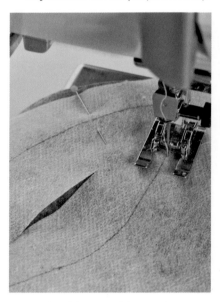

5. Trim both layers of fabric about 1/8 in. away from the sewing line (see below).

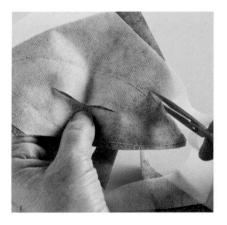

6. Turn the shape right side out through the slit in the center of the interfacing. It's helpful to use a turning tool, a blunt knitting needle, or even chopsticks. Be careful not to poke right through the interfacing (see below)!

7. Place the appliqué shape on the background fabric, with fusible interfacing facing the right side of the background; arrange the shape as directed in the pattern, then fuse the appliqué shape onto the background with a hot steamy iron.

8. Sew around the appliqué shape with a zigzag, satin, or blanket stitch (shown) using thread that matches the appliqué shape or thread that contrasts with the shape, depending on the look you want. Be sure to use an open-toed foot for any of these stitches (see below).

9. For a motif that has multiple shapes, you can fuse, then stitch each shape into place or fuse all the shapes, then stitch around the entire motif, securing all exposed raw edges.

MACHINE APPLIQUÉ USING FUSIBLE WEB

Fusible web is a paper-backed, heat-sensitive adhesive. For fusible appliqué, you want the light, sew-through variety. Be careful—some fusible web shouldn't be used for sewing. The adhesive on the heavier fusibles will gum up your sewing machine! Your quilt shop should be able to help you get the right stuff.

Of the three appliqué methods I've discussed this one is my least favorite, but it has its uses.

For example, fusible appliqué is my method of choice when I'm under tight time constraints to finish a project. It's also great for complex shapes with seams that won't turn under nicely. But some brands of fusible web can make your appliqué shape stiff. To avoid this, follow this little trick.

1. Using a permanent Pigma pen, trace the appliqué shape in *reverse* onto the paper side of the fusible web.

2. Roughly trim the paper around the shape, and cut a slit in the center of the shape. Then cut away the center of the shape, about 1/4 in. away from the appliqué line.

3. With a hot iron, fuse the roughly trimmed shape to the wrong side of the appliqué fabric.

4. Trim the appliqué shape on the traced line.

5. Place the appliqué shape on the background fabric, and the fusible web on the appliqué facing the right side of the background fabric, arranging the shape as directed in the pattern. Remove the paper, and fuse the appliqué shape onto the background with a hot steam iron.

6. Sew around the appliqué shape with a zigzag, satin, or blanket stitch using thread that matches the appliqué shape or thread that contrasts with the shape, depending on the look you want. Be sure to use an open-toed foot for any of these stitches.

7. For a motif that has multiple shapes, you can fuse, then stitch each shape into place or fuse all the shapes, then stitch around the entire motif.

Trim the paper, fuse it to the wrong side of the fabric, and trim.

CURVED PIECING

Oh my! Curved piecing? Seems complicated! Trust me on this: You can do it! Sewing around a curve is just a series of short, straight stitches. It's that simple.

In my mind, the best way to approach curved piecing is to take it slowly, use lots of pins, and practice. Some may disagree with me, and that's okay. It's just another one of those things—find the way that works best for you and run with it.

For **Sweet Revenge**, on p. 102, and **Square Peg, Round Hole**, on p. 110, I recommend Marti Michell's Drunkard's Path Template Set. The templates are super easy to use for cutting the shapes, they can be used over and over again, and they come with a set of instructions. But you can just as easily trace the shapes provided in the pattern onto your block parts and cut carefully with scissors. Once the curved shapes are cut, the sewing steps are the same.

When making traditional drunkard's path blocks and shapes, many pattern writers have used the word *pie* to refer to the pie-shaped part of the block and the word *crust* to identify the outer leftover shape. But, especially considering the size of the Sweet Revenge block, that would be one strange-looking pie, particularly the crust part. So in describing the elements, I prefer to tag the parts as the *bite* and the *brownie*, respectively.

So bake up a batch of your favorite brownie recipe, and pull up a chair. Take a deep breath, follow the steps and tips, one by one, and you'll be fine! (You might even enjoy it! And if you don't, you still have brownies.)

1. First, follow the pattern directions carefully to cut the curved shapes—the bites and the brownies—using the size shape or template as instructed. As a rule of thumb, the bite will be cut from the larger of the two shapes (see below).

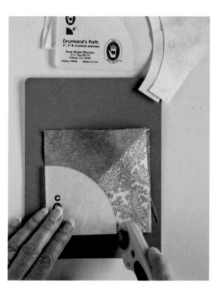

For either of the curved-pieced projects in this book, whether you use Marti Michell's templates or not, carefully cut two layers at once. When using the templates, use a small rotary blade—28 mm or smaller. If cutting without the acrylic templates, use scissors, securing the layers with pins first. Also note that Marti Michell's templates come with paper on one side of the template. I have chosen to leave the paper on the template for a bit more stability as I cut.

2. Save the extra pieces for another project.

3. Select one bite and its coordinated brownie. Find the center of each curve. For both patterns using curved piecing in this book, the curved shape is cut from a half-square triangle unit. So the center of the curve is the seam intersection.

4. With the bite facing up, place one pin on both sides of the seam intersection. The seams should nest.

5. Next, pin both layers of one end. Take extra care to line up the straight edges of the bite and the brownie, and pin with several pin-dips to keep the straight edges aligned throughout the next few steps. Place two or three more pins in between the middle and the end pins. (see below)

6. Turn the unit upside down, so the brownie is now facing up. Sew carefully and slowly one stitch at a time, remembering to ease in any bulk as you sew. Remove pins only as you reach them with the sewing machine needle (see below).

7. Once sewn, the seam can be pressed easily either toward the bite or toward the brownie (see below).

PIPING, AND FLANGES, AND PRAIRIE POINTS . . . OH, MY!

For a bit of drama, a flange, covered piping, or prairie points—or as in **Petal Pushers**, on p. 144, prairie point half circles—can be sewn in between pieced quilt elements like two borders, or in between the quilt center and a border, or in between the quilted quilt and the binding.

1. Make the flange, covered piping, or prairie point element as directed in the pattern.
2. Layer the flange (or other element) in between the quilt top and the binding (see photo above right) or in between the two piecing layers, with raw edges aligned (see below).

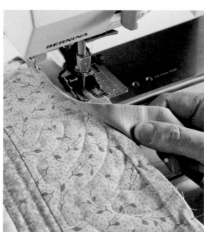

3. Pin liberally to secure all layers.
4. Baste within the seam allowance with a straight stitch set to an extra-long stitch length.
5. Then sew all the layers using a 1/4-in. seam.
6. Take a peek!

ADDING BORDERS

Several of the quilts in this book end with the blocks. No border. If that makes you uncomfortable, feel free to add a coordinated border.

Some quilt instructions suggest that you measure the quilt top in three places and then average the numbers and cut your border to size—a perfectly valid theory. I prefer to skip the math and the rulers and measure the border for larger quilts using the quilt itself as the measuring device. Here's how:

1. If you're adding side borders first, take the quilt and fold it in half, so top and bottom edges are aligned.
2. Lay the folded quilt flat on a large work surface.
3. Find a verticle seam somewhere in the center of the quilt. This will be a line-up guide for the border measurement.
4. Fold the side border, which has been roughly cut a little larger than the suggested border measurement from the pattern, in half.
5. Lay the folded border on the folded quilt, with the folds aligned and with a border edge aligned with a center vertical seam on the quilt.
6. Hold the fold in place on top of the quilt with one hand, and gently smooth the border across the quilt with the other hand, so there's no extra slack in the border fabric. Be careful not to stretch the border.
7. Mark and cut the border even with the raw edge of the quilt (see top left photo on p. 186)

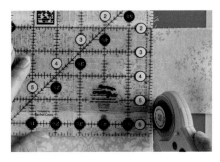

8. Repeat with the second border.

9. Open the quilt and place the quilt top right side up on your workspace.

10. Unfold a side border, and place it right side together along the side edge of the quilt.

11. Pin one trimmed border strip to the quilt. Pin the ends first.

12. Then pin the center and ease the fabric in between until the entire border is pinned in place. Use lots of pins (about one pin at least every 2 in.), and remove pins as needed to reposition and ease out any lumpy or stretchy spots.

13. Move the pinned quilt to the sewing machine and sew, using a 1/4-in. seam allowance to attach the border. Press the border seam per the pattern recommendation.

14. Repeat for the remaining side border and top and bottom borders.

FIXING MISTAKES

Ta-da! Finally! It's done. You've been up late for the last three nights with the end in sight. Your scraps have been obliterated, or at least one or two stacks have been purged from the bins, and they are now part of your newest quilt creation.

You stand back. And there it is— a mistake! A block is sewn upside down, the color is way off, something is definitely wrong. And it's ever so obvious. Disappointed, you put the project away for a few hours and turn to another distraction. After a while, you come back to it, and there it is . . . again. This time, it's all you see and it's bugging you.

One perfectly fine solution to a mistake is to leave it alone. It's there and it's part of the quilt. If that won't work for you, here's how to make things better.

To Fix a Piecing Mistake in a Completed Quilt Top:

1. Locate and mark the mistake (see below).

2. Turn the quilt wrong side up. With a seam ripper, pull out all four seams connecting the misplaced block or block element, plus at least 1 in. of the seams on adjoining

sides, following the original row and block piecing configuration.

3. This will create a square- or rectangular-shaped hole in the quilt, with adjoining seams unsewn (see below).

4. Replace or adjust the mistake in its proper position, and with right sides together, pin one side of the corrected block into place. Sew a 1/4-in. seam allowance. Pull the extra quilt material out of the way; it will be awkward, but workable.

5. Sew the opposite, parallel seam in place in a similar manner, using pins as needed.

6. Sew the remaining two perpendicular seams, pinning and nesting the seam intersections as necessary.

7. Press the repaired seams, first from the back, then from the front of the quilt top (see below).

APPENDIX II: QUILTTING 101: MACHINE QUILTING

Once the quilt is basted, take a step back and decide on a quilting plan. I like to start with some in-the-ditch quilting around borders or blocks. Then spread the quilt out again and take another look before filling in with free-motion quilting. Look for secondary patterns within the play between light and dark. Decide what areas will be quilted lightly so they remain puffy and what areas will be more densely stitched to flatten them.

Consider thread color. Some quilters like to use variegated thread, others like to create contrast. I prefer quilting with a solid-color cotton thread that blends with the main color scheme of the quilt. Truth be known, my most commonly used thread color for quilting is natural.

Position the sewing machine 2-ft. to 3-ft. from the edge of your sewing table, so some of the quilt's bulk and weight is supported on the table. Target a block or section of the quilt and remove a handful of safety pins to free up an area between 8 in. and 12 in. square. Stuff the quilt into the machine with the unpinned area under the foot. Use your fingers to form a pair of parentheses on either side of the needle and gently press outward with the palm of your hand. Gloves with rubber fingertips or palms help you maintain control on the quilt as you gently guide the quilt to create the quilting pattern.

You may jump from one block to the next, removing the pins as you go. Unlike hand quilting, as long as you were meticulous with layering the quilt sandwich and ultra-zealous with pin-basting, you don't have to quilt from the center outward, as is commonly suggested. I often move from one spot to another!

TIPS FOR MACHINE QUILTING

When I quilt, I like to create texture. Less quilting creates puffy spots, more dense quilting compresses an area. The quilting can add a whole new dimension to your project.

General Quilting Tips

* Refer to the batting package for the recommended distance between quilting lines.
* Change to a darning foot and drop or cover your feed dogs. Consult your machine instruction book for details on inactivating the feed dogs.
* Quilting gloves with rubber finger tips and/or palms are helpful for holding and moving the quilt as you stitch.

Straight-Line Quilting Using a Walking Foot

* Use straight lines to define the spaces and set the stage for free-motion fill stitching.
* Find end-to-end and diagonal paths for quilting lines.
* Look beyond the blocks and create secondary patterns not necessarily obvious from the piecing alone.
* Your entire quilt may be quilted using the walking foot and straight-line quilting.

Free-Motion Quilting

* If you're a novice at free-motion quilting, start with a medium-size meandering line. Practice on a small sandwich and strive for smooth lines and gentle transitions from curve to curve. Imagine you're drawing back country roads or Mickey Mouse hands as you move the fabric.
* As your meandering improves, try other patterns, or just doodle. Swirlies, bishop's fan, leaves, and feathers are some of my favorite filler patters.

Some quilters wonder why they struggle with free-motion quilting. Here's my theory: Often the advice to the aspiring quilter is to draw the desired design on a piece of paper, then you'll feel more comfortable when you quilt it on the sewing machine. I don't agree with this. Think about it; when you draw, the paper stays in one place and you move the pencil around with your hand. When you make the free-motion stitches with the sewing machine, the "pencil" is the needle, and it stays in one place, moving up and down making stitches. The quilt moves underneath the needle. No wonder it feels so awkward! In my mind, the best way to learn free-motion quilting is to practice; jump in and do it. Let go. Relax. Remember to breathe!

MITERED BINDING CORNERS

Attach the binding to one side of quilt with a $1/4$-in. seam, stopping the stitching $1/4$ in. before the corner. Pivot the quilt under the presser foot 45 degrees, and sew off edge; cut the threads.

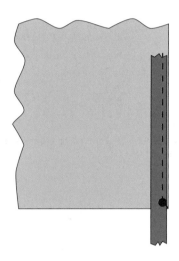

YOU WIN!

Here's my rule of thumb for machine quilting: You and the quilt are gonna' duke it out. And *you* are gonna win! Be bold! It's a pile of cotton and fluff, after all, and it squishes!

It's hard to imagine being able to stuff an entire quilt under the sewing machine arm, and you don't have to. You have to stuff only half of the quilt in there, and only while you're quilting the exact center of the quilt. Quilt one side of the project, then turn the quilt and work on the other side. As you quilt, you remove pins, and the quilt gets lighter in weight and easier to maneuver.

I've tried rolling up the quilt and throwing it over my shoulder to support it—that just didn't work for me. I prefer to loosely fold the quilt, almost like an accordion fold, and gently ease the quilt into place for quilting. I find this squishing and repositioning process allows me to move around more freely.

Place the quilt on a work table, with the sewn binding to the left and the unbound side of the quilt on top. Fold the unsewn binding to the left at a 45-degree angle so the raw edge of the binding makes a straight line with upper raw edge of quilt.

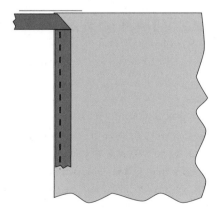

Fold the binding a second time so that the folded edge of the binding is aligned with the left edge of the quilt and the raw edge of the binding is aligned with the top edge of the quilt. Pin to secure the binding in place along the upper edge of the quilt.

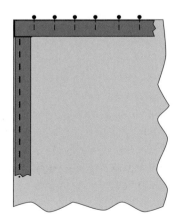

Sew a $1/4$-in. seam to stitch the binding to the quilt. Repeat the same mitering process at each corner.

NOTE: This technique also works to secure the binding to a quilt with an angle other than 90 degrees. Once the binding is secured to the corner, fold the binding away from the quilt to create a straight line along the raw edges of the binding and quilt. Then fold the binding back onto itself, with the fold at the corner, and continue to the next corner.

CONTINUOUS BINDING CLOSURE

As with many methods and techniques in quilting, several options achieve the same result. Here's how I join the binding ends.

1. After trimming the batting and backing even with the quilt top, start along one edge and sew the binding to the quilt edges, leaving about 24 in. of the binding unsewn: 12 in. at the beginning and 12 in. at the end. Place the unbound section of the quilt flat on your work table. Lay the binding ends evenly along the raw edge of the quilt and fold the binding back on itself so the folds meet and "kiss" (see top left photo at right).

2. Make two marks on the top binding layer one-half the width of the binding from the fold. (I usually cut my binding strips 2$\frac{1}{4}$ in., so half of that is 1$\frac{1}{8}$ in.) Make two lines on the binding, each 1$\frac{1}{8}$ in. away from the fold. This calculation works for any width double-fold binding.

3. Fold the quilt onto itself, and pin the quilt layers, creating some slack to allow you to work easily with the binding ends (see top right photo).

4. Bring the binding end from the left above the quilt onto the work table and open the fold. Place the binding rightside up so you can see the marking line.

5. Open the crease, and fold the right binding end, wrong sides together, at the marking line (see bottom left photo).

Fold the binding back on itself so the folds meet and "kiss."

Create slack to allow you to work easily within the binding ends.

Open the crease.

Open the right binding fold, and draw a line parallel to the quilt top.

6. Align the fold from the right binding with edge of the left binding. At the same time, align the marking on the left binding with the edge of the right binding.

7. Open the right binding fold, and draw a line parallel to the quilt top, from edge to edge, as shown. Secure the binding with pins on both sides of the drawn line (see bottom right photo).

8. Sew on the line (see top left photo at right).

9. Trim about ¼ in. away from the seam (unpin the quilt to test it first, if you like) (see top right photo).

10. Pin and sew the remaining binding to the quilt edge (see bottom left photo).

11. It's almost continuous (see bottom right photo).

If you have a basket of binding end pieces from quilts past, a scrap quilt is the perfect opportunity to use them up. Connect leftover binding strips end to end, and attach to the quilt like any other double-fold binding.

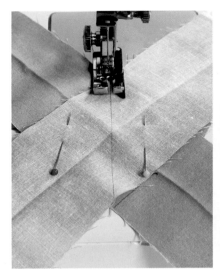
Sew on the line.

Trim ¼ in. away from the seam.

Pin and sew the remaining binding.

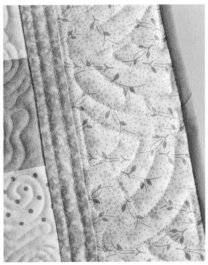
You have an almost continuous binding.

HAND-SEWN BINDING CORNERS

Once I've secured the binding all the way around the quilt, I like to sew the folded binding edge to the back of the quilt by hand. You can sew it by machine, but this finishing touch is one of my favorite parts of quiltmaking—almost like personal time with old friends before you are parted from them.

1. Find a comfortable chair with good lighting.
2. Place the quilt on your lap with the backing up.
3. Thread a needle and knot the end. Insert the thread where it will be hidden by the binding once sewn.
4. Turn the binding fold from the front to the back so it's ready to sew, and secure the fold in place with pins or clips. Secure about 18 in. of binding ahead of where you are working with pins or binding clips. Remove and advance the clips as you sew.
5. The binding stitch is similar to the appliqué stitch. Come up from the quilt, and grab just a few threads of the binding fold.
6. Insert the needle into the quilt backing, just barely behind the spot where the needle exited the binding fold.
7. Travel about $\frac{1}{8}$ in. through the batting layer of the quilt, and come up through the backing and grab the binding fold. Keep repeating until you approach a corner.

8. About 2 in. or 3 in. before the corner, park your needle in the quilt, and fold the binding from the adjacent (left) side of the quilt and tuck it underneath the binding fold to the right (see below).

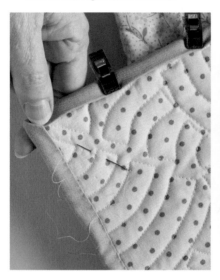

9. Continue sewing to the corner intersection, then travel along the diagonal fold toward the outer most corner of the quilt and up through the fold in the binding (see below).

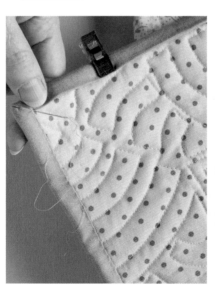

10. Take one stitch through all the quilt layers to the front of the quilt, and secure the mitered fold on the front. Then pull the needle back through all layers and return to sewing the binding along the side to the next corner (see below).

11. These extra steps at the corner will keep the corners crisp over time and reduce the bulk at the corner. Notice that the binding thicknesses on front and back oppose each other (see below).

GLOSSARY

APPLIQUÉ BLOCK

A quilt element that incorporates fabric shapes sewn onto a background fabric. Appliqué may be done by hand or by machine using a variety of techniques.

APPLIQUÉ PRESSING SHEET

A heat-inert synthetic liner placed between the iron and the fabric as a barrier; heat will pass through the liner, but fusible glue will not adhere to the sheet.

BACK-BASTING

A type of hand appliqué technique. The arrangement of appliqué shapes is drawn on the back of the main block fabric; then the pieces are placed on the front of the block in layers and basted from the back. The shapes are trimmed, and seams turned under and sewn to the background fabric from the front to complete the block.

BACKSTITCH

A backward stitch or a stitch on top of an existing stitch to keep the thread from getting loose.

BASTE

An extra-long stitch by hand or machine to hold fabrics in place for the next step in the process, such as piecing, quilting, or appliqué.

BIAS

Fabric cut on an angle, as opposed to straight of grain. Fabric cut along the bias will be more stretchy than fabric cut along the lengthwise or crosswise grain. Also, the 45-degree line on an acrylic quilter's ruler.

BLANKET STITCH

A decorative stitch made by hand or machine commonly used along the edge of an appliqué shape.

CHAIN PIECING

An efficient method for sewing block elements by machine. Sew two pieces of fabric together, make a few stitches in between, and then sew the next two pieces of fabric together. The result can be a long "chain" of sewn units connected by threads in between units.

CORNERSTONE, CORNER-STONE BLOCK

A square of fabric placed between sashing strips. The square can be one piece of fabric or made from several pieces sewn into a small block used as a cornerstone.

DARNING FOOT

Sewing machine attachment used for free-motion quilting. The darning foot is often used with the sewing machine feed dogs in the lowered position, allowing fabric to move freely under the foot to make curved quilting designs.

DECORATIVE STITCH

A machine or hand stitch that is wider and more involved than basic utility stitches, such as the straight stitch.

DIRECTIONAL PRINT FABRIC

A fabric print with design elements that face one or two ways. Depending on how the fabric is placed in a project, some elements may appear upside down.

DOUBLE BACKSTITCH

A short anchoring stitch, with a repeat of a stitch on top of itself in a series of running stitches.

DOUBLE-FOLD BINDING

A method of covering the raw edges of the finished quilt sandwich whereby a long strip of fabric is folded in half, attached to the quilt from the front with raw edges aligned, and the fold is sewn to the back of the quilt, typically by hand.

DRUNKARD'S PATH OR DRUNKARD'S PATH BLOCK

A classic pieced quilt block pattern that includes one curved pieced corner.

DUAL FEED

An integrated sewing machine feed device available on some sewing machine models that allows several layers of fabric to advance through the sewing machine with equal pressure from the top and bottom of the fabric. The dual feed operates similar to a walking foot.

EDGESTITCH

Sewing through a few fabric layers along the extreme rim of the piece, often to keep a folded edge compressed.

FAT QUARTER

A quantity of fabric representing 1/2 yard of fabric that has then been cut in half along the lengthwise grain. A fat quarter is usually 18 in. by 21 in.

FLANGE

An accent for a border or binding, usually made from a narrow strip of fabric folded in half lengthwise, then inserted, raw edges aligned, between two fabrics seamed together.

FLYING GEESE

A block element made from one quarter-square triangle and two half-square triangles. The resulting unit is a triangle within a rectangle that resembles the V-shaped formation made by migrating geese.

FOUR-PATCH OR FOUR-PATCH BLOCK

A classic quilt block pattern that is made by sewing four fabric squares of the same size into two rows of two squares each.

FREE-MOTION QUILTING

A quilting technique using a darning foot with the sewing machine feed dogs dropped below the bed. The quilt sandwich is moved under the sewing machine needle using smooth curvy strokes to create curved stitching patterns.

FURLING

A seam-pressing method. The center of the seam allowance is opened, allowing the remaining four seams to be pressed to one side, rotating around the center in a clockwise or counterclockwise direction.

FUSIBLE INTERFACING

A lightweight fabric similar to a stabilizer that has heat-sensitive glue. The interfacing may be printed with shapes for appliqué or piecing or may be unprinted.

FUSIBLE WEB

A heat-sensitive fabric adhesive that usually comes with a paper backing on one or both sides. Used for techniques like appliqué to adhere two pieces of fabric together without adding any additional fabric like interfacing.

HALF-SQUARE TRIANGLE

The right isosceles triangle that results from cutting a square in half diagonally.

HALF-SQUARE TRIANGLE RULER

A specialty ruler that facilitates making half-square triangle units from strips of fabric.

HALF-SQUARE TRIANGLE UNIT

The resulting square unit made from sewing two half-square triangles together.

IN-THE-DITCH

Straight-line sewing to topstitch or quilt directly along the seamline.

LENGTH OF GRAIN

The direction along the selvage as it comes off the bolt. Also called lengthwise grain.

NINE-PATCH OR NINE-PATCH BLOCK

A classic quilt block pattern that is made by sewing nine fabric squares into three rows of three blocks each.

PIECED BLOCK

A section of a quilt made entirely from geometric shapes sewn together using 1/4-in. seams. A quilt is usually made with several blocks sewn together in rows.

PINWHEEL OR PINWHEEL BLOCK

A classic quilt block pattern that is made by sewing four half-square triangle units so the triangle points meet in the center and the colors alternate within the units. The block resembles a child's pinwheel toy.

PRAIRIE-POINT BINDING

A finishing technique that incorporates squares that are folded in half twice. The raw edge of the folded triangle is incorporated in the seam, creating a jagged-edge appearance on the finished quilt. Prairie points may also be incorporated as a border embellishment.

QUARTER-SQUARE TRIANGLE

The resulting right isosceles triangles from cutting a square in half along both diagonals.

QUARTER-SQUARE TRIANGLE UNIT

The resulting square unit made from sewing four quarter-square triangles together.

RUNNING STITCH

Equally spaced stitches made by rocking a threaded needle from front to back through one or more fabric layers. May be decorative as for quilting or embroidery or functional as for joining fabric pieces or making ruffles.

SASHING

Rectangular strips commonly placed between blocks in a quilt.

SATIN STITCH

A decorative stitch made by hand or machine commonly used along the edge of an appliqué shape. Also a zigzag stitch with a narrow stitch length.

SEAM ALLOWANCE

The area between the stitching line and the raw edge of the fabric when two pieces are sewn together. Seam allowances are typically pressed to one side or pressed open to create a flat finished product.

SETTING TRIANGLE

Half-square and quarter-square triangles that complete the straight edges of a quilt when the blocks are set and sewn on-point or in rows that are at a 45-degree angle. Typically quarter-square triangles are used along the sides and half-square triangles on the corners. The triangles keep the less-stretchy straight of grain along the outside or border edge of the quilt.

STRIP PIECING

A time-saving piecing technique of sewing two width-of-fabric strips together, which are then typically cross-cut into smaller sizes.

TACK STITCH OR BAR TACK STITCH

A satin or zigzag stitch with no stitch length. It can be used at the edge of a seam opening to keep the seam from opening farther.

TOPSTITCH

Sewing through a few fabric layers, often to hold a fold compressed or to keep fabric from curling with use.

UNFINISHED SIZE

The width and length of a block unit, block, or quilt section that includes seam allowances, often provided at various checkpoints in a pattern to make sure piecing and seam allowances are accurate.

VALUE

The relative intensity or absence of color.

WALKING OR EVEN-FEED FOOT

A sewing machine attachment that works in conjunction with the feed dogs to advance the fabric from the top and bottom. Used for straight-line quilting or sewing through multiple layers of fabric.

WIDTH-OF-FABRIC OR WIDTH-OF-GRAIN

The crosswise, selvage-to-selvage direction as the fabric comes off the bolt. Quilting cotton fabrics are typically between 40 in. and 42 in. wide off the bolt.

ZIGZAG STITCH

A decorative stitch made by hand or machine commonly used along the edge of an appliqué shape. A zigzag stitch is also used to reinforce a raw fabric edge.

METRIC EQUIVALENTS

One inch equals approximately 2.54 centimeters. To convert inches to centimeters, multiply the figure in inches by 2.54 and round off to the nearest half centimeter, or use the chart below, in which figures are rounded off (1 centimeter equals 10 millimeters).

⅛ in. = 3 mm	4 in. = 10 cm	16 in. = 40.5 cm
¼ in. = 6 mm	5 in. = 12.5 cm	18 in. = 45.5 cm
⅜ in. = 1 cm	6 in. = 15 cm	20 in. = 51 cm
½ in. = 1.3 cm	7 in. = 18 cm	21 in. = 53.5 cm
⅝ in. = 1.5 cm	8 in. = 20.5 cm	22 in. = 56 cm
¾ in. = 2 cm	9 in. = 23 cm	24 in. = 61 cm
⅞ in. = 2.2 cm	10 in. = 25.5 cm	25 in. = 63.5 cm
1 in. = 2.5 cm	12 in. = 30.5 cm	36 in. = 92 cm
2 in. = 5 cm	14 in. = 35.5 cm	45 in. = 114.5 cm
3 in. = 7.5 cm	15 in. = 38 cm	60 in. = 152 cm

RESOURCES

Visit these websites for additional information about products or events mentioned in this book.

ALICIA'S ATTIC
Qtools™ Cutting Edge
www.online-quilting.com

AMERICAN & EFIRD
Mettler® thread
www.amann-mettler.com

THE AMERICAN FOLK ART MUSEUM
Infinite Variety: Three Centuries of Red and White Quilts
www.folkartmuseum.org

AURIFIL
Thread
www.aurifil.com

CLOVER NEEDLECRAFT
Black Gold appliqué needles
www.clover-usa.com

FROM MARTI MICHELL
Drunkard's path templates, original set
www.frommarti.com

IRIS
6-quart modular boxes
www.irisusainc.com

HOBBS BONDED FIBERS
Batting
www.hobbsbondedfibers.com

MARY ELLEN PRODUCTS
Mary Ellen's Best Press™ starch alternative
www.maryellenproducts.com

OLFA®
Rotary cutters and mats
www.olfa.com

THE ORIGINAL LITTLE FOOT
That Purple Thang
www.littlefoot.net

PIECES BE WITH YOU
Piping Hot Binding tool and book
www.piecesbewithyou.com

QUILTSMART, INC.
Printed fusible interfacing
www.quiltsmart.com

RELIABLE CORPORATION
Digital Velocity iron
www.reliablecorporation.com

STUDIO 180 DESIGN
Wing Clipper, Tucker Trimmer™, and Square²
www.studio180design.net

YLI CORP.
Soft Touch and quilting thread
www.ylicorp.com

SCRAPTHERAPY
Log on for the latest patterns, tips, and news on the ScrapTherapy pattern series.
www.scrap-therapy.com
or
www.hummingbird-highway.com

INDEX

Note: Page numbers in *italics* indicate projects, and **bold** numbers indicate definitions.

If you like this book, you'll love everything about *Threads*.